SMOKESCREEN

SMOKESCREEN

Canadian security intelligence after
September 11, 2001

J. Michael Cole

iUniverse, Inc.
New York Bloomington Shanghai

SMOKESCREEN

Canadian security intelligence after September 11, 2001

iUniverse books may be ordered through booksellers or by contacting:

iUniverse
1663 Liberty Drive
Bloomington, IN 47403
www.iuniverse.com
1-800-Authors (1-800-288-4677)

Because of the dynamic nature of the Internet, any Web addresses or links contained in this book may have changed since publication and may no longer be valid.

ISBN: 978-0-595-50344-5 (pbk)
ISBN: 978-0-595-61470-7 (ebk)

Printed in the United States of America

C ONTENTS

Acknowledgements

I would be remiss if I did not thank certain people for their support, understanding, and patience throughout my intellectual—and oftentimes emotional—journey. First and foremost, I extend my gratitude to my parents, who taught me to always question things and that there are certain moments in one's life where personal security and comfort are less important than standing up for one's ideals of justice. This book is the result of such a philosophy and certainly would never have come into being had they not inculcated those important values in me. It is also the result of a deep respect I have entertained for many years for individuals who, despite the real possibility of risk and damage to themselves and to their families, did what they had to do to abide by their standards of morality in the face of institutional injustice. Jeffrey Wigand, of the movie *The Insider* fame, and Daniel Ellsberg, whose excellent book *Secrets* I quote in this work, immediately come to mind. Too paraphrase Ellsberg, my book is intended to show to the public that even someone who has had access to the classified material can reach the same conclusions as those reached by many rights activists, academics and citizens who haven't.

My parents' respective spouses have also been extraordinarily supportive, and for this I thank them. Many friends, both at CSIS and outside its circle, have been privy to my anxieties and dissatisfactions, and displayed tremendous patience and understanding. I hope that the coffee that usually accompanied these rants managed, in some small way, to mitigate some of their suffering. I offer my gratitude, too, to the dozens of intelligence officers who shared their frustrations, aspirations, and ideas with me. Some of those important pieces of information will inevitably have melded with the narrative of this book, and though these people must remain nameless, their generosity of mind will unquestionably have made this book a better one. All errors in conception and interpretation are mine and mine alone.

I extend my regards as well to the officer who, less than a week after I had handed in my resignation, conducted what I like to call my post-mortem interview: the post-employment debriefing. Despite his warnings against writing a book on my experiences at CSIS, he seemed to recognise that a real conflict exists within the new generation of intelligence officers. Along with the other officers who conduct those interviews, he will have many occasions to hear similar or additional grievances, and I hope that the reports that result from those interviews do not get lost in some database, never to be consulted. There is, I am convinced, a lot to be learned from intelligence officers who are on their way out.

I also would like to thank Dr. David Last at the Royal Military College of Canada in Kingston for his exemplary sense of duty, intellectual curiosity, and sustained encouragement. He is the perfect example of the successful combination of military professionalism and academic pursuit in the service of peace and security. Notes of gratitude are also in order for Dr. Thomas Homer-Dixon of the University of Toronto, Dr. Norman Hillmer at Carleton University for his invaluable support, Sarah-Jane Meharg at the Pearson Peacekeeping Centre in Ottawa, Robert Stewart at McGill University, Maria Banda at Oxford University, Drs. Michael Roi, Peter Archambault and Charles Morissey at RMC, author and former CIA officer Barry Eisler, David Kaplan, formerly at *US World & News Report,* for kindly sharing some of his useful research on US intelligence, and the numerous friends all over the world who, on many occasions, expressed an interest in and support for this project. Special thanks to Jean-Louis and Dieter, who relentlessly pushed me to complete this project, to Patricia, who always supported me and who, sadly, became a victim of what I was becoming, and to A in Japan, who played an important role in how I came to see the world. A big *xie xie nimen* to the wonderful staff at the *Taipei Times,* whose enthusiasm for this project amid my already heavy workload made its completion possible.

Finally, I would like to thank my partner and her sister, both of whom have also had to deal with the suffocating environment from which I escaped. Their assistance, ideas, and patience kept me afloat throughout it all. My partner's implacable spirit of independence showed me that it is permitted to dream of a better life for oneself.

Introduction

To be inhuman in defence of our humanity,
Harsh in defence of compassion,
Single-minded in defence of our disparity.

—John Le Carré, *The Honourable Schoolboy*

We live, we are told, in a dangerous world. More than six years after the Sept. 11, 2001, multiple terrorist attacks against the United States and despite spending billions of collective dollars on the so-called "war on terrorism," states have made little progress in ensuring that our world is a safer place. In fact, it would be difficult to disagree with the conclusion, reached by many, that we are worse off now than we were on Sept. 10, 2001. After a quick ouster of the Taliban regime in Afghanistan, which was accused of harbouring the high-ranking al-Qaeda members who were responsible for the Sept. 11, 2001, attacks, the country has gradually fallen back into a state of insurgency and last year was its most violent in years. Meanwhile, terrorist suspects were arrested in Great Britain, and in the summer of 2006 aviation once again seemed to be threatened by al-Qaeda. Iraq, which as part of its campaign against terrorism the US invaded in 2003, is faring no better and continues to be on the brink of civil war. Many other places are facing similarly dire challenges. In Pakistan, opposition leaders were being killed in bombings and social upheaval was on the rise. At this writing, North Korea, after carrying out its first test of a nuclear device in 2006, remained a regional threat, while Iran continued to defy the world with its own alleged pursuit of militarized nuclear technology. Palestinians were unable to find unity within their own government, and Israel was again pounding the Gaza Strip. During the summer of

2006, Israel launched a vicious war against Hezbollah in Lebanon, a group that, according to some analysts, poses a much greater threat to regional and international security than al-Qaeda. Genocide in Sudan, war in Somalia, which once again risks falling into the hands of Islamists, foreign workers kidnapped in Nigeria, Muslim insurgency in southern Thailand, rebel attacks in Chad, post-election chaos in Kenya—the list of calamities seems endless.

In Canada, the summer of 2006 also brought its scare, with 17 individuals arrested in connection with an plot to bomb multiple targets in Toronto and perhaps even behead the Canadian Prime Minister in Ottawa. The world was a dangerous place. Americans, wherever they were, certainly were not safe. And if we believed the doomsayers in Ottawa, neither were Canadians.

The Canadian agency that is charged with protecting Canadians against this seemingly inexhaustible list of threats is the Canadian Security Intelligence Service (CSIS). Since Sept. 11, 2001, the Service, as it is also known, underwent a substantial growth, both in terms of budget and responsibilities. There was agreement around the world that security intelligence organisations would not only need to become more proactive in this new age of "global terror," but that bigger budgets and more intelligence officers was the solution to those challenges. Consequently, all over the world the agencies involved in security intelligence grew in size and reach, and did so at an unprecedented pace. CSIS was no exception.

Attendant to this growth was a new permissibility arising from the belief that to win the "war," the rules of the game needed to be changed. No comment by a high-ranking government official better encapsulated this new worldview than US Vice President Dick Cheney's contention that "governments needed to work through, sort of, the dark side."[1] Unfortunately, this so-called dark side was not only ill-defined but over time gave rise to many forms of abuse. And while most accusations against illegal government practices were made in the US, other countries followed suit, including Canada, which saw the consequences of such unchecked behaviour exposed, however incompletely, in the O'Connor Commission over the Maher Arar case.

The world is slowly awakening to the reality that greater government power does not make the world safer. In fact, as this book seeks to demonstrate, the frantic adoption of more aggressive anti-terrorism measures after Sept. 11, 2001—added to tremendous pressures from the US to follow its lead in the security game—have made the world more dangerous not only for Americans, but for people everywhere. This includes Canadians, both by virtue of their being from the "West" and as a result of what the Canadian government has done for the sake of its alliance with Washington.

Based on my experience working at CSIS and extensive research into the literature on the subject, this book looks at what has happened within the Canadian intelligence community—from the training of new intelligence officers onwards—and attempts to demonstrate how the path we have engaged ourselves into is creating a world that is increasingly dangerous for Canadians. Not only are some of the decisions our government has made in the name of security increasing the risk of terrorism against Canadians, but our very own adoption of the "dark side" is threatening the very foundations of our hard-earned liberal democracy and whittling away at the system of values that makes Canada such a vibrant society.

Many critics of the Canadian government's involvement in the "war on terrorism" have blamed the Stephen Harper administration for its pro-US and pro-Israel stance on international issues. The truth of the matter, however, is that the slide in favour of Washington had begun well before the Conservatives came to power. In fact, most of what readers will encounter in this book occurred when the Liberals were in office, both under former prime ministers Jean Chrétien and Paul Martin. While it is true that Harper's policies, from his decision to further involve Canadian soldiers in Afghanistan without properly consulting the Canadian public, to his Cabinet's disconcertingly pro-Israel rhetoric during Israel's illegal attack on Lebanon in 2006, represent a shift to the right, the behind-the-scenes system of unaccountability that permeates security intelligence had become institutionalized at a much earlier time and underwent a marked upswing immediately after the September 11, 2001, terrorist attacks in the US. Pressure from Washington after 2001 and in the lead-up to the 2003 invasion of Iraq, therefore, only compounded a philosophy that was already well ingrained in that branch of the Canadian government.

Most of what CSIS and the Canadian intelligence community do in the name of security is carried out in secret. Despite the proclivity of Canadians and the media to take an aloof attitude and the moral high ground vis-à-vis their cousins south of the border, Canadians have done a far poorer job finding out what their government is doing in the campaign against terrorism. With rare exceptions, no one in the media and very few academics have tried to tell truth to power. Consequently, the debate on the value of what the Canadian government is doing in the realm of public safety has been largely, if not shamefully, absent.

The latter is probably the greatest threat Canadians face today. In the following pages, I intend to walk the reader through contemporary security intelligence in Canada and explain why the direction taken by CSIS, and the system of which it is part, is a dangerous one.

The urgency in writing this book was exacerbated by increasing signals in 2007 that the US was readying itself to wage war against Iran, the consequences of which action, like the invasion of Iraq in 2003, could put Canada further at risk. For an organization like CSIS, a US-led war against Iran—and the larger Shiite population in the Middle East—would imply cooperation at all levels and tacit acceptance of the premises used to launch the war. In other words, CSIS intelligence officers would redouble their efforts, as they did when the US went into Iraq and Afghanistan, in support of US objectives. As war against Iran would be far more damaging to international security than anything seen since Sept. 11, 2001, Canadians need to know that their country's security intelligence community would, for all intents and purposes, be doing Washington's work rather than serving Canadian interests. As of this writing in early 2008, Bush was increasing the pressure on the Iranian regime while touring countries in the Middle East; it would take an incident in the Strait of Hormuz involving Iranian Revolutionary Guards Corps craft and US Navy vessels to show us how close we were to escalation, if not war. Weeks later, the assassination of the former head of Hezbollah's Foreign Security Organisation (FSO)—the group's "terrorist wing"—in a car bombing in a suburb of Damascus, Syria, which many blamed on Israel, risked sucking the world into a war with Hezbollah and its principal sponsor, Tehran. No matter what happens, Canadians will feel the consequences.

On at least two occasions while I worked as an intelligence officer, I was warned by my superiors *never* to write a book about my experiences at CSIS. The fact that you are holding a book on the very subject is proof that I did not allow myself to be intimidated by those threats. Such warnings, however, are indicative of the great malaise that exists within Canada's security intelligence apparatus.

The world of security intelligence shares precious little with the adventurous life of the James Bond character type portrayed in film and popular writing, or with that of the protagonists in movies such as *Spy Game* and *The Recruit*. Still, and perhaps ironically, it is to fiction that one turns to obtain the truest approximation of what it is like to be an intelligence officer—not because authors of fiction are necessarily better at explaining things, but rather because practitioners of the intelligence craft are more often than not discouraged by their employers from writing about their work, while those who do are often tempted to embellish the story lest the act of writing make them realise how boring the routine associated with their line of work really is.

The two authors of fiction whose works come closest to providing a true-to-life depiction of the world of intelligence are Graham Greene and John

Le Carré. Both, perhaps ironically, were products of that world: Greene worked for the British Secret Service (MI6),[2] while Le Carré served some time at the British Foreign Office and in military intelligence.[3] The combination of having experienced the dull reality of life as practitioners of intelligence and the freedom that fictional writing gives them puts these two authors in a position where they can provide a fair approximation of what the real thing is like. As such, the true literary richness of their work is beyond the plot and lies instead in their capacity to show what the experience of being an intelligence officer does to the individual, the self, and one's sense of morality. This is where the genius of Le Carré's *Smiley* trilogy is unleashed, when the characters on both sides of the ideological divide—the East and the West during the Cold War—realise how harmful their game has been, not only to their opponents but to themselves and to the world. The harm, one soon realises, did not stem from the threat of nuclear annihilation; it lay inside each and every individual who took part in the looking-glass war.

Despite the seriousness of the topics that these two authors deal with—the Cold War, nuclear annihilation, terrorism in the Middle East, the arms trade, the exploitation of Africa—their work can be read as satires, and once the reader manages to look beyond the story itself, he realises that a great humour lies in the background, smirking at the folly of human agency. While humour and spying may not seem like logical bedfellows, in order to remain sane the intelligence officer *must* maintain his sense of humour. For amid the dullness and the ugliness that an intelligence officer deals with on a daily basis, a certain dispassionate distance must be maintained, as well as the capacity to laugh at oneself and one's situation. Otherwise, one could easily drown (as some do) into the sucking waters of paranoia and depression. After all, as Le Carré writes in *The Russia House*, "there is no such thing … as an intelligence operation that does not occasionally run to farce."

In the long term, however, a problem quite different in nature emerges: The more an intelligence officer laughs at himself and his part in the game, the more difficult it becomes to take things seriously. Having reached that point, the intelligence officer become quite the dangerous weapons indeed: he turns into a cynic. Once an individual with such powers reaches that state of mind, once the farce has been exposed and the seriousness of the religious belief has been abandoned, it probably is time for him or her to start looking for another line of work. As we shall see, most intelligence officers do not make that decision, however, for reasons mostly financial.

However one looks at them, security intelligence agencies can do tremendous harm to people, societies, and constitutions. This book was written with this warning clearly in mind. That world is a circus; it is quixotic in scope, blind in its belief of knowledge, disjointed in its need for unity, and hallucinogenic where firm roots in reality are required.

In the process of protecting ideologies—for in the end this is what intelligence agencies ultimately do—intelligence officers and the institutions of which they are part tend to lose sight of the only unit of reference that truly matters: humanity. Whether one lies inside the illusionary gates of the intelligence world or outside makes no difference. In the game, no one is spared.

What follows is a story of institutional incompetence, obstinate resistance to change, moral aloofness and, in the end, a tale of an intelligence service that, through some of its actions, may be endangering the security of Canadians rather than protecting it. One would rightly expect that Bill C-36, which came into force in response to the multiple terrorist attacks of September 11, 2001, had provided CSIS and its law-enforcement counterpart and sister agency, the Royal Canadian Mounted Police (RCMP), with the necessary increases in power and intrusion to do their job properly. It has. But those increases have not been accompanied by a similar augmentation in the brainpower required to use them judiciously, or the checks and balances to ensure that they do not result in abuse.

After a close look in Chapter 1 at the numerous institutional defects that prevent CSIS from serving the Canadian public in the manner that it should, Chapter 2 puts the agency in its larger contemporary context and demonstrates that since Sept. 11, 2001, Canada has been forced into a war that is not and should not be its own, at great peril to its citizens. Many of the things CSIS does wrong (and wrongly) are largely the result of political pressures—pressures that come both from within Canada and, even more so, from Canada's paranoid giant down south. While, despite claims to the contrary, an intelligence service cannot be completely apolitical, there nevertheless is a requirement that it remain independent of the daily tug of war that exists at the trade and political level between states. When those very different issues are linked, when the softwood lumber trade dispute, for example, is intermingled with a government's decision whether or not to join an illegal war in the Middle East, the danger for the smaller state of losing its sovereignty becomes very real. When a government announces publicly it will not join the so-called Coalition in Iraq while, through backchannels, it promises the full cooperation of its intelligence services, a country endangers its identity. Through a belligerent, right-wing media that, almost seven years after the fact, still cannot stomach the blow that the military giant received on Sept.

11, 2001, the US has managed to force the Canadian government, and others, to adopt security measures that are unlikely to offer better protection for Canadians, but which will almost certainly result in great harm to the values that Canada stands for and has nurtured over the past hundred years. Canadians must take a close look at what they want for themselves. And since our institutions are part of and symbolise that identity, even secretive agencies like CSIS need to reflect—and reflect on—what Canada stands for. State-building cannot be a selective process, with certain parts aiming in one direction while others head in one that is diametrically opposed. States that do so are known as "failed states"—hardly the sobriquet Canadians would want for their country.

Chapter 3 turns to what has been called "Canada's largest anti-terrorism operation since the creation of the *Anti-terrorism Act*" to consolidate some of the arguments that are made in the preceding chapters.

Finally, Chapter 4 proposes a list, by no means exhaustive, of changes that would help transform CSIS and the wider community into an institution that not only is suited to meet Canada's needs but that, should the need arise, could protect Canadian citizens from harm. It is my hope that this book will provide enough information to awaken an interest in CSIS' activities and subsequently encourage people from all walks of life, from ordinary citizens to government employees who really ought to be better informed, to call for change. Ultimately, it is the public that will suffer the consequences of a repetition of avoidable intelligence blunders, and not the civil servants who sit comfortably in their offices in Ottawa. Public inquiries and internal reviews, for the moment the only means of official checks and balance, are a beginning, but so far they have not managed to capture the interest of Canadians to the extent that it should. Canadians must abandon the belief that the activities of their government are beyond their reach, or that government can only be made accountable on election day. In reality, every single day and in everything that it does, governments can and *must* be required to act responsibly.

A note on the *Security of Information Act,* which not long after Sept. 11, 2001, replaced the *Official Secrets Act.* All intelligence officers in Canada are subjected to rules governing what they are allowed to communicate publicly in writing or verbally. Even as a former intelligence officer, I must still abide by those rules and will be subject to them for the rest of my life. As such, readers hoping to obtain "secret" insights into investigations, tradecraft, and so on, will have to look elsewhere, for none appear in this book. What I intend to expose does not rely on the operational—and therefore classified—aspects of CSIS and the greater intelligence community. What the *Act* does not forbid one to write about, however, are the fundamental flaws that lie at the core of the institution, the daily practices, the personalities, the hierarchical pressures, the system of fear, the institutional ineptness, the ideology, the mentality, the philosophy, the intellectual apathy, the skewed morality, the racism. This is what this book is about. There is no need to do what Daniel Ellsberg, of the *Pentagon Papers* fame, did, and to photocopy 7,000 pages of classified documents.

CHAPTER 1

▼

THE TOTALITARIAN
SYSTEM

*Intelligence officers need to address, individually and
collectively, the issues of ethics of their profession.*

—William Nolte[4]

It is perhaps reflective of a strong resistance to institutional change that the great majority of books published in the last few years calling for an "intelligence overhaul," in Canada and elsewhere, still fail to address the *fundamentals* of the processing of information and propose instead changes in organisational structure or in technical applications. In other words, the focus remains largely on who does what, and what with. Rather than look at the human beings who process intelligence, or suggest new ways to think about intelligence, recent writings, with a few notable exceptions, have all been looking at the tools spies use, or the buildings in which they use them.[5] It is quite revealing that the front covers of many of those books usually depict satellites, satellite dishes, laptop computers, or other symbols of technology. The latest recruiting campaign at CSIS is no exception, as it includes a booth display on which two young individuals, a man and a woman, are seen crouching and using a laptop computer, with a satellite in the background. To people who do not know better, the panel conveys the following message: Good looking, young, and tech-savvy. It does not matter whether the fashionable agents know anything about intelligence, or are capable of rigorous analysis—the message is technology.

These images, both on book covers and in recruiting campaigns, create the expectation that twenty-first century intelligence is all about signals and imagery, while in fact the art itself is as old as civilisations and has changed very little over time. Intelligence is about information and how it is used to gain an advantage in decision-making; the manner in which it is obtained—through human intelligence or electronically—matters very little. Whether a name is collected by sitting in a corner of a smoky bar late at night or through an intercepted phone conversation does not change the fact that the information is the same. New technologies offer more possibilities to obtain information, but in the end what counts is the quality of that information and the minds that will be assessing, interpreting and using it. Moreover, in the opinion of many, only human intelligence will ever allow people to learn about the *intentions* of others.

The argument that some sort of organisational restructuring is required buys into the assumption that intelligence was somehow "broken" before the Sept. 11, 2001, terrorist attacks. But was it really? Some have argued it was broken, or defective, because it failed to see the attacks coming clearly enough and early enough to prevent them. But is it reasonable to expect intelligence agencies to be right *all the time?* Furthermore, it is now common knowledge that the intelligence on imminent attacks was there, but that the authorities failed to grasp its meaning or simply chose to ignore it. In other words, the intelligence community did not fail in gathering intelligence on the attacks. It had the raw data, the undigested intelligence. The failure, instead, occurred at the analytical and decision-making level.

Too much attention has been put on structural reform, and too little on the art of collecting, analysing and disseminating intelligence. As William Nolte explains, in the US and elsewhere, "caught between the structural changes legislated at the end of 2004 and the argument that intelligence is not broken, national security managers may be inclined to split the difference, implementing the new structure but not correcting much else."[6]

Some responsible analysts have argued that nothing was broken to begin with, but in the aftermath of the Sept. 11, 2001, attacks, the pressure to change things, to demonstrate that something was being done, was simply too strong to be ignored. Something had to be done. Intelligence needed to be changed. It became more aggressive.

This is where the greatest threat lies. Restructuring may not be necessary, at least not in the way it has been argued throughout the community. The emphasis on the need to act, to change the way things were being done—in effect to do more—may itself be the problem. The sudden expansion, and in many ways the militarization, of intelligence, added to the increased power of the intelligence community following the Sept. 11, 2001, attacks, will in the long term be more deleterious to society than if we had kept our intelligence services, however "broken" they were, in the state we found them on Sept. 10, 2001. In other words, action for the sake of action can, in some instances, be worse medicine than maintaining the status quo.

The reaction of most governments, however, has been to give more, invest more, and do more. Accrued powers and increased activity have come under the guise of reform. When something "fails," people expect there must have been something wrong to begin with. Governments therefore have felt they had no choice but to be seen to be doing something, which has resulted in all the changes that we have experienced in the past seven years or so, and all those books claiming to provide the solutions to the "intelligence failure."

But, as this book will attempt to demonstrate, the intelligence community was not "broken" to begin with. Rather, if something needs to be changed, it is the philosophy of the trade. Having failed to do so while augmenting the powers of intelligence agencies, the faults in the system have only been exacerbated and today present us with a problem that is far more serious than the one we were facing prior to the Sept. 11, 2001, attacks.

Some writings, such as Robert Baer's *See No Evil* and Richard Clarke's *Against All Enemies,* focus on the failures of the Central Intelligence Agency (CIA) and the rest of the intelligence community, and on the intelligence community having become the victim, in their opinion, of politics and commercial interests.[7] While these accusations may be true, it remains that the fundamental philosophical question of *how* intelligence should be fixed, or whether "fixing" is the right thing to do, remains to be answered. Calling for a more aggressive CIA, as Baer and others do, will hardly remedy the situation.

Despite the fact that the great majority of people in US academia, government and the intelligence community have approached the problem from the wrong angle and looked at the wrong things that need fixing, a tremendous amount of time and energy has nevertheless been devoted to fixing what was perceived to have been broken, and most of those efforts were well intentioned.

The same can be said of Canada. Canadians, and CSIS more specifically, have also shown some interest in addressing intelligence deficiencies. Computer systems were upgraded—a quick fix—but those changes would likely have occurred even in the absence of the Sept. 11, 2001, attacks. CSIS hired new intelligence officers at an unprecedented rate and, given the new, more permissive environment, it became more aggressive in its collection of intelligence.

However, for all the talk about "intelligence failures" in the US, CSIS seems to have been utterly uninterested in truly examining and, if necessary, fixing itself. In fact, Canadian society as a whole has failed to take a close look at the changes that are required for intelligence in the 21st century. One cannot dispute the fact that there is, in the US, a debate going on, and that this debate, through the publication of books, magazine articles, TV interviews, and various think-tank Web sites, is readily accessible to the public. Whether this debate is looking at the right issues is another matter, but at least there is an interest in questioning things, and this is a very healthy development. Unfortunately, no such thing is happening in Canada, and the little intellectual effort that has gone into rethinking intelligence matters has largely been confined to the halls of academia, at such institutions as the Royal Military College of Canada and civilian universities like the University of Toronto and the University of British Colombia.

This lacuna means that the intellectual rationalisation for the use of intelligence, along with a critical assessment of the manner in which the intelligence community operates, is beyond the reach of most Canadians, in whose name CSIS and its counterparts are acting. In this respect, Canada lags behind its US cousin, and as a result it could be argued that CSIS is able to operate with even less scrutiny and more impunity than the CIA or the Federal Bureau of Investigation (FBI). Consequently—and this may come as a shock to Canadians—CSIS is far more secretive than its US equivalents. While accusations that the CIA is responsible for all the ills of this world are preposterous, the fact that the Agency is constantly being exposed, talked and written about has engendered an interest within American society. There is an urgent need for the Canadian media and publishing industry to play their role in making sure that the impact of intelligence activity upon Canadian lives is also exposed. The time has come for Canadians to admit to themselves that even if this is un-Canadian, the country *has* an aggressive intelligence agency, with upwards of 2,400 employees.

The 9/11 Commission in the US identified four principal failures within the intelligence community: imagination, policy, capabilities, and management.[8] In the present volume, I intend to address the three that, in my opinion, are the most pressing in terms of how they affect the Canadian intelligence system: *imagination, management, and policy*. Imagination and management are issues that lie mostly within CSIS and are therefore addressed in this chapter. I turn to policy, which lies at the strategic level rather than at the tactical level, where CSIS operates, in Chapter 2 and in the concluding remarks.

New recruits come from varied academic and professional backgrounds. Some have worked in banking, in security departments at convenience stores, while others have been teachers, worked at embassies, served in the military or exhumed bodies in mass graves in the Balkans. Many come from the Province of Quebec, on par with the customary overrepresentation of Quebecers within the Federal Government.

Very few recruits, however, have the academic and/or professional background that would make them "naturals" for security intelligence, and a great percentage of recruits is simply too young to play that role, coming straight out of university. This makes the claims that "CSIS has an extremely capable workforce, thanks to rigorous recruitment and continuous learning" and that "a large number of employees have impressive qualifications," as advertised in the 2004-2005 Annual Report, ring hollow. What makes matters worse, as we shall see, is that those officers who do have impressive qualifications are rarely used to the fullest of their abilities, and in many cases those individuals are the first to leave the Service.

While diversity can be a force for change, it should nevertheless not come at the price of lack of basic knowledge about the issues that intelligence officers will be looking at. It is therefore alarming that the majority of new recruits have, for the most part, a very tenuous grasp of geography, history, and conflict analysis.

A few weeks into training, recruits are assigned an ongoing world conflict, on which they are asked to write a one-page summary and give a five-minute overview. Many know next to nothing about those conflicts, even the better-known ones like that pitting Israelis against Palestinians. Since a large part of the work of an intelligence officer is linked to conflicts overseas, this reality is understandably worrying. But then again, Canadians might find solace in learning that new intelligence officers go through a 14-week-long training program, during which, one would assume, whatever knowledge gap a recruit might have will be thoroughly remedied. Unfortunately that is not the case.

Intelligence agencies and police forces take pride in the length of their training courses. In many ways, the duration of training seems to be equated with quality. At 14 weeks, the Intelligence Officer Entry-Training course (IOET) at CSIS is one of the longest in the world.

With IOET begins what I like to refer to as the long process of "waiting for Godot." Though, as far as we know, playwright Samuel Beckett, author of the tragicomedy *Waiting for Godot*, never worked in an intelligence service, his depiction of Vladimir and Estragon, the main characters in the play, who sacrifice the present and await the arrival of Godot, who will fix everything, provides an apt description of the lives of intelligence officers at CSIS. Within the Service, every step along an intelligence officer's career, beginning with the entry training course, is nothing more than a stepping stone to the next. Things always get better, officers are told.

Most, if not all recruits are miserable during the 14 weeks of training. Even the trainers, who often look demoralised, will admit that it isn't, to put it generously, the most exciting thing in the world. Classes who have just completed training will, despite being asked to refrain from doing so, share bits of advice with the following class, along with warnings that boredom is the rule rather than the exception. There is a running joke concerning people who do not drink coffee—IOET is sure to make a coffee drinker out of you.

Within the training department, the rule is to encourage the new recruits to look beyond the immediate and to focus on the goal: The end of training and the beginning of "real" work on a desk. Once you've completed training, you'll see how exciting it is! The problem is that this rule does not end with IOET; in fact, it applies to an entire career. If an officer is unhappy in Security Screening (the branch that deals with immigration and the vetting of government employees, and where a large number of recruits begin their career), he or she will be told to swallow the pill. Do the twelve to eighteen months, and wait until you move on to something really exciting: work on a "real" operational desk. When an intelligence officer is unhappy on an operational desk, or has to work for an undesirable supervisor, the same psychology is used: Do your two to three years, and then you'll be on the investigator's course, the six-week course that prepares intelligence officers for investigative work in the field. And so on, from headquarters to the region, within the region, and from the region back to headquarters. There is always something better, something more "real" out there. Only you have to be patient.

Also, looming distantly, is the possibility that one day an officer will be granted one of the few coveted postings overseas. CSIS has a number of posts abroad, most of which, to this day, remain undeclared, although as we shall see later high-ranking officers occasionally slip and reveal posts that, on paper at least, should have remained secret. These postings, too, are used to justify misery in the present. For example, Security Screening is often looked down upon as a non-operational and generally boring branch filled with intelligence officers who ostensibly "need more time" to learn the ropes. As a result, very few people want to work there, and new recruits dread being sent down to SS after they complete their training, as it may not reflect well upon their skills. Nevertheless, officers are often told that working in SS is a prerequisite for obtaining a post overseas, as if 12 to 18 months of misery earned one enough karma to unlock the doors to paradise in some exotic spot.

Thanks to this process, the entire body of intelligence officers, from recruits to supervisors, is fixated on the future. Misery becomes acceptable, and many lose sight of the importance of dealing with, let alone enjoying, the present. Those who are "in the know"—that is, intelligence officers who have been there long enough—are the voices that tell the new recruits to swallow the bitter pill, to wait for Godot. After all, if these people managed to tough it up for fifteen, twenty years, with the pin on the lapel to prove it, surely I, too, can do it, the recruit tells himself.

Training is death by Power Point. Over the course, recruits are visited by every branch and almost every operational desk within the Service, as well as by people on the administrative side, lawyers, and other government agencies. Although an understanding of who does what in the building and within the intelligence community is of the utmost importance, weeks on end of such vapid presentations tend to blend into each other, often leaving the audience more confused than informed. While the quality of the presentations varies as much as the Ottawa weather in April, overall they are of poor quality. Some agencies will skirt pointed questions, such as when I asked whether the port of Vancouver has been infiltrated by criminal gangs and what a certain agency, aware that this is the case, intends to do to remedy the situation. Others will show condescension and visible contempt for the Service, or give the impression that they have better things to do than to spend a couple of hours with 20-odd green recruits.

From the very beginning, it is obvious that the various agencies that constitute the Canadian intelligence community are highly territorial and suspicious of each other.[9] Feelings of superiority mix with the counterpart of inferiority, as if there existed a hierarchy of agencies, in which CSIS likes to think it is at the pinnacle.

By the end of the course, the recruits' knowledge of conflict will not have improved by much: In the fourteen weeks that are spent in the classroom, only one, two-hour overview of current world conflicts is provided. To be fair, the operational desks provide a snapshot of their respective investigations, but the final result is far from thorough, as the investigations are presented in a way that isolates the tactical issues from the strategic causes of the conflicts. Most recruits, therefore, end their training just as they began, with no understanding of current conflict. Their perception is that we have individuals in Canada who, through their allegiances and actions, represent a threat to security—that much is understood. But nothing is said, or learned, about the environment in which those individuals grew up, or the reasons why they picked up arms in the first place and why Canadians should care.

How can we expect an analyst just assigned to a desk, therefore, to be able to understand the nuances of what constitutes a war crime, for example, if one does not have the necessary basic training in conflict analysis and history? None of this is ever touched on during the more than three months of training. The result, therefore, is not unlike what an intelligence analyst in Iraq told the Iraq Study Group, in that "[intelligence officers] too often don't understand what is reported back because [they] do not understand the context of what [they] are told."[10]

No wonder that some supervisors with years of experience still have difficulty locating certain countries on the world map.

What recruits get during IOET, however, includes team-building exercises such as constructing the tallest building with marshmallows and straws, afternoons of laser tag, billiards, as well as an entire day on table manners, which way to point one's feet when trying to break into a conversation in a bar, and how to colour-coordinate one's shirts and ties. Judging from the amount of time spent on these, it seems that team-building and bonding are more important than knowledge of history, geography, and current events. A newly-arrived Muslim from, say, Somalia, whose file is being reviewed by a new recruit in SS would doubtless be confident that his file is in capable hands, knowing that the officer in charge is quite capable of building a tower with marshmallows and straws, or to match his tie with his shirt.

Another concept that from the onset is hammered into the consciousness of new recruits is that idealism has no place in the world of intelligence. Idealism, recruits are told, is nothing more than the daydreaming of people who don't know better, like all the useless artists, rights activists, reporters, historians and philosophers out there. It is acceptable—in fact recruits are encouraged—to belittle those people and to treat them as if they were nothing more than a nuisance. The media in general is reserved a similar treatment. Intelligence officers just "know better."

During the second-to-last week of training, class members are dispatched to various regional offices within the country. Throughout that one-week assignment, recruits are exposed to the various functions of the regional offices. Most regional offices, being closer to the "real" world than headquarters, exude a sense of superiority, and it doesn't take long for recruits to pick up the hatred that the regions feel vis-à-vis Ottawa.

The regions enjoy a certain amount of freedom and like to do things their way. Policy and the green light on operational matters, on the other hand, comes from Ottawa, which on occasions when HQ and the region do not see eye to eye can lead to battling of the ugliest kind. Very early on, therefore, recruits are given the impression that headquarters is not a good place to be in, that it is too caught up in red tape. And that it is boring, that "real" work is only accomplished in the region. Given that more than half of an intelligence officer's career will be spent at headquarters, the revelation that Ottawa is not a good place should make one pause early on, during that very week.

Aside for meeting the different players in the region, the regional visit also allows recruits to take part in mock surveillance. After being equipped with radio transmitters and briefed on how to use them, the recruits are released into the city with the objective of shadowing an individual, the "mock target." Recruits soon discover that the analogue transmitters they have been given do not operate well in dense urban areas filled with concrete and competing electronic transmissions—places like Toronto, Montreal and Vancouver. Most of the time, transmission gets cut off, and strive as they might recruits cannot make out the information they are being given. As most recruits don't know the city they have been sent to, it is not unusual for a few to get lost.

During the last two days in the region, recruits are teamed up with regional investigators in order to give them an idea of what a day in a field investigator's life looks and feels like. During that time, recruits are driven to landmarks of the investigation, including places that individuals of concern—that is, "targets"— are known to frequent. Many become excited at the sight of a mosque that is allegedly frequented by a target, or a store where another does his groceries. It is amazing to see how the targeting of an individual can transform what would otherwise be a normal suburban residence into a location that holds almost mystical attraction.

With rare exceptions, after returning from their regional trips recruits are informed that the entire class has "passed" the IOET course. Although it is supposedly pass-or-fail—a revelation that creates no small amount of apprehension among the recruits—one would probably have to declare his allegiance to Osama bin Laden to actually fail.

After completing the fourteen weeks of training, recruits can be assumed to have a general idea of how to do their job. In other words, by then most will know how to use the tapestry of software they will be working with for the duration of their career.

One thing recruits *do* spend a lot of time on during training is writing reports and how to upload them into the Service database. Emphasis is duly put on the Service standards for writing—how to write names and dates, for example—so that information stored in the database can be easily accessed using Boolean searches. Unfortunately, the standards are seldom respected, and supervisors throughout the country have different interpretations as to what those standards are, or will invent their own as their little fiefdoms grow. This means that obtaining 100 percent returns on a search, however proficient one is at making Boolean queries, is a near impossibility. Information, therefore, gets lost.

While recruits are taught how to use the various custom-made software involved in report writing, they are often told about the sense of accomplishment they will feel upon uploading their first report into the database. The reality, however, is far less glamorous. The act, which follows a painful and sometimes weeks-long process of approval up the chain of command (reports often slumber in a supervisor's in-box), is accompanied by the realisation that it will get lost in the sprawling database and will likely never be accessed by anyone. Soon, officers begin to take greater pride in the *number* of messages they upload into the database—often nothing more than reformatted, copy-and-pasted foreign agency reporting—than in their investigative utility.

While some supervisors spend an inordinate amount of time correcting grammar (sometimes making the final product worse than the original), very few will refuse a report because it lacks analytical value. In fact, many supervisors discourage analysis, as they fear an analyst's comments might not reflect the institutional view. What this means is that analysts are not to be trusted to make sound arguments. This anti-analysis spirit also stems from the fact that many supervisors simply do not have the knowledge or the cognitive capabilities that would allow them to assess an investigator's analysis. It is safer, therefore, to simply remove all analysis and stick to the hard information, the facts. In the end, the principal rule is the Process. As former CIA "China Hand" James Lilley wrote in his memoirs, the institution "focuse[s] on process over substance."[11]

As we have seen, the great majority of intelligence officers have not made the intellectual journey to prepare them for the investigation, or desk, they are assigned to. Upon arriving on a desk, they are usually given an overview of the investigation, which consists of either a summary document prepared for management, or a copy of the most recent affidavit presented to the Federal Court for the renewal of warrants. From those documents, along with the occasional verbal briefings by fellows on the desk, the recruit learns about the targets and their recent activities. Depending on the supervisor and the other analysts on the investigation, certain open source (that is, unclassified) texts—newspaper articles, books—or overviews prepared by the Research, Analysis and Production branch (RAP), may be provided, but it is largely the responsibility of the new officer to do his homework. More often than not, he will have to find the information on his own, with little or no encouragement from his supervisor.

Few intelligence officers who start on a desk, however, will choose to spend additional time reading up on the background of an investigation. For some, this is the result of a lack of intellectual curiosity. For many, it is simply a matter of not having enough time to do so. The body of knowledge an intelligence officer relies on, therefore, is mostly restricted to the hard data on sources and targets, with no context.

In spite of this, there is the assumption, both within the Service and outside, that intelligence officers know more than everybody else. This phenomenon is exacerbated by the questions from friends and family about "secrets." They will be asked, over coffee or during dinner, if they know where bin Laden is hiding, or if Iraq did in fact have weapons of mass destruction. Some recruits, as I was, will be asked these questions merely weeks after completing training. The assumption is that by virtue of being an intelligence officer, one magically gains access to all the secrets in the world. The truth is that intelligence officers rarely know more than the rest of us, and as we shall see, their focus is so narrow that they often-times know less than what one could learn from reading the newspaper, even about the subject matter the IO is supposedly a specialist on.

Secrecy, however, allows the intelligence officer to mask his ignorance. It's need to know. That information cannot be shared. Even when the more humble admit to not knowing the answer to a question, people on the outside will assume that the IO knows something but simply cannot tell them. Consciously or not, this reinforces the myth of the intelligence officer as the all-knowing. Over time, it exacerbates what George Packer, author of *The Assassins' Gate*, calls the "theology of confidence."[12] It would be dishonest to claim that the assumption that intelligence officers know more than the rest of humanity is not pleasing to them, or that some of them do not exploit that belief to make themselves sound more interesting.

For some officers, getting a higher education is a way to obtain the kind of knowledge that is so desperately lacking in the intelligence community, even more so at CSIS. However, in many situations the Service will make an officer feel that being allowed to go to school is actually a favour it is doing him. Some officers have to beg their supervisor so that they can take half a day off every week to complete a Master's Degree or other training—even if the courses are directly related to one's responsibilities on an investigative desk. After all, the last thing uneducated and narrow-minded supervisors want is for their ignorance to be highlighted through the superior knowledge of their underlings. Still, supervisor permitting leave of absence and provided one writes a short blurb on a legal form explaining why they want to enrol in a course and what it would bring to CSIS, the Service will usually pay for tuition. Many analysts at CSIS are therefore spending Canadian taxpayers' money on their academic pursuits, but the organisation that is paying simply does not tap into this knowledge. It is not an investment. Learning and making contacts within the community and in academia, let alone furthering one's knowledge on conflict theory, is often not considered to be a part of an intelligence officer's responsibilities. Meanwhile, CSIS employees who participate in the frequent golf tournaments or hockey games use the rationale that they are making contacts, and consolidating bonds, to avoid having to work longer hours to compensate for their absence.

Now that CSIS has more money than it ever had in its twenty-four-year history, people are discovering the many ways in which to spend it. More often than not, sadly, the disbursements are for personal gratification rather than operational needs or investment in knowledge.

One area where there has been tremendous abuse is operational travel. Much of the travel that intelligence officers do in the course of their work is perceived more as good fortune and vacation time than an opportunity to provide something that is truly valuable to an operation. Some officers, usually supervisors, collect trips abroad like trophies, and after returning to Ottawa some will spend countless hours describing the shopping, the food, and the other attractions of the places they visited to an envious audience that only dreams of doing the same one day. The information obtained in the course of those trips, meanwhile, is often treated as secondary. (Trips to Washington, the centre of gravity, inevitably result in the acquisition of CIA and FBI paraphernalia. Mugs, T-shirts, plaques and pins are in high demand. Some collect them with a passion that by far surpasses that for their work.)

This is not to say that travel abroad has no value. When the proper people are sent to meetings with specific operational needs, precious information can be obtained. But without the proper oversight mechanisms in place, it is far too easy to exploit the system and spend thousands of dollars on travel abroad with little return for CSIS.

As evidenced above, the acquisition of knowledge through academia or travel is seriously lacking. Sought and regarded properly, both would help provide the historical and cultural context that is difficult, if not impossible, to acquire via the dry intelligence reports officers work on and read at their desk. Budgets permitting, every intelligence officer should spend at least a few weeks visiting the countries whose groups or intelligence apparatuses he will be investigating. Since it is at present unlikely the Canadian government and Canadian taxpayers would be willing to foot the bill for such an endeavour, the second best thing, therefore, is education. But as we have seen, given the disdain the Service has for academia, there is no system in place to ensure that investigators will obtain the knowledge they need to do their job properly. As such, officers limit themselves to memorizing the biographical data about their sources and targets, which leads to the targeting of individuals in isolation of the history, culture, geography, and religion that shaped them.

This is how Arabs, Muslims, Asians, Colombians, become uniform, monolithic entities. Terrorists. Extremists. Narco-traffickers.

Absent a thorough knowledge of the historical forces that give rise to conflict, operational reports can only provide the kind of information that leads to a narrow view of the situation: name, date and place of birth, political affiliations, employment, and so on. To which is added the description of all the incriminating "evidence" that, over the years, was gathered against an individual. But everything is kept to a bare minimum and there is no room for complexity. Officers are often told that an individual from a certain age bracket born in a certain village in a certain country having had a certain education *must* be an active member of a terrorist organisation. Only a mechanical view of the world, one that does not take history and individuality into account, can generate teleological thinking of this kind. The operational documents from which recruits obtain their introduction to the investigation leave little room for the grey areas: Individuals are targeted, they were selected at some point in the past, ergo they represent a threat.

After only a few days on a desk, an analyst will be heard referring to "his" targets—not individuals, but targets, with a file number attached to them. The language used among investigators when discussing their targets is often dehumanising, with references to "scumbags," "idiots" and "pieces of shit." It doesn't help, as we saw during the War in Lebanon in July 2006, that then minister of foreign affairs Peter MacKay would be heard referring to Hezbollah as a "cancer on Lebanon,"[13] language that harkens back to the Nazis' dehumanisation of Jews.

Once an analyst feels he knows his targets well enough, the "we know best" syndrome kicks in: Although the new officer lacks the background and the experience to make his own judgement on whether a target indeed represents a threat, the digested assessments are deemed to contain all the conclusions one will need, which obviates thinking. Worse, the conclusions cannot be questioned and are regarded as sacred. To do so would put the credibility of an officer's predecessors into question, as well as the long chain of command that approved the targeting of an individual or organization.

There probably is not better example than the 1996 bombing of the al-Khobar Towers in Saudi Arabia to demonstrate intelligence officers' unquestioning adherence to intelligence "truths." In the literature, both classified and unclassified, two broad investigative areas—one on al-Qaeda and the other on the Iran/Hezbollah nexus—simultaneously claim that the group they are investigating was responsible for the attack, in which 19 US servicemen were killed. Both claim to have solid, incontrovertible intelligence linking their respective group to the bombing. After nearly three years working on cases related to both these investigations, and after reading reams of open-source literature on the subject—including works by retired intelligence officers—it is still impossible for me to state which organisation was behind the bombing. When two investigations claim, without leaving any room for doubt, to be right, it also means that one of them has to be wrong, if not both. Yet nobody in the intelligence community seems to mind the paradox. For the Hezbollah desk, Hezbollah conducted the attack, independently or at the behest of Tehran. The same applies to the al-Qaeda desk.

The documents that comprise the bible of an investigation, or the reference point, and which are handed to the new analysts upon their arrival on a desk, by and large consist of recycled material, with assessments rarely changing over time. In fact, thanks to word-processing, most documents display a distinct paucity of new thinking. From one year to the next, the assessments are copy-and-pasted, meaning that a document made five years ago will hardly differ, if at all, from the current one. During the six months that I worked preparing a Federal Court affidavit for the renewal of a warrant against a certain Middle Eastern organisation, I saw many examples of paragraphs that had become carved in stone, and any attempt to rewrite them, were it only for a fresh rephrasing, was met with incredible resistance. Attempts to revisit certain conclusions, assessments, or positions met a similar fate. As Josh Kerbel, an analyst at the Strategic Assessment Group at the US Directorate of Intelligence, recently wrote: "It has always been safer to predict that the situation tomorrow will be like it has been for the past dozen years than to say that it will change abruptly."[14] Based on my experience at CSIS, I would tweak Kerbel's observation and argue "change *at all*."

New analysts are also told that for the information to have made it into an affidavit or any other legal document attached to an investigation, it must have gone through a rigorous process of writing, footnoting, and levels upon levels of approval. But in reality that process is anything but rigorous. It certainly is lengthy, involving months of preparation and dozens of people, but man hours is no assurance of intellectual thoroughness. In fact, as we have noted, the resistance to reassessing prior conclusions is symptomatic of the intellectual laziness that characterises the entire drafting of an affidavit. For the recruit who bases his assessment and knowledge on such documents, the result is a skewed and altogether incomplete picture of an investigation and an inability to question the validity of those conclusions.

Rather than abide by a system of truths delivered top-down, investigators should be able to "reverse engineer" the preordained conclusions, which would allow them to really see how a group or an individual came to be targeted, and whether they should remain on the list of targets. Doing so would force investigators to make the intellectual journey and to accumulate the building blocks of a case on their own. Pieces of information that were overlooked, or missed, could also be gathered in the process. Unfortunately, new analysts are not given the time to do this. Instead, they are expected to hit the ground running, which can only be possible if they are told what to think. This approach to information ensures that anything that does not support, or in fact demolishes, a case is not retained, if at all considered.[15]

Analysts are told at the onset that certain groups and individuals represent a threat. That information is swallowed abjectly, synthesised, recycled, and repeated until everybody sings from the same page. Why make the effort to understand the realities and complexities of human phenomena when one can, with little effort, obtain all the necessary conclusions to play the game and please his superiors? Why think when a pre-packaged assessment is one read away? If readers ever wondered how millions of people could follow homicidal maniacs like Adolf Hitler, Pol Pot, or Shoko Asahara into murderous folly, they should look no further. The power to sway the masses—even the elite—is no dark art. It is easier than it seems, and intelligence officers are certainly not impervious to its lure. It rises from the ashes, in institutionalized form, of the uncritical mind.

The language in which reports, bulletin notes, and even Federal Court affidavits are written is also revealing of the absence of intellectual rigour that goes into the process. It is simple, and formulaic. Furthermore, once it has been approved, it becomes the root out of which all further reporting will emerge. Terminology and phraseology is not only adopted, it is copy-and-pasted, literally. Whole sentences are lifted from one document and pasted into another—not just from the previous year's affidavit to the current year's, but also from affidavits to reports, memoranda, and overviews for domestic or foreign consumption. Few intelligence officers can claim they actually write their own reports. Those who do are quickly told to stick to the prefabricated wording. Even after a supervisor has left a unit and his replacement has been assigned, the old style is retained, meaning that even the new supervisor will not feel the need to make the intellectual journey necessary to fully comprehend the nature of the investigation he or she will be leading.

This mechanism, which perpetuates conformity for the sake of conformity, partly explains the intellectual shallowness that characterizes many of the supervisors within the organisation. In many ways, the Service is doing its utmost to ensure that the world does not change, hoping that by repeating the language, its preconceived views will not need to evolve—an alternative that, of course, would require more effort.

The writing style, meanwhile, is overwhelmingly sub-par, with a tendency to dumb down the language, which leads to a loss of flavour, precision, and character. Correct word usage is not the prerogative of published authors alone; it is, rather, a sign of precision and organisation of thought. As analysts spend little time outside their office, accurate language represents one of the very few tools at their disposal to paint as complete a portrait as possible of the world out there and the individuals who inhabit it. By lowering the linguistic standards, much of that precision is lost. (I was once asked by my supervisor to change the term Caucasian to "white people." There were, therefore, very few "white people" in the Middle Eastern country I was writing about.)

As George Orwell so eloquently put it in his essay *Politics and the English Language*, "bad usage can spread by tradition and imitation ... this invasion of one's mind by ready-made phrases ... can only be prevented if one is constantly on guard against them, and every such phrase anaesthetises a portion of one's brain."[16]

The problem is that intelligence officers are strictly told not to be on guard against ready-made phrases; in fact, every form of encouragement is given to ensure, purportedly in the name of efficiency and standardization, that intelligence officers adopt the same style of writing. Within the unit, supervisors spend a lot of energy enforcing writing standards. As those standards are mediocre, so is the mental energy that goes into the preparation of reports.

Only through such mechanical and uncritical learning and resistance to change can the assessment of a target remain the same over more than a decade, which happens in some instances. This is where the lack of understanding of the strategic forces and history, as we discussed above, can be of such danger to the intelligence officer who works in this secluded environment: The world changes, and historical currents inevitably bring certain adjustments in how groups, individuals, and countries behave.

The Hezbollah organisation, which came into existence in 1983 during the Israeli occupation of Lebanon and the daily pummelling of Beirut by US warships, provides a good example of this phenomenon. Since its creation, Hezbollah has undergone a series of changes. It began as a Shiite resistance group using methods, such as devastating car bombings, that resonate today, especially in Iraq. Years after the invasion, the Israeli presence on the ground in Lebanon—with the exception, of course, of its invasion of the country in the summer of 2006—is now largely limited to disputed areas in the south, as well as the occasional intrusion by its military aircraft. Adjusting to the times and yielding to domestic and regional pressures, the organisation has remodelled its image and fundamentally altered its strategy. Hezbollah entered the political mainstream in the early 1990s and won seats in the 2005 general elections that followed the February 14, 2005, assassination of Prime Minister Rafic Hariri. This is not to say that Hezbollah no longer represents a threat to regional security, as it remains a significant military force within the country. But to look at the organisation today the way we looked at it in the 1980s, at a time when it was participating in sectarian war within Lebanon and trying to oust foreign occupiers, is intellectually criminal. Distinctions must now be made between parts of the organisation that engage in indiscriminate use of force to achieve political ends, those that are part of a legitimate political system, and those that are responsible for the maintenance of schools and hospitals in the poor Shiite areas of Lebanon—responsibilities that for various reasons the Lebanese government has been unable to fulfil. To simply see everything Hezbollah as intrinsically and immutably evil—which CSIS, the US and Israel do—can only be counterproductive, leading, for one, to acts such as the Feb. 13, 2008, assassination, most likely by Israel, of Imad Mugniyeh, the organisation's former chief of the FSO, which will surely undermine efforts by the "moderate" Hezbollah members to turn the organisation into a true political party, if not to its disarmament, as has been requested by the international community.

The same principle applies to a variety of individuals, groups, and states that the Service investigates. And yet, year after year, the affidavits read as if time had stopped, as if organisations were organisms that one looks at in a lab, in isolation from everything else. One consequence of this institutional failure to move on is that it gives rise to self-fulfilling prophesies, just as the misreading of the Soviet Union's nuclear arsenal during the Cold War led to an arms race that brought us to the brink of extinction.

Another example of this phenomenon was provided in late 2005, with the case of Bhupinder S. Liddar, whom the Jean Chrétien Liberal government had picked to become Canada's consul general to India. For months, CSIS provided assessments that prevented Mr. Liddar from obtaining the security clearance he needed to do his work. In their review of the case, the Security Intelligence Review Committee (SIRC), and later its former chairwoman, Paule Gauthier, declared that CSIS had conducted a "hasty, slipshod investigation," had based its assessment on "inaccurate, misleading and uncorroborated sources," and had "a regrettable attitude that supporting Arab causes can be suspicious."[17]

While it was true that Mr. Liddar, who was born in Kenya, had supported Middle Eastern causes in the 1970s and 1980s, and as a parliamentary assistant had on certain occasions been in contact with the Palestine Liberation Organisation (PLO) and various Arab lobby groups, what CSIS failed to take into account was that those activities took place *thirty* years ago. Apparently, in Mr. Liddar's case time had frozen, and support, three decades ago, for organisations that had changed over time and whose causes were now markedly different, was interpreted by CSIS as threatening to Canadian security in the twenty-first century.

Young analysts, who as I have mentioned tend to be terribly ignorant of history, also fail to realise that history and politics are not static. These young analysts have a fixed image of the world, and television may have something to do with that. After all, the mention of Hezbollah or the PLO usually summons images of the bombed-out Marines barracks or the US embassy annex in Beirut or, in the case of the PLO, bombed civilian aircraft or the Munich incident. But all these events, along with the mental images they conjure, are decades-old. As with these cases, Mr. Liddar's was the casualty of the Service's constant laziness in assessing and reassessing history and what historical change means to us in the present. In a way, Mr. Liddar probably was the victim of the tendency to recycle the primary documents that give direction to the various investigations carried out by the Service. To the "junior analyst" who dealt with Mr. Liddar's case (and who later allegedly destroyed his notes), the acronym PLO was probably sufficient to raise flags, which subsequently led to linear thinking along the lines of

Liddar + PLO + Palestinian extremism + names of people Mr. Liddar had been in contact with = recommendation (for in the end this is the extent of what the Service does in such a case) that his security clearance be denied.[18]

Without an understanding of history and how it changes, the officer would fail to distinguish between what those associations meant thirty or twenty years ago, and what they mean now. It takes far less effort to fix the PLO and other Arab political beliefs in time than to make the intellectual journey that would allow an analyst (let alone an entire desk of officers) to clearly determine if an individual was a threat at the time and, more importantly, remains so today.

I remember being approached on more than one occasion by a grim-looking new intelligence officer who worked in the Security Screening branch, the same branch that had dealt with the Liddar case. Going through his files, he had come across information linking an individual to an organisation that was nominally related to a group I was investigating. Sure enough, that individual *had* supported the organisation. But the problem, I told the officer, was that the organisation had ceased to exist fifteen years ago. It is one thing to link an individual to a group, a cause, or an acronym, one of those small "eureka" moments one gets by searching the convoluted database; it is quite another to follow the progression of those movements and to understand what they mean in a contemporary context. Recycling is prevention against change. It is the path of least resistance. Never mind that it leads to individuals being accused for having lived in different times.

Understanding of the type that is required will never materialise absent an institutional requirement, as well as an individual thirst, for historical background information—both the past that shaped individuals, groups and countries, and what journalist Timothy Garton-Ash calls the "history of the present," or current history. At the moment, other than the unusual intelligence officer who reads up on history and stays up to date on political developments in his area of investigation (let alone outside of it), much of the indispensable data that history offers us is lost on analysts and their supervisors. The further we go up the chain of command, the thinner is that knowledge, as cadres are swamped in paperwork that has little to do with operational matters, if at all.

The responsibility to keep up with and understand history, therefore, rests on the desk officer. Those (and there are some) who do that intellectual homework usually have to do it outside of regular work hours, or in school. The daily rhythm of meetings, report writing, uploading of information, and other mind-numbing tasks provides the officer with little time and energy to do that extra effort. Moreover, an organisational culture that shrugs at intellectual pursuit can be a very discouraging environment for those who would like to bring more rigour to their work. I recall once going back to my office late at night so that I could read up on a threat that a terrorist organisation had published on the Internet and do the required data mining in the database. Had it not been for this unpaid overtime, it is unlikely that the information I came across would ever have been found. Lack of time and a culture that discourages intellectual pursuit are two elements ensuring that relevant information will fall through the cracks.

If, as some critics of the US intelligence system pointed out after the "intelligence failure" of Sept. 11, 2001, the inability to use intelligence that we have in our systems resulted in a failure to prevent the attacks, then the way our intelligence officers are overloaded with information and other clerical tasks can only lead to future such failures. What is even more worrying is that a large part of the information that piles up on an analyst's desk (or in his in-box) is outdated and often irrelevant.

Weeks into my first operational assignment I realised that I knew less about what was going on in the world *after* I joined CSIS than before I was hired. I no longer had the time, nor the mental energy, to absorb information outside that which intelligence officers are bombarded with on a daily basis. Like everything else, the human brain has a finite storage capacity, and when much of that storage space is wasted on reams of mostly useless or outdated information, the ensuing overload, what University of Toronto professor Thomas Homer-Dixon calls "info glut," results in the brain no longer being capable of assimilating, let alone synthesising, additional information.[19] Publications such as *Foreign Affairs, Foreign Policy, Current History,* and *The Economist*, gold mines of information under normal circumstances, pile up, and remain unread.

While the institution gives little value to open source information, there is something almost mystical about classified material, with analysts holding it in such regard that after a while anything that is not classified is deemed a waste of precious time and hard disk space. As we have noted, intelligence officers are already bombarded with great amounts of information. In this context, the reflex is to give precedence to classified materiel over open source. Given this, intelligence officers spend the little time they have to do actual reading on classified material only. Unfortunately, as we have already seen, the classified information found in the database is often recycled material that is bereft of historical value, poorly written, and devoid of outside information that does not support the organisation's assumptions. The consensus, nevertheless, is that if information is not classified, it is not worth reading. As Chalmers Johnson writes in his book *The Sorrows of Empire*, information is often classified "because it would [be] embarrassing to have it known that … conventional journalism pass[es] for strategic thought."[20]

But "many policymakers and intelligence officers mistake secrecy for intelligence and assume that information covertly acquired is superior to that obtained openly,"[21] writes Stephen C. Mercado in a paper on open-source intelligence (OSINT). What most intelligence officers fail to understand is that background material is by default open source, as it comes from local newspapers, history books, and even film. In fact, Mercado contends that "open sources often equal or surpass classified information in monitoring and analysing such pressing problems as terrorism, proliferation, and counterintelligence."[22] Furthermore, much of the classified information one finds in a database will be available, in unclassified form, somewhere. Those who choose to acquaint themselves with the historical background of a conflict—in other words, who consume OSINT—will not reap any benefits professionally, as that information will be deemed of no value by the institution. Consequently, the rich information obtained by consulting alternative sources seldom finds its way into the operational reporting, a situation that is compounded by an unwritten rule that, mainly for reasons of storage space, the database should not contain any unclassified information.

The individual who defies the organisational opposition to open source will nevertheless gain a fuller understanding of his subject matter, but as there is no venue for that information to be stored and disseminated, after that officer has been transferred to a new desk or a region, all that knowledge will be lost. Nothing stays behind, except that which supports the thesis or has been recycled from earlier reporting. As a result, the Service database remains bereft of all the information that makes living history, that ties individuals, groups, and states to events. Officers are therefore given a tool—and instructed to rely on it—that is, at best, myopic.

The institutional defect runs deeper. Due, as mentioned above, to time constraints and an attitude of professional condescension vis-à-vis the rest of the intelligence community and non-intelligence officers, the "experts" in the department within CSIS charged with providing the much-needed background material are also often ignored. The Research, Analysis and Production (RAP) branch generates documents of variable quality that nevertheless attempt to put investigations into their historical context. The branch has a mix of new intelligence officers and experienced academics and former politicians. Their knowledge, if it were ever tapped into, could be of great benefit to the organisation. In reality, however, most intelligence officers have little time for RAP publications, and the "experts"—some of whom actually do the intellectual journey to understand a conflict—are almost quarantined and treated as annoyances.

Exacerbating the problem with RAP is the fact that under the current system, a number of recruits are sent straight from training to RAP, which makes absolutely no sense. Some of the individuals who are transferred there have no idea what they are doing there, as the great majority know nothing about the area in which they have spontaneously become "experts." Others, meanwhile, have no training in history or conflict analysis, or have expressed their disdain for writing. Still, many are sent to the branch, where they will spend the next twelve to eighteen months writing university-level papers whose benefit to the organisation is questionable.

Dispatching recruits to a unit where they will languish for more than a year and produce nothing of value also puts into question the Service's argument, following the Sept. 11, 2001, attacks, that it urgently needed to recruit an unprecedented number of intelligence officers. Surely, if the need were so urgent, those officers would have been put to better use.

To fulfil its mandate, RAP should only be comprised of experienced intelligence officers, academics, and former diplomats who, because of their experience, can bring value added to the branch and to the Service.

Sadly, the few specialists in the RAP branch who are actually qualified to do the job are usually ignored, as their informed views oftentimes go against the assumptions upon which operations are based. As a result, rather than sit down with the RAP analysts to learn from them or defend their different opinions, desk supervisors often resort to personal attacks against the RAP specialists, making new victims of the "we know best" syndrome that characterises intelligence officers. During my fourteen months on an operational desk, my supervisor would relentlessly insult a RAP analyst who, by virtue of where he was born and his academic pursuits, was much better informed about the subject matter than she was. Still, in front of her subordinates, that supervisor would treat the RAP specialist as if he were an idiot. Over time, as unit cohesion is strongly encouraged, the entire desk was treating the analyst with something close to contempt.

With a whole series of documents vying for an intelligence officer's attention, this discriminatory approach to RAP specialists means that their voice suffers a serious handicap and is often ignored.

The operational desk's contempt for divergence of opinion also extends to other agencies within the Canadian intelligence community. One can imagine how unlikely an intelligence officer groomed to look down on a RAP specialist—part of the CSIS family, after all—is to take seriously an assessment by, say, the

Department of Foreign Affairs. Very occasionally and when a threat to the CSIS position is perceived, a high-ranking CSIS officer will prepare an official rebuttal, which will be sent back via official channels. But in most situations, the information is discarded, accompanied by remarks that the agency in question is either "high on crack" or that it simply "doesn't get it"—two expressions that I have actually heard during my time at CSIS concerning other branches of the Canadian government.

That the Service may have a different opinion on a subject is understandable, and in fact it is healthy. After all, its view of the world and its institutional priorities differ from those of other government agencies. But when difference of opinion is treated as treason or proof that the other is, for all intents and purposes, "insane," and that disagreement is not addressed in collegial debate, the Service does itself and every Canadian it pretends to protect a great disservice.

The world of intelligence can be a very frustrating place. With most investigations, intelligence officers rarely see their efforts lead to a satisfactory conclusion; rather, investigations keep on going, with no resolution on the horizon. The Service's philosophy of grooming generalists rather than specialists who have the skill set and interest necessary to work on a specific investigation also means that an officer will be rotated—in other words, moved to another investigation—every two or three years. One consequence of this system is that all the effort an individual has put into an investigation, all the knowledge acquired from getting to know the sources, the targets, and so on, is lost. Worse, once the investigator has left a desk, the rule is that he is no longer in the loop and will not know what happens next, as this is "need to know," and once out, the analysts doesn't need to know. There is no closure, no sense of continuity, which in the long term affects the analyst's sense of accomplishment. As such, intelligence officers are perpetually in a professional limbo, always in transit. Referring to this factory-like approach to intelligence, a Vietnamese Lieutenant Colonel once told a former RAND and Pentagon analyst, the US war in Vietnam was not one war, but the same war fought seven times.[23] The same applies to CSIS investigations.

All of the above goes counter to logical long-term case building. For the Service, especially since the substantial increase in funding it received after Sept. 11, 2001, hiring new intelligence officers has become coterminous with action, which in effect has deceived Canadians into believing that it is, in fact, doing more to ensure their safety. At no other period in its twenty-four-year history has the Service hired so many new employees, with nearly 100 new intelligence officers trained every year. The problem, however, is that Canada cannot produce enough qualified people to sustain such hiring, and by the time I left the Service in fall 2005, it was already becoming clear that most of the recruits lacked the intellectual capacity and educational background to do the job—the job that real intelligence officers in a real professional agency ought to be doing, that is. Very few had the advanced educational background, let alone the intellectual capacity, to do inductive reasoning, gather material and make the appropriate connections to build a case. Only an institution that does not perceive the value of advanced education, that does not fully understand what an intelligence agency should ask of its employees, would hire the type of people that, with some exceptions, it has been hiring in recent years.

Exacerbating this problem is the fact that intelligence officers are not trained in the art of cognition. This is not only wrong but also potentially dangerous, for we cannot expect twenty-three year-olds, or people who do not have the appropriate training in logic, to know how to avoid the numerous intellectual pitfalls that will emerge while a case is being built. Nevertheless, this is exactly what the Service does, and it seems to hope that somehow its intelligence officers will develop those skills on the job. As we have seen, a great deal of time is spent on mundane items such as coordinating one's tie with his shirt, but not once during the 14 weeks of training is cognition discussed—and this despite the fact that books have been written on the subject, including an excellent one by someone from the CIA,[24] available both in book format and on the Internet.

Building a case against a potential target involves much more than accumulating evidence through covert means. In fact, gathering facts is the easy part. The more challenging aspect of case building is to make a sound assessment of the "evidence" in a logical manner. Intelligence collection should be akin to being given pieces of a puzzle without the player having any idea what the complete picture looks like. Unfortunately, the way intelligence agencies proceed turns this logic on its head: A complete picture is provided at the onset, whereupon the player is given the pieces, which he is expected to make fit. George Packer, writing about the Office of Special Plans (OSP), which before the US invasion of Iraq in March 2003 was charged with collecting data to support assumptions on the presence of weapons of mass destruction in Iraq and its links to international terrorism, writes that its members were "working deductively, not inductively; the premise was true, facts would be found to confirm it."[25] It didn't matter that most of the raw intelligence the OSP was obtaining came from Iraqi dissidents who knew exactly what to say to gain an ear at the Pentagon and in the White House, and in the process obtain large sums of money.

It would be invidious, however, to claim that the OSP is alone in this. As with the OSP, intelligence agencies tend to disregard whatever piece of information does not confirm the established truth. This process is the very antithesis of cognition. It also compels the intelligence officers within a unit to conform to the accepted knowledge, leading to what is known as "groupthink," a phenomenon whereby the individual's views cannot depart from those of the unit. Cultivated long enough, groupthink becomes invisible, like the devil, whose greatest trick was to convince the world that he doesn't exist. As Will Hutton, paraphrasing Cass Sustein of the University of Chicago, explains it in his book *The Writing on the Wall*: "the societal pressure to conform stifles the multiplicity of voices that are needed to articulate views other than the group norm."[26] Groups, he continues, "tend to reach the lowest common denominator decisions acceptable to all that are either second best or downright wrong." Once groupthink becomes insidious, it is extremely difficult to address it because those who suffer from it are unable, or simply refuse, to see it. The path of least resistance is therefore to keep things the way they are. Those who stand to gain from maintaining the status quo (usually the supervisors) will lash out at whoever tries to import a worldview that threatens to rattle the hermetic confines of the unit.

While the Service systematically uses the anti-cognitive approach, the process is reinforced by the very lacking qualities mentioned above in terms of background knowledge and the will to question established conclusions. Compounded by a tendency for intellectual laziness, it comes as no surprise that officers, along with their supervisors, will choose the easy approach by beginning with the premise and then making whatever piece of information they have in their possession fit the model while discarding whatever doesn't support the consensus.

Oftentimes, the premise hinges on a single piece of information provided by an allied agency, or a single source. Whether that information comes from a reliable source or has been corroborated by another makes no difference: Once an individual's name is the object of a query, the cognitive damage is done. Sometimes, a report whose assessment reads "We have no adverse information on this individual" will be sufficient for another intelligence officer to write, in a subsequent report, something like "While we have no new information to suggest that this individual represents a threat to the security of Canada, it should be noted that his name appears in the context of the XXX investigation in report XXX dated XXX." No tangible information exists against that individual, only negatives. Nevertheless, through recycling that individual's name is now mentioned in the context of a specific investigation. This, on occasion, will be enough to create problems for those people whenever they want to visit Canada, travel abroad, or seek employment with the Canadian government or in a sensitive sector such as an airport. Furthermore, the sharing of negative intelligence—"we have nothing but his name appears in the context of an investigation"—may be enough for more aggressive foreign intelligence services to justify questioning, if not worse.

Without the proper intellectual defences, careless officers will allow cognitive biases to taint their perspective, even when the Service has nothing against an individual. Pushed to an extreme, cognitive bias leads analysts to interpret absence of activity as meaning that an agent or suspected terrorist is in "sleep mode," "inactive," or so proficient that he has yet to be caught in the act.

This worldview is not without its precedent. One of the most notable demonstrations of this intellectual failure is the infamous Team B group of experts (which included Paul Wolfowitz, one of the architects, thirty years later, of the US invasion of Iraq) that, after its creation in the 1970s, was given the mandate to revisit the conclusions reached by the CIA on the status of Soviet strategic forces and, using the same data used by the CIA, to reach altogether different conclusion. One of those conclusions was that absence of evidence, as the CIA argued, that the Soviets were developing a submarine fleet that could endanger US subs, didn't mean it didn't exist. Rather, Team B argued that the Soviets must have developed submarines that simply couldn't be detected, which came to be known as anti-acoustic submarines.

Needless to say, the scientific Occam's razor principle, which stipulates that "when faced with two hypotheses that explain the data *equally* well, [one ought] to choose the simpler,"[27] certainly does not apply to the world of intelligence, though it should. In certain cases, absence of activity is just that: absence of activity. But by creating monsters out of that which cannot be demonstrated, the Service ensures its survival. When even evidence of inactivity is interpreted as threatening behaviour, an organisation will never go out of business. When the absence of activity is seen as irrefutable proof of superb tradecraft, the enemy becomes something intangible, that lurks in the shadows, waiting to be activated.

While intelligence officers build their cases in much the same way scientists attempt to prove a theory, the difference between the two lies in the fact that in the scientist's case, his findings will only be published following peer review. In the world of intelligence, however, there is no such mechanism to ensure intellectual rigour and honesty. As peer review, in its critical approach to conclusions, is the antipode of "groupthink," whoever dares to make a critical assessment, or to attempt to "peer review" an investigation's position, is either accused of committing something close to treason, or of being a bad team player.

The review process, the chain of approval that allows the Service to legally target an entity or an individual, *should* in theory be the equivalent of scientific peer review. Unfortunately, that process, which involves employees with higher pay grades and tons of paperwork to deal with, as well as committee reviews and various bureaucratic lawyers, is also subject to the cognitive bias trap: Every individual involved begins with the conclusion, which is provided by CSIS. What this means, therefore, is that the only things that the process looks at are supporting facts. As long as those facts are seen to support the theory—and facts have a remarkable elasticity, I discovered—the targeting of an individual or organisation will be approved. Without their knowing it, however, the people involved in the approval process never get to see information that *does not* support the case. In other words, the review committees only get to scrutinize and approve a biased argument, determined by CSIS, that is supported by biased information also hand-picked by CSIS. This is akin to a judge being asked to decide on a case where information showing that the suspect was outside the country at the time of a crime is kept secret. All the other possibilities, all the other interpretations one could reach based on the facts, are ignored.

Based on my experiences at the Service the entire warrant approval process is nothing more than an exercise in rubberstamping, the result of a biased view going up the chain of command all the way to Federal Court, compounded by mental laziness, again all the way up to Federal Court. Given the tendency of the management at CSIS to equate quantity of targets with the quality of an investigation, the norm is to approve as many targets as possible, regardless of the operational value of, or the quality of information that supports, doing so.

Such a quantitative philosophy can only result in a drop in the value of the individuals or groups being targeted, which needlessly overburdens the finite resources of the various units that provide coverage on those targets.

I remember, about six months after joining an operational desk, sitting in my office with another analyst, contemplating the investigation. "What do you think would happen if we were to drop all our targets, right now?" I asked the other analyst, who had been on the investigation far longer than I had and was considered the "star" analyst on the desk. "Would Canada be more at risk?"

The answer stunned us both: It wouldn't.

Later, as I was preparing the affidavit for the same investigation, I literally struggled to find information that would justify targeting those individuals. If, as the law stipulates, intrusive investigation should be the *last resort,* how could we explain the paucity of information I had at my disposal to prepare the documents that made the investigation legal in the first place?

This, I came to realise, was but one of the many examples of how low the threshold for targeting individuals had become.

Such intellectual and institutional sloppiness ultimately represents a failure to abide by the mandated commitment of the Service to make Canada a safer place for *all*. If, as a result of institutionalised intellectual laziness, the targeted individual's chances of making a living in Canada are ruined, then we could argue that our intelligence service is not fulfilling its mandate. The problem largely lies in lack of accountability. Individuals are often targeted for reasons that are, at best, tenuous, and the targeting is, in most occasions, a fait accompli, in that there will be little resistance to, and often encouragement for, the targets being added to an investigation. For most intelligence officers, the above dysfunctions do not pose a moral problem, as they likely will not have done the intellectual, let alone the emotional, journey to build a strong, airtight case. Facilitating this is the fact that the target will have been emptied of his historical background and will, in effect, have been dehumanised through the use of language. Quite often, targets are just names and file numbers in a database. This approach ensures that intelligence officers do not connect emotionally with these people. What they are, however, is the object of resentment and ridicule, a verdict rendered, as we have seen, even before an officer has begun acquainting himself with a case. Whether intelligence officers are aware of it or not, there is a tendency to commit racial or religious profiling against certain types of individuals.

Readers will not be surprised to learn that people of Middle Eastern or Southeast Asian origin, and people of the Muslim faith in general, are largely representative of that group. Official declarations that *the Service* does not do racial profiling are not entirely wrong. Rather, it is at the individual level, in the unconscious mind, that this phenomenon rears its ugly head. On several occasions I heard otherwise responsible analysts make such a claim as "individuals with such a last name in Canada and in the US are all members of that organisation, are all into fraud, cigarette smuggling, contraband, etc ..." While the above is akin to cognitive carpet bombing, it does happen. It is also reflective of a lack of understanding, of knowledge, on the part of the intelligence officers. And it is racist, to which we will turn later.

There is no knowledge at CSIS as to which last names are common in Iran, for example, or in Afghanistan. Heaven forbid that an intelligence service in the Middle East were so inept as to think that, because one individual with the family name Smith committed adultery, all Smiths are therefore adulterers, so let us therefore lynch all the Smiths! There is not place for such syllogisms in the intelligence world; it is sloppy, inexcusable, and criminal. But the Service commits this error on a regular basis. People have been denied entry into Canada because of such behaviour—and it is an accepted practice: Intelligence officers openly talk about it at work, and will joke about "not being in a good mood" when they were reviewing an individual's file and therefore decided to recommend that his entry visa be denied. Again, this is hardly the type of reasoning Canadians would expect from the intelligence officers who are charged with protecting them, and hardly an argument in support of the belief that "CSIS knows best." Those misguided few who allow their "bad mood" to influence their decisions would not represent such a threat to Canadians were there a system in place, somewhere up the chain of command, to check their biases. But, as we have seen, the universal sloppiness that characterises the targeting process ensures that bad judgment will no be remedied before it starts affecting people's lives.

This assumption that CSIS knows best prevails both within the halls of the headquarters building in Ottawa and outside—even if at times CSIS has absolutely no information on a subject. Over time, I came to understand why certain agencies within the Canadian government are hesitant to deal with the Service; after all, sustained contempt can only generate reciprocal contempt. Internal memos stating that another agency should "go suck eggs" cannot but be reflective of an environment that brooks no opposition to its views. Left unchecked, misguided elitism leads to a siege mentality. The symptom becomes all the more obvious when, out of a constellation of agencies, a single one invariably disagrees with all the others. Either that agency is wrong most of the time, or, alternately, all the other agencies are. In either case, Canadians and immigrants hoping to start a new life in Canada should be worried.

Some of those agencies, such as Foreign Affairs, do provide information that, were it ever used by the Service, could be useful. But the contempt at CSIS for anything that does not consist of "pure" intelligence, as it understands it, runs deep. CSIS does this at its own detriment, for, as we have seen, one of its worst weaknesses lies in knowledge. This is the result, mostly, and beyond all the shortcomings discussed above, of CSIS having been intended as a Canada-centric intelligence service, one that operates and investigates *within* Canada. Initially, the organisation wasn't meant to look from the inside out, although the writing in the CSIS mandate is sufficiently open to interpretation as to allow for flexibility on that issue. Up until recently, CSIS would not admit that it engaged in the collection of information abroad, and recruits were often told during IOET to avoid discussing that issue with other people. This position, however, has changed recently, with its spokeswoman saying that "The CSIS Act allows us to collect security intelligence anywhere in the world, and we've always done so. But in the past few years, certainly, we've done that increasingly."[28]

Before Sept. 11, 2001, the institutional view was that threats occurred within Canada, and therefore the focus was, for the most part, inside the country's borders. But with Sept. 11 the perception of the threat has changed, and so has its origin. Within less than a day, someone from Southeast Asia can now be in Canada, or to paraphrase Stephen Gaghan, the director of the movie *Syriana*, one day I was shooting in Dubai; the next, I was sitting at the airport in Los Angeles. Furthermore, through hand-held devices, the Internet, and other modes of communication, information—plans, orders, etc—can now be transmitted instantaneously. All of this means that threats to Canada are no longer limited to individuals who are in Canada. Nowadays, with the exception of the occasional clash with Aborigines, white supremacists in Western Canada and the cyclical flare-up in hardcore Quebec separatism, threats to Canadian security are rarely the result of conflict within Canada.

Conflicts are exported the world over, and clashes are no longer local: they are, in potential reach (though not necessarily in nature, as we will see later), global. CSIS, which until 2001 remained an inward-looking organisation, remains ill-prepared to understand the changing realities of the twenty-first century. It is frighteningly thin on the ground, and oftentimes analysts at headquarters have to rely on the news (if they can be bothered) to know what is going on in another country. The Service is unable, at present, to generate its own reporting on the political situations in other countries. More than once I was required to prepare reports outlining the political situation in country X, as developments there could have an impact on a certain community in Canada. Despite my efforts, I could not find a single piece of Service reporting on that country. True, allied foreign agencies—agencies with a agents on the ground—were sharing some of their information, but usually the nature of the reporting spoke to the national requirements of that country rather than Canada's. I had no choice, therefore, but to turn to the news. We were totally blind, and the Service was not in a position to provide added value to Reuters, CNN, the BBC, and the other news organisations whose articles we mined. In other words, the Service was unable to fulfil its role as an organisation that augments what everybody can learn from the news with information of its own. Moreover, as we have noted, given the institutional aversion to non-classified material, this meant that even the little information we had at our disposal about that country was likely not being read.

A presence on the ground, on the other hand, would allow CSIS to better understand the culture, the history, and the religion of its potential opponents.

Many of the targets within Canada come from outside, either as immigrants or visitors. Their way of seeing the world, their moral codes, grievances and so on, are products of those societies. How can the Service hope to understand them—the motivation, the fears and aspirations behind the decision to use violence for political ends—if it does not know the first thing about their country of origin? The failure lies in the long-held belief that Canada, and to a certain extent North America, is an island. It took the trauma of Sept. 11, 2001, to make us realise that it no longer is, and perhaps never was. Additional funds alone, however, will not be sufficient to remedy the current lack of knowledge at the Service. If CSIS is to seriously begin collecting information abroad, a sea-change in how it trains its officers and treats information will be required. In the most optimistic scenarios, it will take years before the institution becomes capable of making those principles a *modus vivendi*.

In the short term, and while the debate in Ottawa rages on as to which agency is best suited to accomplish the difficult task of collecting intelligence abroad, CSIS could fill the knowledge gap by accepting that other Canadian agencies are present on the ground and may be able to help. The Department of Foreign Affairs, the Canadian International Development Agency (CIDA) and National Defence all have personnel deployed in other countries. Their officers have a better chance of understanding the reality on the ground, for instead of sitting in an office in Ottawa, they are there, in situ. Moreover, many of them have received language training or lived in foreign countries long enough to get a better understanding of the situation. It is one thing to get the story from the news or on FBIS, the FBI's foreign news gathering system; it is quite another to live it, to be immersed in it, and to assess it from a Canadian perspective. As long as the various agencies that comprise the larger Canadian intelligence community refuse to talk to each other and fail to understand that despite the institutional differences they are all serving the same purpose, the community as a whole, as well as the individual parts, will remain half blind.

For the moment, CSIS collection of information abroad is accomplished through its own interpretation of the mandate. The debate on which agency should *legally* be responsible for collecting intelligence abroad has been going on for a long time and was reinvigorated after 2001. CSIS claims it already has the know-how to achieve this, and that all that it requires before it can commence operations are (hold your breath) more funds, and more employees. The Department of Foreign Affairs, on the other hand, argues it already has the architecture and the global footprint to accomplish this task. Furthermore, it has history on its side, and before CSIS even existed Foreign Affairs (back then known as External

Affairs) was doing that the world over. In fact, evidence has emerged that in the 1960s and 1970s, the Canadian embassy in Havana, Cuba, was gathering intelligence about the regime for the US, with the full support of Ottawa.[29]

CSIS, for its part, is already struggling with its domestic intelligence collection, and its presence abroad is limited. Its intelligence officers are not ready, let alone trained, for deployment overseas. Furthermore, for CSIS to accomplish the task of intelligence collection in foreign countries, a substantial investment of time will be required for the implementation of a chain of command, the training of officers, language acquisition and other aspects, meaning that the Service would only be able to begin actual collection of intelligence abroad five to seven years from now. According to the Canadian Press, an internal blueprint for plans to increase CSIS activities abroad was delivered to the Director in December 2005.[30] Given that during the elections campaign Conservative leader and now Prime Minister Stephen Harper had promised to expand the collection of intelligence overseas, the management at CSIS must have seen this as an opportunity to increase its operational budget. Indeed, in order to achieve this, the blueprint task force asked for a fresh injection of resources, which shows us, once again, that the top echelons at CSIS are unable to think other than in quantitative terms. Absent, therefore, is serious discussion on how it should proceed or a re-evaluation of the manner in which CSIS trains its officers in preparation for deployment abroad.

Meanwhile, other voices within the Canadian government have called for the creation of another agency, one that, like the CIA, would only focus on matters outside Canada. The jury is still out as to which approach would provide the best reporting on foreign matters, but the creation of an entirely new agency would require a lot of time and investment and would only add another layer to an already complex system of agencies. Furthermore, a new service would likely result in a brain drain from existing agencies, including CSIS.

When it comes to deployment abroad, an intelligence service must treat with caution, as lack of preparation could have deadly consequences for an intelligence officer who is sent to a war zone or an unstable country—which, unsurprisingly, is where the requirement for intelligence collection is most pressing. To name a few, deployments would be in countries like Afghanistan, Iraq, Iran, Lebanon, Saudi Arabia, Uzbekistan, Pakistan, Colombia, the Democratic Republic of the Congo, Sudan, Somalia, Haiti. Errors in judgment or commission by an intelligence officer who has not received the appropriate training for the mission could have dire ramifications for the officer himself and could even result in a diplomatic incident. Given the Service's current modus operandi, if it were to engage in activities of this nature today, dangerous blunders would certainly be committed. What this all means, therefore, is that in light of the possible consequences of error, there is no room for the kind of amateurish operations that CSIS is only capable of mounting at the moment.

In the interim, Foreign Affairs could accomplish foreign collection with the least amount of federal money. It already has a presence all over the world, and has a history of providing intelligence on other countries. Its reciprocal disdain for CSIS, however, could make information sharing difficult.

A consequence of the way intelligence officers are forced to think—or not to think, that is—is that absent a full understanding of a conflict, or of a case, and absent the intellectual effort to reach one's own conclusions about a case, the Service will have great difficulty making forecasts, which in the end is the very *raison d'être* of intelligence services. Over time, desk officers who are beaten into recycling information will shut down mentally, and such a shutdown means that bits of information will be missed, and precious clues will slip through the cracks. There is also very little place for imagination at CSIS; scenarios are dismissed. Events are treated in a vacuum, and little thought is given to what the consequences of doing something might me. Will the target attempt to flee? Stop his activities and go underground? Retaliate? The Service acts when it does, but often fails to look over the horizon. In other words, it is not very good at forecasting the consequences of its actions, as if the individuals or organisations targeted were like characters in an ancient video game that act independently of the player's actions. No action-reaction.

This results in a very reactive intelligence service, one that chases after events rather than sees them coming. What this means is that the unit that is responsible for providing threat assessments will provide a report *after* a bombing has occurred, *after* is has been reported on CNN and in the press. In fact, whenever something happens somewhere in the world, the entire CSIS building comes to a full stop and everybody crams into those offices that are equipped with a TV set. Who needs an expensive intelligence service if all we need is a television set, the *Globe and Mail*, or a link to the Internet? Why should we want an intelligence service that recycles news material while providing very little in value-added assessment? True, there is much to be done in terms of investigation after a terrorist incident has taken place. But this is mostly the remit of law enforcement, not that of the intelligence apparatus, whose mandate is to warn of possible threats *before* they occur—in other words, to protect Canada rather than explain to them, post facto, who did what and how. There is something quite illogical to naming a document a "threat assessment" *after* an event has occurred. And yet, this is the kind of advice that CSIS provides, on a daily basis, to the rest of the Canadian government. In all fairness, one cannot expect an intelligence service to *predict* events, for in the realm of human behaviour there is no such thing as prediction. However, what every taxpaying citizen in the country has a right to expect from its spooks is that they be allowed to do some thinking and that they keep their eyes, ears, and brains open. As things stand, most officers are busy with either the very present, or the past. (I remember, to give just one example, spending weeks working on something that had happened *nine* years earlier.) The future is a concept that simply does not exist. What's more, trying to conceive of possible futures—scenario playing, something the military does on a frequent basis—appears to be too much of an intellectual effort. As with dissent and difference of opinion, those intelligence officers who, out of a sense of duty, try to come up with possible scenarios, were it only for discussion, for the intellectual exercise, are patted condescendingly on the head and told to stop wasting their, and other people's, time.

Exacerbating the tremendous deficiency in the Service's system of learning is the stove-piping phenomenon, whereby information is not shared between units, desks, and individuals. The "need to know" principle, as it is known, is a very powerful force within the intelligence community. It occurs between agencies—CSIS is loath to share its information with the RCMP, or Foreign Affairs—and it also occurs within the Service. From the onset, intelligence officers are told to guard their information with their lives. File cabinets must be locked upon leaving the office. One should avoid leaving Top Secret documents on his desk when he leaves his office for lunch. In certain cases, the principle is even active *within* the unit, leaving officers on an investigation wondering what is happening in another section of the same investigation. (I was once asked by my supervisor to be on standby to prepare an overview of the political situation in a certain Middle Eastern country once part of the investigation to which I did not have access had reached a certain point. Weeks later, when I asked an analyst who was privy to the leg of the investigation I was excluded from if she knew when I would be expected to prepare my overview, she told me that the operation had taken place days earlier and that my overview was no longer necessary. Most shocking was the fact that she and I shared the same two-desk office.)

The "need to know" can be taken to certain extremes. Analysts who run into each other in the elevator will immediately press whatever document they are holding against their chest, or slide it into a folder, lest prying eyes catch a glimpse of the information they contain. Over time, this type of behaviour gives intelligence officers the impression that they are not really part of a team, as if the objective—protecting Canadians—were not a common one.

Why such secrecy? Ultimately, the "need to know" principle is self-defeating and further weakens institutional learning, for even if the subjects of investigation differ from one desk to the next, lessons learned are usually similar. If desks are not allowed to discuss these matters among themselves, how is the information on tradecraft to be distributed? What if a desk attempted something new, something that worked well? Shouldn't other desks be told something about the tactic? Conversely, should not other desks be informed of a methodology that failed or endangered the life of an officer, blew a source, or exposed the Service's interest? Overprotection of information goes counter to the open system of the 21st century. What gives the Internet its immense power is the sharing of open code, of information. In other words, it allows for a plurality of ideas. As Will Hutton explains:

> Pluralism ... improves the quality of deliberative decision-making; as a process it also provides crucial safeguards for the whole system by offering insurance against mistakes, Decisions are made in a context of uncertainty, fallibility and complexity, which grows more uncertain and unpredictable when consequences depend on events in the distant future. Some decisions have nearly immediate consequences, other may take years to prove their worth, but decisions all require delicate judgments about whether the supporting conditions will hold, or whether or how the world might change to alter them. The value of plural decision-making ... is that although one individual decision is almost certain to be wrong, one decision among a multiplicity is likely to produce the right answer.[31]

How can an organisation evolve if it goes in the opposite direction and instructs its employees to hold on to their secrets with a dedication bordering on paranoia, in a manner that is reminiscent of the closed system of totalitarianism?

The protection of information within the Service goes even further: It smothers the self-criticism, at both the personal and institutional level, that would allow officers to learn from each other. During training, a few people in my class asked the inevitable questions about John Farrell, the former CSIS employee on whose whistle blowing account Andrew Mitrovica's book *Covert Entry* is based. Some also asked about former intelligence officers who had left the Service and were now making public criticisms of CSIS in the media. In every instance, such questions were met with disdain by our trainers or whoever was giving the presentation that day, and we were promptly made to understand that these issues had better be left alone. Pejorative references were made; whoever had quit or been critical of CSIS was either an opportunist or an "asshole." Questions relating to blunders, allegations of malpractice and so on also backfired. Even if we could learn useful information from past mistakes so that we could avoid repeating them, it soon became obvious that is was in our interest not to ask. So we stopped asking. (I wouldn't be surprised if future intelligence officers asking questions about this book were served the same dose of dismissal.)

Attendant to this stove-piping phenomenon is the elitism that inspires intelligence officers. From the very beginning, they are told that the entire Service gravitates around them, that every employee of the Service is supporting staff for the hundreds of intelligence officers who comprise the overall workforce. While this serves to reinforce egos, it also exacerbates the sense of isolation. There are certain non-intelligence officer sections, such as communications intercept, that play a crucial role in investigations. In spite of this, intelligence officers know very little about this part of CSIS. Ironically, a major complaint coming from that section is that intelligence officers do not consult them often enough, or at all. There is a strong desire on the part of communications analysts to share their knowledge—after all, who knows the most about a target's daily life and routine than the people whose job it is to listen in on their conversations?—but that desire, unfortunately, is not reciprocal. In fact, their calls are often not returned. For some reason, intelligence officers seem to be under the impression that intercepts, and the reports that are based on them, appear out of nowhere. Once, while I was drafting an affidavit, I was strictly forbidden from contacting communications specialists in a region for information that I needed. Even if those people were by far the best placed within the entire organisation to provide me with what I needed, I was instructed to search for fish in the ocean, without knowing which species of fish to look for, and without knowing which ocean to drop the line in. Obviously, what I came up with was nowhere near what the communications analysts could have given me—and far more quickly.

A slight variation upon the "need to know" principle is the military-like approach to communication that exists among CSIS officers. As it is a very hierarchical organisation, this tends to create various strata that over time congeal into a fixed structure. One repercussion of this is that communication occurs on different levels simultaneously—in other words, horizontally. Certain supervisors regard this hierarchical system as if it were a religion, and consequently subscribe to the belief that only officers of equivalent levels are allowed to speak directly to each other. Put differently, a new intelligence officer would not, for example, be allowed to communicate directly with a supervisor in a region. Very often, this leads to voicemails or e-mails wasting away in a supervisor's in-box for days, if not weeks, before he or she opens it and transfers it to his or her counterpart. As a result, timely, perishable information becomes obsolete due to the inherent slowness of such a system.

Practitioners of the intelligence trade hold the firm belief, as we have seen, that the higher the classification, the better—or "sexier"—the information. The consequence of this system-wide belief, however, is that a great number of individuals need the proper security clearance to access information. At CSIS, no intelligence officer could do his job without at least a Top Secret clearance. Given that the allocation of a classification level for a piece of information is sometimes random, and that there is not community-wide standard on how information is classified, Top Secret for CSIS does not necessarily mean the same thing as Top Secret for an allied agency, or another branch of the Canadian government. I have seen replies to "trace checks" (when a service asks another agency for information on an individual) come back to us, classified Top Secret, in which the only piece of information was "we don't know." How can a negative response be Top Secret, especially when the initial document, our trace request, was only classified Secret? Since not everybody has access to Top Secret information (e.g., non intelligence officers, employees in other branches of government), some people within the Service could not read the document, stored in the gigantic electronic database, that said "we don't know." Moreover, Top Secret documents are often given an "eyes-only" distribution list, meaning that only individuals whose name appears on that list are able to access it, regardless of whether they have the appropriate clearance or not. We can all imagine what happens when, years down the road and following a few rotations, new investigators, or a new supervisor whose names obviously do not appear on that "eyes-only" list, attempt to access the report. No one will be able to find out that the reply to the trace request was "we don't know." This can only result in a waste of time as analysts will either need to find a way to access the information or, as is more likely, make a new request to the agency that provided the information in the first place.

The problem of over-classification of information runs deeper and encounters further problems once the information needs to be shared among Canadian agencies. At CSIS, the standard, rule-of-thumb classification is Secret. Everything is Secret. Most items, however, do not warrant such a classification, and if an officer were to dig enough, nine times out of ten similar information could be found at a lower classification, or with no classification at all. But there is the belief, as we have noted, that if information is not at least Secret, it doesn't deserve to be read. So documents are made Secret, even if it is nothing more than a euphemism for "please read." As long as the information remains within CSIS, this is no a problem, as all intelligence officers have clearance for Top Secret-level information. But not all other agencies do. In fact, first-line responders, such as law enforcement or customs officers, do not have Secret-level clearances and even use an entirely different system of security clearance. How, then, can CSIS share information if the people who need to know the information cannot access it? How can a police officer in Montreal know what to look for when he is not allowed to see the information that led CSIS to contact Montreal police in the first place? Admittedly there are, in certain areas, liaison and exchange officers who can act as a bridge between services and who will filter the information in a way that allows individuals who do not have high enough a security clearance to nevertheless receive the information they need. But this is time consuming, ad hoc, and in emergency situations requiring immediate action—a bomb is about to explode—this could be quite problematic.

Other Canadian agencies impose even higher classification levels on their information. This creates incessant headaches at CSIS, in that the information coming from another agency is of such classification that it cannot be used. If that information is to be usable (to be included in a Federal Court Affidavit, for example), the Service needs to apply for "sanitisation," a lengthy and increasingly complex process of removal of certain elements of information which can take up to a few weeks. This is not to say that some information, or sources of information, should not be protected. But this demonstrates how the numerous layers of classification, added to the different security clearances attributed to the vast number of people who comprise the intelligence community, can lead to problems and slow down the process of distribution to a grinding halt.

But officers and agencies do not simply over-classify for the sake of over-classifying, nor do they do this only to ensure that their reports will be treated seriously. Ultimately, as Chalmers Johnson writes, "Agencies classify things in order to protect themselves from ... scrutiny or from political or bureaucratic rivals elsewhere within the government."[32] Secrecy is protection. It prevents, as Daniel Ellsberg cynically writes in his excellent book *Secrets*, "uninformed (uncleared), shortsighted, and parochial individuals and institutions [from intervening] in matters that were too complicated for them to understand, and to muck them up."[33] As we shall discuss later, high classification is part of a system that shields CSIS and other services from public scrutiny, which comes in very handy when errors had better not be made public or when it is not in the government's interest for the public to know of certain things it is doing in their name, things that perhaps should never be permitted in a democratic society.

CSIS is far too tolerant of incompetence, which again makes secrecy such an important tool. Like any big organisation, it is a lumbering beast, slow to react, and its operations are heavy on the paper and overwhelmingly time consuming. Officers spend a substantial share of their time uploading reports, writing bulletin notes, and preparing altogether useless and painfully insipid replies to a series of documents coming in from the regions or from allied agencies. These tasks are excruciatingly mind numbing. Thus burdened, intelligence officers will slowly become de-motivated; their attention to detail will invariably suffer, and a sense of carelessness slowly installs itself. So much energy is spent on the process that aside for becoming mere robots in a long chain of data-processing, analysts lose sight of that which they were hired for in the first place: to do analysis.

Mediocrity spreads. If it is not treated swiftly, if it is not perceived as a threat to the system, it replicates. For someone to be fired from the Service, he or she needs to commit something akin to treason. Incompetence, laziness, even alcoholism, are not only rampant, but are also nearly accepted types of behaviour. Problem employees, rather than being selected out like in the normal world, are shunted aside or moved to another desk or region, where they will become a nuisance to another group of employees.

Can we, therefore, as citizens of a liberal democracy, trust CSIS to legitimately use the vast powers of intrusion it has been bestowed? Can we safely assume that CSIS does its homework effectively and honestly before it starts intruding into people's lives? There is too much information to process, combined with too much politics, paperwork, and institutional weight, compounded by too much incompetence and aversion to dissent, for the process to be an efficient one. And given that the targeted individuals are seen in Manichean terms—that is, in black and white—the institution is incapable of processing the nuances, the grey areas of human behaviour, that are necessary to make a complete assessment. Consequently, as a result of the long chain of imperfect systems, from the initial targeting to the approval in committee, individuals will be targeted who should not. The expression *fog of war* is used to describe the imperfect vision of decision-makers in wartime. Given the incomplete picture that intelligence officers have, added to the numerous levels of approval that exist under the current system, we could argue that there is a similar phenomenon at work in the world of intelligence. We could call this phenomenon the *fog of intelligence*.

In light of this fog, of the complete incapacity to see the full picture, belief takes on a special value. The work, therefore, gains the quality of the religious. The gathering of intelligence and, after years of building a case, the possibility that the conclusions may have law-enforcement implications requires faith, a belief in the cause and in the fact that years of effort will avail to something. This world also shares common traits with the grand, sweeping ideologies, whether they be Communism, Capitalism, and now, Freedom, that have defined history.[34] Cognisant of this or not, by joining the game, the intelligence officer chooses an ideological position, or what is akin to a religion. One cannot doubt the truthfulness of the religion; when one does, he gradually begins to feel like an outcast—and we know what this environment does to outcasts: the sense of belonging, so important to this kind of work and constantly reinforced by management, evaporates. Like religion, the intelligence community forbids one to look too deeply into the sacred texts or to question the overarching ideology. To hint at altering this view is nothing short of blasphemous. One is therefore compelled to put blind faith before intellectual inquiry. As we saw earlier, the Knowledge is handed to the officer upon commencement of his work. This Knowledge is biblical.

Rather than having a healthy dose of agnostics—people who believe in the cause but who nevertheless manage to maintain a certain level of scepticism—the world of intelligence expects nothing less than abject gullibility from its practitioners. This, of course, is contrary to the way people should think about terrorism and security in the 21st century. In fact, during a speech in 2004, Canada's then-deputy prime minister Anne McClelland emphasised the need for self-criticism when she stated that "we must continuously review our plans, update our systems and test our people."[35] There lies the paradox: intelligence officers are supposed to be free, critical thinkers, with a mild sense of paranoia. How can an organisation expect its employees to abandon all forms of criticism when these same individuals are simultaneously expected to be paranoid? Isn't paranoia a belief that something out there is not altogether right, suspicious?

The manner in which CSIS deals with this paradox is to redirect the paranoia. By forcing paranoia out of the internal system and re-channelling it outwards, an island is created whose inhabitants are the Truth, the all-knowing, while everything that lies outside—in other words, the rest of the world—is wrong, to be doubted, unwholesome. This inevitably leads to an institutional descent into racism, to which we now turn, as it plays an important role in security intelligence.

How the phenomenon of racism influences the behaviour of intelligence services cannot be emphasised enough. Whether by design or accident, the CSIS view of the world is a racist one. CSIS is an organisation made of individuals whose sense of morality and responsibility has been dimmed. The organisation changes its officers in other ways, too, and the results are no less troubling. It actually alters how intelligence officers view people around them, and makes them *assume* that everybody they encounter, especially members of certain ethnic groups who believe in a certain religion, are threatening. Sunni Arabs (or, increasingly, Shiites, as the Middle East realigns itself, with the predominantly Shiite Iran emerging as the new alleged threat to international security), have a major handicap, one that comes close to that of the black-skinned people in Orwell's *Burmese Days*. After enough exposure to the institution and the paranoia that it encourages in its employees, the individual in turn feels under siege: The enemy is out there, lurking, plotting, and under various guises he will come at you.

These views are encouraged by claims such as the one made by the Director of Operations in spring 2006 that generations of Muslims who were born and grew up in Canada were increasingly becoming radicalised. They look like us, talk like us and behave like us, the DO said, but deep inside they have a hatred for who we are. Repeated often enough, this view of the world becomes a law within the organisation, a page taken out of the security intelligence bible. Over time, everybody believes it—even the great majority of officers who, because of the "need to know" principle, have no access to the intelligence that would allow them to determine for themselves whether individual X indeed poses a threat or not. It is common for an analyst on a desk dealing with Northeast Asia, for example, to parrot the claims made by individuals on a Middle East desk, even if the former has no access to the information. Paranoia and racism become an article of faith, and as with everything else, those who fail to sing to the tune at mass face a formidable battle.

Unusual clicks on the phone, letters coming in the mail with a corner torn off, people inquiring about your line of work, the recent Iraqi immigrant who moved next door with his veiled wife, holes in the walls—everything is now a potential threat to your person, and to your organisation. Girding all this is the insidious reality of racism: The same question asked by a Caucasian and an Arab will elicit different reactions. In the former instance, it is simply misplaced curiosity; in the latter, it is a threat.

I was shocked when, during a weekly desk meeting, our supervisor informed the unit that a week earlier, an intelligence officer from another desk had been approached in an amusement park by three veiled women who, after starting a discussion with her, had apparently attempted to "convert" her to Islam. Internal security had been advised, and it was decided, with no small amount of alarm, that the intelligence officer could have been the target of extremists or terrorists (the two terms, though they mean different things, are often used interchangeably). History is replete with instances of people attempting to convert other people to their religion. The Catholic Church has done this for centuries, often through the use of force. Jews and Jehovah's Witnesses do this routinely as well. But somehow the fact that Muslims were engaging in the same type of activity represented a threat. In a way, this kind of reaction is similar to that experienced by people sitting in an airplane that is about to take off and who will become alarmed upon seeing that the person sitting next to them is nervously flipping through the pages of the Koran. Hand that person a bible, or a paperback novel, for that matter, and his behaviour will be ignored, the nervousness a perfectly normal reaction to people's fear of flying. Give him (or her) a Koran, however, and immediately people will react differently. It would be invidious to blame the general public too harshly for reacting in such a manner, for since Sept. 11, 2001, through the news and the discourse of many politicians, people have been conditioned to react this way, to fear the "other." But for an intelligence service to go to the extent of informing Internal Security—in other words, to institutionalize the reaction—is something else altogether. By encouraging this behaviour, and in fact making it an employee's responsibility to report contact with people from a specific ethnic background or religious belief, the Service makes racists out of its employees, or exacerbates the racism streak that already exists in some.

As George Orwell presciently wrote in *Burmese Days*: "When a man has a black face, suspicion *is* proof."

The use of language also leaves little doubt that since Sept. 11, 2001, racism and xenophobia have crept into the intelligence community. What is worse is that they seem to have become acceptable. As Kent Roach notes in his book *September 11: Consequences for Canada*: "although no manifesto explaining the rationale for the events of September 11 has been issued and there is evidence that the terrorists did not live their lives in America as devout Muslims, it is widely believed that their suicide mission was motivated by what is commonly called *Islamic fanaticism* [my italics]."[36] As we shall see in Chapter 2, Roach is wrong when he claims that no manifesto for the Sept. 11, 2001, attacks has ever been issued, for there is in fact one, and it was very clearly stated. Nevertheless, his comment is useful in that it demonstrates the frequent wedding of two concepts, Islam and "fanaticism," that results from a failure to think of conflict in terms other than ethnicity and religion (a similar failure, for example, marked the great majority of reporting on so-called "ethnic" conflict in Africa and the Balkans during the 1990s, which though it made the storytelling understandable to the general audience, hid the many other proximate causes that led to war). Hence the unit names, such as Sunni Islamic Terrorism and Shiite Extremism, that one encounters at CSIS. Concepts are put into boxes, and at the unconscious level analysts make the connection between "Islamic" and all the isms that have a negative connotation. But terrorism is terrorism, no matter what motivation lies behind the act. If terrorism were something more than what it is in reality—a technique—then intelligence services would have desks like "Jewish terrorism," and "Animist terrorism" or even, as many would argue, "Freedom terrorism." Admittedly, there are more terrorist attacks coming out of the Middle East, Central Asia and Southeast Asia nowadays than in, say, Latin America, Northeast Asia, or Western Europe. But to hint at a correlation between Islam as a religion and terrorism, that there is some intrinsic proclivity to violence, to terror, in Islam is a dangerous fallacy, dangerous in that through repeated exposure one risks equating one with the other.[37] Since, for the sake of organisational charts, everything has to be put in a box, there is nothing wrong with using geography, or the type of conflict, to describe what an operational unit is investigating. It would be much preferable to see a desk named "al-Qaeda Unit," "Middle East," "Afghanistan" or "Saudi Arabia," than Sunni Extremism. Furthermore, as there are Sunnis all over the world, we cannot expect an analyst to fully comprehend and keep track of the Sunni experience in, say, Indonesia and Iraq. A "Sunni" desk, in principle, would have to look at these two countries, among others, simultaneously, but through different lenses, which would strain even the most dedicated of intelligence officers.

In all fairness to the Service, there are indications that it is moving in the direction of geography-based investigations—at least nominally. But it will take years before a shift occurs in thinking, if one occurs at all, and the renaming of boxes in the organisational chart alone will not suffice.

A racist view of the world carries another danger. It lies in the moral flexibility that the dehumanisation of the "other" gives to the organisation. What will motivate democracies to enforce the ban on torture if we fail to see the opponent, the "other," as a human being worthy of the same rights as we? This is reminiscent of the Nazi Germans debating how to deal with the Jewish "problem" by saying that German Jews, though they need to be exterminated, are much more intelligent than Polish Jews, or Czech Jews. Put people into categories, use, as we have seen, terms such as "cockroaches" or "cancer" to describe them, and very soon it becomes easier to do things that no one in his right mind would ever conceive of doing to the rest of humanity.

Racism works in subtle ways, and if we are to stick with the question of torture for a moment, we can see it at play in the discourse, mostly on the right of the political spectrum, that terrorists cannot be protected by international law because their chosen course of action makes them bandits. The debate on the permissibility of torture harkens back to the pre-Vatican II Catholic school dilemma of the "lesser of two evils" argument, and many people have used it to justify the treatment of "non combatant" prisoners in Guantanamo Bay, Cuba, a treatment whose very legality is now, at last, being challenged. The argument is a luring one, but it threatens to lead to moral slide: where do we draw the line? Will only *known* terrorists be subject to torture? What about suspected terrorists? Supporters? This course of action is also contingent on how we define terrorism. After all, as has been argued many times before, one's freedom fighter is another's terrorist. As such, if the definition of terrorism were limited to the *technique*, then perhaps we would have less reasons to be worried. But in a world where terrorism has become coterminous with "Arab" or "Muslim," the moral slide is all the more worrying.

There is no indication that CSIS has engaged in the torture of suspected terrorists, nor has the O'Connor Commission looking into the Maher Arar case found any connection between CSIS and the role the Canadian government played in his being deported to Syria, where he was allegedly tortured. But the Service's racism-based, dehumanising view of the world would provide little protection against its committing actions that could result in the torturing of a suspected individual. In fact, if it believed it could get away with it, in extreme cases we can assume that it would. Which raises the all-too-important issue of oversight and accountability, to which we will return later.

What the concept of torture illustrates is that it is always easier to treat another human being with inhumanity when the latter is seen as less than human. So is the targeting of a suspected individual and all the ramifications that such an operation will have on him and his relatives. Given, as we have seen, the language used by CSIS personnel to describe their targets, along with the numerous allusions to "cancer," "vermin," and "disease" used by heads of state and certain media outlets in reference to certain groups, it is easy to understand why for many, al-Qaeda and those who subscribe to a similar ideology are perceived as less than human.

Whether a state practices torture or limits itself to intrusive investigation, there is always a chance that an individual will be mistakenly suspected of having engaged in activities that can be defined as terrorism or are in support thereof, the latter now being sufficient in Canada to target an individual. What if the assessment made about that individual is erroneous? What does it say about a society if it not only condones the use of torture against suspected criminals but also allows for the torture of individuals who are blameless? In some people's opinion, the type of confinement that the suspects who are currently held under the Security Certificates borders on torture. The pith of the argument is this: The more a society slides toward a radical approach to treating a suspected group of individuals, the more likely it will give itself permissions. The more permissions we give as a society, the likelier it is that individuals will be subjected to injustice. If Western societies have reached a point where it is even acceptable to debate whether torture should be allowed or not, then they may already have become too radicalised. What this means is that even societies like Canada, where the choice not to use torture was made long ago, have undergone a shift in attitude. There is no doubt that since Sept. 11, 2001, Canada has done just that: Its targeting of individuals has become more aggressive, and the threshold for targeting has been substantially lowered. A racism-based view of the world—from within society all the way to the upper echelons of government—has made this possible.

Recently, in its public relations campaign to improve the image of the Service—especially with the Canadian Muslim community—high-ranking employees at CSIS, including its current director, sat down with Muslim community leaders in order to appease their fears that Muslims are the target of racial profiling in Canada (attacks upon mosques and community leaders, as occurred in June 2006, would certainly help to inspire that sense of siege). While these efforts, if they indeed represent a desire to engage in honest discussion with representatives of the Muslim faith, are commendable, they still fail to address the real issue of racism, which lies with Service employees. Nothing that the CSIS director can discuss with Imams and Sheikhs will change the fact that racism is now part of the fabric of intelligence officers. It is programmed into them, and by dint of repetition, the racist view becomes something of a reflex. And it works in subtle ways. The progression usually goes as follows: Initially, only the designated targets are seen as "scumbags." Over time, whoever the targets associate with, their friends, family, come to be seen under that light, until all have become "scumbags." Not only is this guilt by association, it is also dehumanisation by association. This, ultimately, is how it becomes easier to destroy an individual's life while knowing that doing so will also have immediate consequences for that person's relatives. Friends and family members, by dint of association with the target, start appearing in reports, their names are repeated from one report to another until, for the sheer number of times the name is repeated (and shared with allied agencies), that person has virtually become a target, if not a real one. Once the unit, the ethnic or religious group, is made less than human, one's moral qualms about affecting the lives of a large group of people are invariably diminished.

Attendant to a racist view of the world, a spirit of tribalism exists within the halls of the Service. It is "us" against "them" or, to put it in racial terms, it is mostly "white" against "non-white." Tribalism in the campaign against terrorism is by no means less archaic or unacceptable than it is in the many war-torn regions of the world where, using ethnicity to explain wars, we shake our heads at how "backwards" these people are. As with racism, the tribal-based view of the world allows individuals who share certain traits to dehumanise the other and to treat him with far less respect and compassion than they would their kin. Over time, as Muslims feel singled out and as their institutions are vandalized, this can lead to the destruction of the ties that have made the Canadian experiment in multiculturalism a largely successful one. But this success is now at risk. As author Salman Rushdie noted in an article: "If people do not feel included in the national idea, their alienation will turn to rage."[38] If we maintain the spirit of tribalism that seems to have caught the imagination of many in the West, there is no guarantee that Canada will not suffer the same kind of riots that struck France and Australia in late 2005. This is not to say that Canada must blindly tolerate every type of imported behaviour in the name of multiculturalism. After all, a state is an evolving project and as a society we must make choices on what we deem acceptable and what should be abandoned at our shores. But at the same time we cannot expect members of a visible minority to feel that they are less part of the project because of their origin, religion, or the colour of their skin. Sadly, in light of recent events in Toronto and elsewhere, some Canadian Muslims could be excused for starting to feel that Canada is not the welcoming place they imagined it would be.

Sometime in 2004, a scholar from a certain religious group was invited to give a presentation to intelligence officers to explain to them what Islam stands for and what it means in the twenty-first century. Standing at the lectern, his first reaction upon looking at the audience was how few visible minorities there were. And he was right. The Service is still very much a white, Anglo-Saxon organisation with precious few representatives of the multitude of ethnic groups that comprise the fabric of Canadian society (according to the CSIS Public Report 2004-2005, 8.2% of the organisation's intelligence officers identified themselves as belonging to a visible minority). This is shameful. Knowing that the great majority of the targeted individuals in Canada fall within the visible minority category, having less than one intelligence officer out of ten issuing from a visible minority is not enough. Moreover, out of those, even less are Muslim. This is no coincidence. The Service (as do other agencies) justifies this by claiming that Muslims and Middle Easterners in general are "more difficult" to screen, and that their reliability and patriotism are more difficult to assess, than that of "ordinary" Canadians. This even applies to generations of Canadians born to immigrant parents, as if they, too, were somehow genetically tainted by their origins and that despite the fact that they were born in Canada, their allegiance would nevertheless lie with a country that, in many instances, they will never have visited, let alone associated with its culture.

Not only is this practice indicative of the racism that is inherent to our intelligence service, it also denies the Service a much-needed source of knowledge—cultural, linguistic, religious—that it can ill afford to do without. By hiring more employees who come from different ethnic and religious backgrounds, the Service could mitigate the negative effects of the lack of worldly education and travel that its current workforce suffers from (not to mention the quasi-total lack of interest in foreign movies, literature, and music, from which intelligence officers could gain an understanding of other cultures). But so far there is no indication that it intends to do so, or that it has realised the importance of putting together a workforce that is truly representative of the rich cultural fabric of our country. Otherwise, how could the Public Report vaunt that 8.2%, in a diverse society like Canada, constitutes "a diverse workforce that is increasingly representative of Canadian society"?

How can we expect a white, English-speaking-only intelligence officer driving a Ford Taurus, to avoid drawing attention to himself when he drives into an Arab community in northern Toronto, or a North African neighbourhood in Montreal? Not only will that officer stand out like a sore thumb, he will also be ill-equipped to deal with the different culture, languages, and mores that are at the heart of that community. How will he or she manage to obtain the information the Service sent him to collect? The best intelligence officer in the world, with years of experience, training, and a steeled dedication to the cause, would still fail, despite the best of intentions, to open doors in such an environment. Not to say anything about the danger that standing out like this represents to officers as they go around knocking on doors. Everybody recognises this—except CSIS. Not only does this represent a futile, almost Quixotic exercise, but furthermore it irresponsibly puts unnecessary pressure on intelligence officers, and in some occasions puts them at risk.

Canadians should hope that the white, elite mentality that governs the selection of new intelligence officers would be revised. Recent trends, unfortunately, are less than encouraging. Out of the 16 individuals who made up the last class of recruits before my resignation, not one spoke French as his first language. Only two were of a different ethnic background, and only three spoke languages other than French or English. In my class, only one person came from a different ethnic group, and very few spoke other languages. Given the Service's post-Cold War reorientation toward terrorism from the Middle East and Northern Africa, it is hard to explain why there has not been a similar adjustment in terms of the kind of people it hires. Does it really believe that Canada-born English or French speakers will pick up the complexities of the Arab language, or Farsi, or Pashto, or that it can avoid tapping into the rich pool of Canadians who speak those languages fluently? Why ignore them? And why, finally, will the Service refuse to pay for an intelligence officer who wishes to learn Spanish—a language that nearly half of the American continent speaks as its first language, including large sections of the US—arguing that she should learn Arabic instead? It is myopic to focus on the Middle East only, and the refusal to invest in an employee's language skills is short sighted. After all, wouldn't we all be better served if ten, fifteen years ago, CSIS had had the foresight to start training officers in Middle Eastern languages, when the "in" thing was learning Russian? Who is to say where the next hot spot will be? Wouldn't we want to have more Spanish speakers if, ten years from now, Colombia, say, or Venezuela, were to become sources of global threats? Or Mandarin speakers, if the US, mostly of its own doing, continues on its collision-course with China?

Like surgeons, law enforcement officers and prison guards, intelligence officers must create an emotional distance from their subjects if they are to remain sane. To take everything personally would lead to certain demise by paranoia, or depression. After all, the job of intelligence officers, especially those who are working in counterterrorism, is to monitor and hopefully lead to the arrest of groups and individuals whose intention it is to kill people. There is nothing uplifting about the motivations of terrorists or, when they are successful, to the results of their actions. In order to protect themselves, intelligence officers therefore distance themselves from the subject. As we saw earlier, this is also a means by which to dehumanise the opponent and to avoid feeling empathy for people against whom one is conducting an aggressive operation. This in fact leads to a feedback loop: The more distance or detachment one creates, the more dehumanised the opponent becomes; the more dehumanised he gets, the more distance is created. As William Nolte, the Deputy Assistant Director of Central Intelligence for Analysis and Production, observed:

> the reality is that most American intelligence professionals deal in analysis or technical collection, not in the "up close and personal" world of HUMINT collection or prisoner interrogation. Back at the far end of the collection process, many of us could, even up to the recent past, feel that we were comfortably removed from the manipulation of assets or the direct application of lethal force. In some respects, the analogy is that of killing in combat with a bayonet versus dropping ordnance from 30,000 feet: The effect may be the same, but with a decent interval attached.[39]

The problem is that oftentimes the emotional distance becomes too great, and this is partly the result of the lack of education and world experience that characterises intelligence officers new and old. Seated in a windowless office at the headquarters building in Ottawa, it is very difficult for intelligence officers to feel threatened. Moreover, as many of them have never travelled, they have no emotional attachment to some of the countries where the realities of war and terrorism are part of the daily lives of people. As the current workforce is mainly white North America born, the affinities and links with other ethnic and religious groups are almost inexistent. This, therefore, results in detachment whenever something goes wrong somewhere on the planet. With a few exceptions, intelligence officers become increasingly isolated, less worldly, and lose the link that ties them to the world they are purportedly protecting. How can intelligence officers be expected to responsibly carry out their mandate if they shun people from other ethnic groups, or see them as somewhat less than human, a threat?

One instance clarified this reality for me, and it was seeing a neighbour in Ottawa, a broad-shouldered Iraqi who had fled northern Iraq to build a new life for himself and his family in Canada, sitting in the lobby of my apartment building, crying his heart out. If I had done what most intelligence officers routinely do and treated this person with suspicion, if I had not become acquainted with him as normal human beings usually do, I would have ignored him and continued on my way. Instead, since I saw him as an equal, I took the time to find out what was wrong. As it turns out, he had just received news that a friend back home had been killed in clashes. For this man, a past he had tried to get away from had followed him all the way to Canada. This was a real man, with real suffering. This drove home the fact that there are consequences—especially in this

line of work—to our actions, and only when we realise this and connect emotionally to the people who are affected by what we do can we begin to act responsibly.
Otherwise it's just like a videogame, where the enemies are virtual, a view that
shares many similarities with the fire-and-forget attitude of aerial bombing begun
in World War II and refined in recent years, whereby killing is rendered virtual,
the distance between perpetrator and victims so great that the commission of the
act will cause the doer no compunction, no second thoughts.

During my graduate studies at the Royal Military College of Canada, I also
came to know many Canadian soldiers, many of whom have since been deployed
to Afghanistan and Haiti. If only intelligence officers left their little white clique
behind—which the Service creates during training and reinforces over time—
they would realise that it doesn't take much to widen one's social circle and feel
part of the real world outside the suffocating confines of the Service. Doing this
allows an individual to feel the pain and to imagine the consequences of war and
other atrocities through someone else's eyes. It makes the reality of our world pal-
pable, not an abstract that one looks at on a TV screen, or reads about in a dry
intelligence brief. One consequence of the enlarged social circle that, despite the
Service, I have created for myself is that every time I read about a roadside attack
in Kandahar, Afghanistan, I fear that among the victims will be people I studied
with at RMC, or one of the 40-odd brave humanitarian workers with whom I
took a course in New York City mere months before Sept. 11, 2001. The Service
should encourage its intelligence officers to develop such links rather than force
them into isolation. Knowledge of the outside world carries with it responsibilities, and it is those responsibilities that keep intelligence officers honest and, in
the end, human.

But how, one wonders, can otherwise educated, intelligent individuals either
not be aware of the many deficiencies described above, or be so uncaring as not to
bother trying to remedy the situation? How can the abuse of the law, absence of
due process, rampant racism and drop in morality become an accepted norm?
How can dedicated intelligence officers come to accept that organised incompetence and dishonesty lie at the core of the institution they sacrificed so much to
be a part of? The answers lies in the fact that CSIS is very much like a small totalitarian state within the state.

By looking at leadership and institutions and their impact on followers' decision to engage in large-scale violence, one can see how an individual can commit
actions that, under normal circumstances, he would never consider doing. The
totalitarian apparatus owes its survival to the combination of the deresponsibilisa-

tion of the individual and a system of fear. In such regimes, including the one at CSIS, the choice for the individual is binary: either one conforms, or he is chewed up by the system of which he is part. In his brilliant book *House of War,* James Carroll describes a similar phenomenon at the Pentagon, a process that, as others have, he likens to the "Niagara current toward war" that of its own momentum obviates the individual and carries us all to what seems to be an inevitable conclusion.[40]

As in Arthur Koestler's *Darkness at Noon,* the system "denied [the individual's] power to distinguish good an evil—and at the same time it spoke pathetically of guilt and treachery."[41] Good and evil, as concepts, are simultaneously weakened and reinforced at CSIS. They are weakened in that as long as one follows orders, no action can be evil, regardless of the consequences. Evil can only describe the actions and motivations of the other, of the enemy. Of course, CSIS does not literally chew up its recalcitrant officers, nor does it send them to the Canadian equivalent of the Gulag in the Great Canadian North. But the intellectual, emotional, and physical ramifications on the disillusioned individual are nevertheless devastating, ranging from sleeplessness, loss of appetite, disgust, self-hatred, de-motivation, alcoholism and other manias.

Careerism and the vertical race within the system also make an individual look the other way when he knows that speaking up in the face of injustice can only have a negative impact on one's chances of career advancement. Unfortunately— and we will touch on this more deeply in the next chapter—many officers at CSIS put career progression above the duty to serve Canadians justly.

The psychological map that is drawn of potential intelligence officers during the recruiting phase is a way to ensure that only those with no extremes in their personality will be selected. In his book *Vengeance,* author George Jonas writes of the Mossad, Israeli's intelligence service: "It is evidently not desirable for [intelligence officers] to be overly imaginative, fanatical or daring: too much imagination is conducive to doubts." Instead, Jonas argues that the Israeli service comprises "average, ordinary people," individuals who "should be ... very clever ... but without an idea in [their] head."[42] It makes a lot of sense to select individuals who are unlikely to question authority if, as is the case at CSIS, the system is one that brooks no criticism. Of course the psychologists cannot be entirely certain that their assessment will be the right one; a two-hour session, during which the candidate talks about his relationship with his parents, among other things, and is asked to answer thousands of "yes" or "no" questions ranging from "do you like to hurt animals?" to "do you prefer tall women?" can only accomplish so much. Consequently, there will be, on occasion, recruits who, given their profile, should not have been admitted into the Service. I believe, now, that I was one of them.

If conformity is what CSIS seeks, it should stick to the appropriate personality type. But this also means that exceptional individuals—individuals with imagination—will be excluded from the country's intelligence service. The "war" on terror, therefore, is not being fought by the best minds in the country; instead, what we get are the average, ordinary people with no ideas in their head, those who will prefer not to think imaginatively, and who will avoid questioning the way things are done. This seems to be the type of individuals who have been recruited over the past twenty years, and judging from the majority of new recruits, it is evident that the same type continues to be sought. As there is no shortage of average individuals out there, the unprecedented hiring we have seen since Sept. 11, 2001, could continue apace for years to come. A few exceptional candidates will, on occasion, be hired, but it is highly unlikely that they will thrive in this environment. Chances are they were hired by mistake or, to be fair to some recruiters, with the hope that they could change the system from within.

In light of this, it comes as no surprise that most intellectuals and academics who find themselves within the walls of the CSIS building are generally miserable. Eventually, they will come to doubt the utility and value of their knowledge, which more often than not remains untapped and, with no outlet, will eventually rot, either for the sake of conformity or through disuse. But management at CSIS is quick to instil the notion that discontent is the result of a problem with the employee rather than the organisation. With this comes a sense of ostracism, of there being something wrong with the employee. Worse, the individual is made to feel that the reason for his malaise is that he just doesn't "get it." Since pressure from the first day encourages conformity and a sense of belonging to the group, those officers—Jonas's "average, ordinary people"—whose personalities are not strong enough to break out of the institutional shackles will gradually abandon their individuality by admitting that there was, indeed, something wrong with them. "Getting it" usually comes at the cost of one's intellectual ambitions, one's sense of morality, and much that is intrinsic to the individual. It happens gradually, and the worst part is that the individual is usually aware that this is taking place. In a way, the person becomes schizophrenic, like a Dr. Jekyll and Mr. Hyde—human and moral on the outside, but inhuman and amoral at work. The result of this conscious attack on one's individuality and system of beliefs is that a large proportion of the workforce is subconsciously disgruntled and demoralised. Discontent is widespread. Over time, however, the initially recalcitrant intelligence officer repents, sacrifices the self at the altar, and joins the flock. Officers become intellectually and emotionally empty, as in T. S. Eliot's poem *The Hollow Men*:

> We are the hollow men
> We are the stuffed men
> Leaning together
> Headpiece filled with straw. Alas!
> Our dried voices, when
> We whisper together
> Are quiet and meaningless
> As wind in dry grass

For the majority of intelligence officers who, either at the onset or, as we have seen, after eradicating critical thinking from the self, choose to conform to the system, they will inevitably be transformed by it, and their sense of morality will slowly be eroded. The worst part, as I have said, is that this partial abandonment of one's individuality is not something that occurs at the unconscious level; for the intelligence officer is very conscious of what is happening to hid *id*. It is like the sheep sauntering willingly into the slaughterhouse, convinced that salvation lies in oblivion. As a character in John Le Carré's novel *The Honourable Schoolboy* says: "I think it safer to stay with institutions ... that way we are spared the embarrassment of personalities. After all, that's what institutions are *for*, isn't it?"[43] Totalitarian systems have no morality and therefore spare those who participate in them the embarrassment of personality, of responsibility toward humankind.

The moral relativism that prevailed during the Cold War and that is woven into most of John Le Carré's novels set during that period implied a semblance of diplomacy, if not of good conduct, between the belligerents. None of these niceties exist in the present campaign against terrorism, and in many ways we could say that the state of the world's morality now is worse than it was during the Cold War, mutually assured destruction notwithstanding. As many civilians were killed in the vengeful military campaign the US and a handful of countries launched in Afghanistan as died in the Sept. 11, 2001 attacks, and many more have died since. Countless more have been killed and displaced as a result of the US invasion of Iraq, which Washington and London sold the world by linking with the terrorism problem. As *New York Times* reporter James Risen exposes in *State of War*, suspected terrorists have been secretly flown to third countries where brutal interrogation tactics are still used, and secret prisons have been established all over the world, through which Western intelligence agencies hope to obtain useful intelligence. In the US, hundreds of individuals were arrested for no other reason than having the wrong last name or for having been born in the wrong country. Anyone who has seen the documentary *Person of Interest* can see how risible, and simultaneously aggravating, was the treatment of certain visible minorities in the US after the terrorist attacks.

Sadly, little by little Canada has been building its own list of wrongful or erroneous targeting. Under certain circumstances, due process has been abandoned, the result of the erosion of the boundaries of morality. In other instances, incompetence—another thriving species in totalitarian systems—has taken a life of its own, so much so that the actors have become unaware of it. Meanwhile, security certificates emitted against alleged terrorists have allowed the state to incarcerate individuals for years on end without those individuals or their defence lawyers being apprised of the charges made against them or having access to the damning evidence. Like in Franz Kafka's *The Trial,* "legal records of the case, and above all the actual charge-sheets, were inaccessible to the accused and his counsel, consequently one did not know in general, or at least did now know with precision, what charges to meet in the first plea."[44] (One should be alarmed when he feels the need to quote Kafka when writing about the activities of a liberal democracy.) All these elements become part of the toxic environment that changes the individuals who operate in it, the intelligence officers, and transforms them into numbers, part of a machine.

The idea of the individual as a number, as a cog in the machine, is certainly not a novel one. Both Aldous Huxley in *Brave New World* and Arthur Koestler in *Darkness at Noon* write about the loss of the individual into the greater organism. Interestingly, both works are concerned with different forms of totalitarian regimes—Huxley's a scientific utopia that strives to achieve homogeneity, Koestler's that of the Soviet Union. In both novels, the protagonists are initially part of the system, and their actions, however immoral, are the result of one's subsumption into that system. Only when they realise that participation in the greater scheme involves the denial of their individualism do the protagonists chose to oppose that system, and thence emerges the source of their travails and the great value of these works of literature. It is at times frightening to see how many similarities there are between the institutions in these two novels and organisations like CSIS. Somewhere along the way, something has corrupted the system, and over time that mutation spreads everywhere, infecting whoever comes into contact with it. Carroll's Niagara river, flowing.

For those who make the choice of becoming one with the institution—in other words, who accept to be transformed by the machine—deresponsibilisation becomes the coating that shields them from the knowledge that, in the course of their function as intelligence officers, they will be forced to commit actions and make decisions that, provided they have good moral foundations to start with, should at modicum make them pause. In addition to what we have described as the gradual process of dehumanisation of the other, adherence to the institution involves what behaviour scientist Konrad Lorenz calls the "anonymity of the flock"—the great liberating power of not having to make a hard decision, combined with the knowledge that, should things go wrong, one will not have to suffer the consequences of one's actions. The approval process that lies behind an actual action by the Service is such that one can always blame a lower or higher echelon, or the system itself, or claim that he was merely "following orders," which is what most war criminals throughout history—from simple soldiers to generals to Adolf Eichmann—have used to defend themselves. Such claims of innocence were made by ordinary Germans after World War II as well as participants in the murderous Soviet apparatus (or, for that matter, at the Pentagon when harmless Vietnamese peasants were being napalmed into oblivion by the thousands). Through indoctrination and, in the German and Soviet cases, a system of fear, individuals created enough emotional distance between themselves and the people they were murdering or informing on that they would feel little, if any, regret at the results of their actions. Only under extreme circumstances, after the regime were toppled, were the crimes exposed.

While it is online, the system is only accountable to itself and the existence of the system is all that matters. Consequently, anything that could undermine its existence is silenced. As we have noted, the use of dehumanising language and the transformation of individuals into file numbers opens the door to grave abuses, which are then silenced through a system of unaccountability. Sadly, even if an internal inquiry or a leak to the media were to expose wrongdoing at CSIS, it is highly unlikely that anyone would suffer the consequences. Whether errors resulted from slackness, mere contempt for the people of a certain ethnic group or religion, or institution-wide failure, the institution is so isolated from the rest of the world that the result will be the same: unaccountability. In the most punitive of cases, SIRC will briefly mention the inadequacies in its annual report, but recommendations alone cannot address the fundamental problems that gave rise to those errors in the first place. When the individual is free to act and knows that, thanks to his position as an intelligence officer, he stands above the law and is therefore beyond its reach, he is unlikely to see the value of making the extra intellectual effort to ensure that every action is warranted, that every suspicion is based on solid, irrefutable and logically analysed evidence. And thus up the ladder.

It may be that the popular image of the intelligence officer, an image that, for the great majority of us, comes from movies and literature, compounds this problem. After all, we all grew up watching special agents committing the full spectrum of action—from intrusion to killing lots of people—for which there were no consequences to the agent and the organisation he worked for. It was all right to kill, to blow things up, to break the law. The fictional special agents did what they did in the name of their country or some other creed such as Freedom, Democracy, Anticommunism or Capitalism. Even if suspension of disbelief is required to actually *believe* in the story, might not that suspension, by dint of repetition, lead to an erosion of that disbelief, in much the same way that one's repeated exposure to scenes of violence will burn his ingrained responses of aversion to such scenes? Unconsciously, might not intelligence officers, whose view of themselves and their newly acquired profession is informed by the same, if skewed, popular images, also see themselves as beyond the reach of the laws that apply to the rest of humanity? Since landing a job with CSIS feels like one is stepping into another world, the world behind the curtain, can we blame the individual for assuming that the laws that govern the real world do not apply to this other world? This is the grey landscape in which intelligence officers are able to play, their wiggle room, and where their sense of being above the law allows them to do things that, as normal citizens, they would never dream of doing.

Of course this is all compounded, as we have already seen, by secrecy. As Ellsberg writes in his memoir:

> Once I was inside the government, my awareness of how easily and pervasively Congress, the public, and journalists were fooled and misled contributed to a lack of respect for them and their potential contribution to better policy. That in turn made it easier to accept, to participate in, to keep quiet about practices of secrecy and deception that fooled them further and kept them ignorant of the real issues that were occupying and dividing inside policy makers. Their resulting ignorance made it all the more obvious that they must leave these problems to us.[45]

Under the current system, errors are simply forgotten, and those who suffer as a result of those blunders are treated as mere annoyances, not worthy of compassion. Anyway, in most cases the victims will be members of a minority group, with very few social and financial resources to make a formal appeal. Moreover, given that members of the targeted minorities do not want to endanger their chances of remaining in Canada, they are unlikely to expose the case and will instead elect to suffer in silence.

We must remember that many of the refugees, immigrants and individuals striving for status in Canada come from countries where security services are all-powerful, a law unto themselves, and symptomatic of everything that is wrong within their society. In many instances, the knock at the door in the dead of night signifies disappearances, jail time, and sometimes torture. Even if the perception of CSIS as using the same techniques is wrong, the newly arrived will accept, however begrudgingly, that they were mistakenly targeted, and the story will die with them. Given this, whoever at CSIS wrongfully targeted an individual from a minority group—in essence the organisation as a whole, given the number of people involved in the approval process—will not suffer the consequences. The problem will disappear on its own, and little, if any, thought will be given to the damage, both financial and emotional, that the wrongful actions will have caused to the individual who was investigated. Since there are no perceptible consequences, not even a slap on the wrist, to the erroneous targeting of an individual, and absent a corrective system, the organisation simply continues the wrongful targeting of minority groups.

This is, in the long run, a recipe for catastrophe. While so far the Service has been lucky and, except for a few embarrassing blunders, has managed to avoid public scrutiny, a day will come when the error of its ways will be brought to light. We should not expect, however, that SIRC or the Inspector General (IG)—the two bodies charged with overseeing the Service's activities—will be at the origin of such revelations. These bodies exist mostly for cosmetic reasons, and while the principle behind their existence is a laudable one, they are, at present, ineffective, political, and virtually useless. SIRC and the IG do not have the means to fully get to the heart of things; it is much too easy to tell them what they want to hear, and to dissimulate that which a desk wants to remain hidden.[46] A good example of this comes from Inspector General Eva Plunkett's comments on the IG review of CSIS operations for 2004-2005, that CSIS "violated operational policies on three occasions" and that it had provided inaccurate information to the review body, including a "misstatement" on the number of joint operations it had engaged in with foreign agencies. The IG added that "the director's [Judd's] report last year also contained inaccuracies which [the Inspector General] identified" while pointing out that these inaccuracies could be "symptomatic of a broader issue of overall information management."[47] Despite all these, the IG concluded by saying that Canada was well served by the Service. On the issues of concern, Plunkett gullibly mentions that "appropriate corrective action" has been taken, while making the recommendation that the Service ought to be more diligent. This is, to say the least, hardly the kind of hard-nosed review that will ensure that the rights and liberties of Canadians are not infringed upon.

The IG is only partly right when she refers to problems with overall information management. While some of the mistakes identified by the IG may indeed have been the result of institutional shortcomings, it neglects to mention that in certain cases the IG and SIRC are being mislead through conscious blurring of, or outright refusal to submit, information by the operational desks. The concluding remarks about Canadians being well served are little more than political politeness intended for public consumption, and the very reason why the existing review bodies will remain ineffective.

The events of Sept. 11, 2001, can only have made the job of overseeing CSIS' activities even more onerous. Indeed, in the 2004-2005 Annual Report's Statement from the Committee, SIRC admits that "for the first time in many years, [it] finds itself in the unhappy position of not being able to review comprehensively certain activities by the Service—responsibilities that have been conferred on CSIS by the Criminal Code, as amended by the *Anti-Terrorism Act*." Under the current system, it is the operational desk that, at the request of the monitoring bodies, provides its files. It is extremely easy for the desk to conveniently "forget" to provide some information, or to manipulate the context in such a way as to completely alter the meaning of what is being provided. In other words, to conceal errors.

Unless someone high up sets his foot down and gives SIRC and the IG unlimited access to the Service files, the many deficiencies at CSIS will never be exposed. Or, that is, they will be exposed, in the form of a catastrophe. This catastrophe—both real and in terms of the Service's image—will come when, as a result of irresponsible targeting, a person will have been unjustly investigated, kicked out of the country, denied entry, and perhaps tortured. That individual, now radicalised and betrayed, will blame CSIS—and perhaps Canada as a whole—for his predicament. Certain, if not most, of the individuals whose names appear in the CSIS database originate from countries that have been torn by war, and where violence is a daily occurrence. For individuals who fled their countries with the hope of finding security and justice to see those dreams crushed yet again may be too much to bear. One day, an individual who is predisposed to violence will act on that injustice, and the consequences for the security of Canadians will be serious. This, in the language of the trade, is called "blowback." The tool of terror will be used not because that individual, for religious or ideological reasons, is against what Canada stands for—the usual George W. Bush and Tony Blair rhetoric, which many Canadians have swallowed—for he wants those for himself and is hoping to enjoy them by relocating to Canada. No. The tool of terror will be used because that individual will feel that he has been betrayed and discriminated against by the one country where he hoped he, and possibly his family, could live peacefully, with the protection of a system of justice. Thanks to sloppiness at the Service, terror will come not out of hatred, but from desperation. As a result of incompetence, lazy practices in collection, commission and review, the Service may very well be sowing the whirlwind.

In addition to being unaccountable to the public, the management at CSIS, along with its public relations officers, build upon the unknown to justify not only their actions but the very existence of the Service. Ghost hunters and exorcists will never run out of a job, for that which they are after, illusion, and what cannot be disproved, cannot be abandoned. The shroud of secrecy that envelops the activities of the Service, and its ability to avoid revealing information by claiming that to do so would endanger protected sources, electronic means of collection or the Service's relations with allied agencies, is, to say the least, very convenient.

There are, in fact, tactical, or operational, reasons why certain types of information cannot be revealed, but these limits should only apply to *how* intelligence is collected. In other words, names of sources, whose security could be at risk were their identity revealed, need not be made public. However, it is unacceptable for these very valid reasons to be cynically used to conceal mistakes, fail to explain *why* an investigation has been launched, or to simply remain aloof of Canadian constituents. Especially under the Stephen Harper government, CSIS and the rest of government have tended to distance themselves from, and to look rather contemptuously upon, the media. The need to protect certain aspects of a case from public knowledge cannot be used to skirt accountability. As we shall see when we turn the case of the 17 individuals who were arrested in Southern Ontario in early June 2006, the marked slide toward a total disregard for the free press—including a request by the Crown for a total publication ban on the court proceedings—and the increased reliance on secrecy that characterizes the Harper administration, does not bode well for Canadian democracy or the accountability of government.

Never has this shroud of secrecy better served the Service than when it requests additional funding to protect Canadians from terrorism.[48] Since Sept. 11, 2001, the official line of the Service, often repeated in interviews, workshops, and conferences by the former director of the Service, Ward Elcock, has been that it no longer is a question of "if" Canada will be the target of a terrorist attack on its soil, but "where" and "when." In fact, in May 2004, the director said before the House of Commons National Security Sub-committee that it was "safe to assume" that Canada would be targeted by terrorists. Compounding this assertion was media reporting that used irresponsible language such as "inevitable" and "clear that Canada will be targeted."[49] At a security and intelligence conference in October that same year, the Prime Minister's National Security Advisor, Robert Wright, stated that "it would be absurd to believe that terrorists will not target Canada."[50] With such comments, Wright was making anyone who disagreed with the scope of the threat that terrorism represented to Canada—including former intelligence officers like me, who not only had had access to all the intelligence on the so-called threat but had in fact spent more than a year writing CSIS threat assessments—"absurd." These harrying statements received a needed boost when, around the same time, a group allegedly linked to al-Qaeda released a statement on the Internet in which Canada was listed among the five Western countries that should be targeted for terrorist attacks. To date, it is true that the only country from that list that has not suffered a terrorist attack on its territory is Canada. This notwithstanding, there is no indication at present which would suggest that Canada is in the crosshairs of terrorist organisations. Furthermore, there were no clear signs that the group that released the warning was in fact legitimate or that it had any concrete ties to the al-Qaeda organisation.

The tradition was continued in spring 2006 when the Service's Director of Operations, Jack Hooper, warned that "home-grown terrorists" who are "virtually indistinguishable from other youth" and who "blend in very well to our society ... speak our language and ... appear to be—to all intents and purposes—well-assimilated" are increasingly looking inside Canada for terrorist activity. By adding the "threat from within" element to the list of possible terrorists, Hooper had effectively closed the gap: anyone, anywhere, was a potential terrorist—your grocer, the Lebanese teenager your son goes to school with, your husband's barber. The sense of imminent, unknowable danger had been raised a notch, and more than ever CSIS needed additional budgets so that it could accomplish its mission. (Remember Team B and its "findings" on the invisible Soviet submarine program? Soon after the release of its report, the US was embarking on the greatest militarization program in the country's history.) Furthermore, Hooper added, budgets cuts in the 1990s had, among other things, prevented the Service from properly screening immigrants. More money was needed, and immigrants were the threat, people who wanted to be like you and me, to hide in our midst.

With help from the media, the Canadian government upped the ante on Jan. 2, 2007, via a Canadian Press report based on a document released by CSIS through an Access to Information request.

According to the CSIS study, the report said, it is "quite surprising" that terrorists have not yet detonated a "dirty bomb"—known in the trade as a radiological dispersal device (RDD)—given that making such a crude weapon is, according to CSIS, relatively easy and the materials required to make one are readily available to ordinary citizens.

"The technical capability required to construct and use a simple RDD is practically trivial, compared to that of a nuclear explosive device or even most chemical or biological weapons," the study continued, adding that the Sept. 11, 2001, attacks had raised fears that terrorists would try to crash airliners into nuclear power stations or find ways to disperse radioactive material with the intent of causing economic damage by rendering an entire area off limits.

CSIS, the report said, claims that the detonation of an RDD is "undoubtedly the most likely" terrorist scenario involving radioactive sources, adding that "it is quite surprising that the world has not yet witnessed such an attack."

This, again, is mere fear-mongering on the part of the authorities, as it uses that which cannot be demonstrated to create a monster on the wall. A closer look at the phraseology and choice of words in the report shows how groundless the assessment is. By saying that a dirty bomb is undoubtedly the most likely terrorist attack involving radioactive material, it is simply stating that other methods—breaking into a nuclear power station and somehow finding a way to cause a detonation, or building a nuclear device and managing to smuggle it to a targeted area—are more difficult to achieve, which they are. Putting a rifle in one's mouth and pressing the trigger is also undoubtedly the most likely way someone would end his life—more likely, surely, than achieving death by waiting for UV rays from the sun to cause a fatal skin cancer.

What the report conveniently fails to mention—and this is the reason why it expresses surprise at the world having yet to suffer such an attack—is that physical aggression is contingent on two factors: *capabilities* and *intent*. Clearly, if building and detonating a RDD were so easy—after all, the materials required to build one are at hand in medical laboratories and universities—the variable that has been missing is intent. What the report also fails to mention is that would-be terrorists could also easily build conventional explosives using ammonium nitrate (a fertiliser) and other available chemicals to commit a deadly attack. That this hasn't occurred in Canada is also a result of lack of intent.

The CP article then mentions that certain parts of the report were too sensitive to have been released through the Access to Information request. This likely is nothing more than the means by which CSIS leaves doubt in the public's mind. What is that material that is so secret it cannot be made public? Could it be information about individuals known to CSIS who have been building such a device? By leaving black holes inviting wild speculation, CSIS ensures that the information it gives is just enough to feed nightmares. In reality, however, this so-called sensitive information is probably little more than foreign agency information on which the CSIS report is based. The truth is, it is not the information itself that is of a sensitive nature—after all, everything in the report can likely be sourced in open—that is unclassified—material. The sensitive information, rather, is likely the name of the foreign agency that provided the information, some of which are even more paranoid than CSIS and therefore even more inclined to report every threat. In the name of good relations with its allies, CSIS is bound not to reveal the identity of the foreign agencies it deals with, and any reference thereto for public disclosure will consequently be sanitised.

Despite this renewed attempt on the part of Canadian authorities to increase the level of fear that there are terrorists out there picking apart a discarded X-ray machine to build a radiophobic's worst nightmare, Canadians need not worry. There is a multitude of means and ways by which people with bad intentions can wreak physical, human and economic havoc. Modern society is filled with technologies that can be turned against us. In fact, certain martial artists make it their specialty to transform everyday objects into deadly weapons. Murders can be committed using a pair of scissors, a pencil—even a door stopper would do the job. Are the daily front pages plastered with such stories? No. Why? Lack of intent.

Following the same logic, the fact that a RDD attack has not materialized is not for lack of opportunities. It simply is lack of intent.

To this day, CSIS and the Canadian government continue to harp on the "when" and "where," and in the process their budgets continue to grow. One cannot prove, or disprove, the warnings emitted by CSIS, so shrouded are they in layers of secrecy. Yesterday's invisible Soviet submarines, or communists waiting to pounce on us at a signal from Moscow, are today's sleeper terrorist cells. The Service knows best, but it cannot tell the public why. Faith is required on the part of the population. If there is one secret ammunition in the intelligence world, this is it: Use fear, but hide the fact that the monster on the wall is nothing more than an illusion.

In spring 2004 I was asked to give a presentation at the Lester B. Pearson building in Ottawa, where the Department of Foreign Affairs is located, and to provide, in front of some 200 department security officers (DSO) at the various branches of the Federal Government, a Secret-level CSIS overview of the current threats to the security of Canada. I shall refrain from elaborating on how difficult it was to convince the organisers of the biannual meeting that we did not need a Power Point presentation, nor will I belabour the fact that despite the Secret nature of the information I was sharing with the audience, the backdoor to the conference room remained wide open and unguarded, meaning that at any time anyone without a proper clearance could have walked in, for there was another problem—a much more serious one—that had been nagging at me ever since I had received the request to give the presentation. On that day I was, for all intents and purposes, asked to lie. Back then, I worked in the Threat Assessment Unit, the small cell at the Service that is responsible for monitoring the threats to the security of Canada. Despite spending every day at work reading up on the various alleged threats to the security of Canada, I could not find evidence that Canada was currently being targeted by terrorists. Nothing. And yet, there I was, echoing the vague threats of the all-knowing, "it's not a question of if, but when" before a half-awake, half-alarmed audience. I had nothing to base this assessment on, but still, I had to deliver the message. I stood at the lectern, feeling like a fraud, doing my best to put on an air of officialdom. Of course, had any question been asked by the audience on the nature of the threat, I would have had to reply that the Service had information corroborating the threat but that I could not share that information with them. This, as always, was the escape route, the assurance that no question, however well-formulated and argued, can ever pierce through CSIS' armour. But no one asked. Everybody had bought the lie.

Looking back on this travesty of a briefing to government officials, I regret not having told them the truth, which is that based on the information we had at the time, there was no credible threat to the security of Canada. But I could not. Back then, my career at CSIS still mattered too much to me, and I was not strong enough to say something that would have affected my progression within the organisation. So I lied. This is how the system survives, through silence, or how, despite all the evidence that nothing was working, no one in the US intelligence and defence community said anything about the Vietnam War before Daniel Ellsberg released the 7,000 pages of the Top Secret Pentagon Papers, a history of decision-making in the lead-up to and during the war. Or why the invasion of Iraq in 2003 was allowed to take place, given the lies that were told to justify the act.

By the same token, CSIS makes enough vague predictions that sure enough one day something may happen to support those claims. Cassandra turns into the all-seer, and once something happens, the constant warnings emitted by the Service are finally interpreted, with hindsight, as foresight. If—and let us hope that this never happens—a terror attack is committed on Canadian soil, CSIS and the Public Safety apparatus at the Federal government will be able to say, "see, we told you so." It would not be surprising either if that claim to perfect eyesight were accompanied by requests for additional funding, based on the assumption that more money would lead to even better foresight. Of course, anybody can make predictions, and in the distant future some of those predictions are bound to be substantiated by events (especially if, as we discuss in Chapter 2, Canada continues along the dangerous road it has chosen for itself). But so far, the "predictions" made by CSIS officials have not been based on access to special intelligence or the work of great minds. In fact, all those warnings of "when" and "where" haven't been supported by an "if," and the only reason they have been made is to give CSIS a sense of importance, to maintain a level of paranoia and, as we have noted, to inflate its budget.

Despite its shaky relationship with the media, CSIS nevertheless receives help from them on occasion. Journalists such as Toronto-based Stewart Bell, author of *Cold Terror* and *The Martyr's Oath,* encourage the perception that Canada is infested with terrorist organisations and that the clock is ticking. Echoing the language of Jack Hooper, his books and news articles give the impression that Canada is a log that is being devoured from the inside by termites. But his writings serve a function: They provide fuel for the Canadian government, and more so for CSIS. Terrorists are everywhere, they live amongst us, and over the years our government has done nothing to address the problem. Of course, the bottom line of these arguments is usually that CSIS needs to do more, needs more people, and therefore needs more money. A more deleterious consequence of such writing is that it exacerbates the sadly uninformed belief held by many in the US that Canada indeed is some sort of Club Med for terrorists. Look, the average American could reasonably think, even Canadian journalists admit that Canada is like a perforated sieve: Its immigration laws are too lax, its security and law-enforcement agencies too kind, and its border insecure! Please, Mr. Senator. More pressure on those Canadians.

Another way, though this time inadvertent, in which the media assists CSIS in its exploitation of fear is its coverage, usually accompanied by wild speculation by so-called "experts," of incidents. The June 2006 arrests of the seventeen individuals who were suspected of planning multiple terrorist attacks within Canada led to a few weeks of wild media speculation, fed by little doses of information by the authorities, as to the nature of the alleged targets. From the CSIS regional office in downtown Toronto to the Toronto Stock Exchange (TSX), the Canadian Broadcasting Corporation building to the Prime Minister in Ottawa, the only thing the media accomplished as it uncritically broadcast this information was to engender irrational fear within the population. Without having any concrete information to base their reporting on, and without giving the authorities the time they needed to gather and analyse the facts, the media started naming every conceivable target. All of a sudden, Canadians were unsafe, everywhere. CSIS, aloof as ever, did nothing to allay those fears, however baseless, for the panic played to its advantage (and it may itself have begun to believe some of that speculation).

The success of the instrument of fear stems from the assumption, as we have seen, that intelligence services know everything, a belief that agencies like CSIS do nothing to dispel. Unable to ascertain whether an intelligence service really is privy to the mysteries of this world, taxpayers have little choice but to hold on to the myth that their money is going toward an organisation that knows more than the rest of us and that in the process it is ensuring our protection.

Conversely, this false sense of security can have its drawbacks, for when the Canadian government, based on material provided by CSIS and other members of the intelligence community, says it has no indication of a threat, those who know how incomplete that information is may have reason to feel insecure. Intelligence agencies, stuck in their old paradigms, overwhelmed by paperwork and slowed down by rampant inefficiency, can be just as surprised and caught off guard as anybody else. In fact, in many ways CSIS and its kin use the system of fear to mask the fact that they just don't know what's around the corner. This way, when and if something happens, they can point to earlier warnings and say: "We knew all along." In the not so eloquent language of the trade, this is called "covering your ass."

This explains why the net that has been case against suspected terrorists has become so wide, including just about everybody, foreigners and citizens alike, or any terrorist technique, from conventional bombs to radiological devices. When you don't know, everything is possible, and everything is a potential threat. To protect their interests, intelligence services start naming everything, which also serves the purpose of keeping the fear level high enough to manipulate people's irrationality.

Ironically, the London bombings of July 2005 were preceded by a *lowering* of the threat level against British interests, an assessment that resulted from a lack of intelligence reporting to suggest a threat. In fact, so little do the British authorities know about the perpetrators of the attacks that, more than two years later, important facts like motivation remain unknown. Aside from providing a minute-by-minute rendition of the events of that day, the British government has had precious little to offer in terms of substantive information. The London bombings were not solely the result of a "failure" in intelligence: They were a signal that the alleged all-seeing can indeed be quite blind. This results from a series of factors, from the immense quantity of intelligence material that needs to be digested, to incompleteness of intelligence, the hubris attendant to the "we know better" view of the world, and the reality, however disconcerting this may sound to intelligence officers, that human activity is oftentimes unpredictable.

There may have been dissenting voices within the British intelligence community, and arguments against lowering the threat level many have been made, but once a group of individuals or an institution has made up its mind, information that does not fit that model is treated with the swift knife of intellectual condescension. Whether someone takes a position against a threat that doesn't exist, or, conversely, is fighting the general view that there isn't one, the consequences for the intelligence officers and analysts who refuse to adopt the prevailing view, who pit themselves against "groupthink," are the same. As *New York Times* reporter James Risen notes in his book *State of War*, in the lead-up to the 2003 invasion of Iraq "Agency officials who appeared to be unenthusiastic about Iraq soon mysteriously found themselves sidelined."[51] Careers are made, or unmade, largely based on an officer's willingness not to oppose the established belief.

As we have seen, the impact of the Service culture on its intelligence officer workforce is by most measures a negative one, and there are no indications that this is about to change. This is mostly the result of a structure that has been in place since the Service was created in 1984. In fact, 24 years after it came into being, CSIS is still run by the those who were present at its inception. Many officers who now are in positions of management at CSIS were former RCMP employees who were transferred from the force to its new civilian counterpart.

Before 1984, the RCMP was the lead agency on counter-intelligence and other spying activities in Canada. Following grave abuses and public inquiries, the Federal government decided to divest the RCMP of all spying activities and to create a new agency responsible for intelligence matters in Canada, CSIS. A fresh start, with a clean slate. As journalist Andrew Mitrovica points out in his book *Covert Entry*, however, the upper echelons at CSIS were soon filled by former senior RCMP officers, who resigned from the RCMP one day and were hired by CSIS the next.[52] Given this mostly cosmetic shake-up, it was unlikely that, with the RCMP mindset still so prominent, the abusive practices of old would end. In fact, little has changed, and the rigid, top-down, hierarchical mindset that existed at the RCMP still prevails at CSIS.

The police mentality that became part of the foundations of CSIS carries social ramifications, such as the manner in which women are treated. There have been instances of sexual abuse, or gender-based authority, involving very high-ranking managers and female officers. In fairness to CSIS, nearly half (47.7%) of its workforce are women (the figure among intelligence officers is slightly lower, at 39.5%).[53] But this does not mean that there is no discrimination, and all things being equal, when it comes to promotions women remain at a disadvantage. Moreover, incidents involving groping and other inappropriate acts have occurred, but given the system of fear that exists within the Service, and the fact that to draw attention to such an act could have negative repercussions on one's career progression—even the victim's—very few of those cases are ever exposed, let alone made public. It is a world in which authority is not to be questioned; one merely follows orders and suffers in silence.

This is a world where the individual loses his intrinsic value: You are part of a force, a mere number on a page, and the Service can move you anywhere, anytime, whether you like it or not. Everything is contingent on operational requirements. There is no logic to it, and from my experience the human resources department in charge of career moves, deployments, and other changes has no idea what it is doing. As a rule, many officers, once they have completed their initial period at headquarters in Ottawa, will not be deployed to their region of choice (there are signs that this might be changing, however). In fact, in addition to being a cause of sleeplessness, wild speculation, and tremendous amounts of stress, the regional deployment process oftentimes leads to discontent. Months before the deployments are announced, lists are drawn, bets are made, and one's submission of desired regions, in order of preference, is an exercise in alchemy. Many officers—and their families—are moved to regions where their quality of life will suffer, as they can ill afford, on the salary of an intelligence officer, to rear a family in some of the more expensive Canadian cities. Most intelligence officers with two or more children simply cannot afford to live close to work in a city like Toronto, for example, which is where the largest proportion of officers is deployed. Consequently, they have no choice but to rent or buy on the outskirts of the city, which often entails an hour or an hour and a half of commuting in the morning. There are numerous instances of the Service losing employees because of the mobility clause. Officers will complete their two to three years at headquarters and, come the time for regional deployment, they will apply for jobs with other, better paying branches of government in Ottawa. This partly explains why so many former CSIS officers are now working for Transport Canada, among other agencies, where not only is the pay better, but also where employees do not face forced deployment. For officers with young families, the need for stability may trump one's dedication to CSIS. The loss of so many employees after three years of employment is hardly a good investment of taxpayers' money, given how expensive it is to train an intelligence officer.

Recruits who do not expect this kind of treatment are in for a big surprise. As one progresses through the hiring process, he is made to feel unique. I remember being told, for example, that for every officer hired in the province of Quebec, which is where I filed my application, 1,000 were rejected. Throughout the hiring process and during the initial weeks of training, recruits are made to feel that they are the cream of the crop. You are unique, the best and the brightest. You cannot be replaced.

Soon afterwards, however, a few classes of new intelligence officers (including mine) were told during an extemporary meeting that our initial stay at headquarters had been inflated by a year, meaning that rather than spend two years in Ottawa, we would be spending three. The discontent was universal. Some, with the knowledge that they would only be in Ottawa for two years, had chosen not to buy property and to rent instead. A few would have made a different decision had they known that their stay in Ottawa would be a longer one.

After a couple of classmates manifested their anger, the human resource sacrificial lamb who had been sent down to meet us said, quite undiplomatically I must add, that if we were so unhappy, we knew where the exit was. After all, he added, for every officer in the room, there were thousands of Canadians who were just dying to get our job. We collectively recoiled. In a matter of months we had gone from the indispensable one in a thousand to the utterly replaceable. We all swallowed our anger, no one quit, and life continued. We had just been told who was boss. All illusions that we were "special" were shattered at that meeting, and the treatment that was reserved us from that moment on provided all the confirmation that we needed. We were anything but indispensable.

Some of us, not satisfied with the answers we had been given, kept asking why, all of a sudden, were we being told to stay an additional year in Ottawa. Operational requirements, we were told. But the more we dug, the more obvious it became that human resources had screwed up and had found itself with too many officers in the regions, and too few at headquarters. Simultaneously, though, the regions were screaming for more resources, claiming that they could not do their job due to a lack of field officers. Schizophrenic claims such as the one above are routine at CSIS, to such an extent that they become the norm, something to be expected. Had we been told, rather than be taken for idiots, we would have understood and accepted that someone, somewhere, had miscalculated. That they failed to do so and chose to lie to us instead was a demonstration of the lack of consideration, if not outright contempt, the management at CSIS has for its employees.

One soon finds out, therefore, that managers run the show, and that officers are mere instruments. Ironically, everybody covets those managerial positions. It's all about the pecking order, and it's a brutal fight. In many ways, what is currently going on at CSIS is very much like the ugly careerism that former CIA operative Robert Baer, in his book *See no Evil*, blames for the effective demise of the Agency. In order to make it in this environment, one need not only be able to swim among sharks—he has to become one.

From this emerges one of the ugliest types of behaviour at the Service: covert backstabbing. People wear masks, the static smile reverting to a grimace the moment a potential opponent has turned his back. No opportunity is lost to make another officer look bad. Despite the alleged sense of brotherhood at CSIS, it's everyone on his own. Rarely will the drowning officer be extended a hand of compassion. The incentive is for self-promotion. Intelligence officers are there only to make their supervisors look good. I, along with the other analysts on my desk, were often asked to write documents for our supervisor, after which she would simply add her name at the bottom, and send it to other recipients using her own e-mail address. That way, no one would ever know that the writing wasn't hers. Whatever makes the supervisor looks good is good for the investigation, recruits are told.

CSIS is made of little islands of accrued power, of intelligence fiefdoms. Blunders are inevitably the young officer's fault, the result of inexperience. Mistakes are papered over. As David Halberstam wrote: "In secret organisations, a subordinate's failure reflects badly upon his superior as well, so there is a very strong instinct on the part of both to cover it up; it is only when knowledge about such failure is out in the open that a superior himself becomes responsible."[54] When it suits their needs (in other words, when something goes wrong), supervisors can have a surprisingly bad memory. "I never said this," "I never ordered you to do this." Deniability, deniability, deniability.

Promotion, on the other hand, is rarely the result of one's performance. True, the annual performance evaluations (PERs) are taken into consideration, but supervisors are often moved from one area to another—with a promotion—simply because they have done the time, or because they needed exposure to a certain field before they can move up the ladder of power. Never mind that many are not qualified for the new position, or that they have no interest in the subject of the new investigation they are being moved to. As long as the title attached to their name changes, and along with it the pay bracket, employees buy into the illusion that they are doing well. What this means, therefore, is that CSIS is not a meritocracy. What it is, rather, is a gerontocracy: Do the time, play the political game well, and you will move up, regardless of what impact you have had on the security of Canadians. Because this process denies the otherwise natural selecting out, as in the private sector, of incompetent employees—where the rotten apples are either kicked out or left to stagnate at the bottom, where they can be a nuisance to as few people as possible—incompetent CSIS employees move up to positions of authority where they negatively affect an increasingly large number of employees and, by rebound, Canadians.

Another aspect that has an incidence on one's chances of getting promoted is the "do not rattle the cage" principle. Supervisors are discouraged from changing the status quo; as we noted, it is recommended that they perpetuate methodologies and ideologies. This, of course, also means that supervisors need to ensure that the intelligence officers who are under their wing are also toeing the line. "Problem employees" are therefore a nightmare for supervisors, as they can potentially make them look bad. So, from the top down, one can hear the ruler slashing the knuckles of the insubordinates. "Make me look good," they say. "Do not rattle the cage, and you, too, in time, will obtain your coveted promotion. Otherwise …"

Under the current system, therefore, spineless intelligence officers are the dream employees: They do not question things, do not propose new methodologies, do not express their discontent, and as a result they do not threaten a supervisor's chances of getting a promotion. And they do not act as whistleblowers when they see something wrong. In fact, to do so would go against everything the Service stands for. This system, as we saw, is reminiscent of what went on in the Washington defence apparatus at the height of the Vietnam War: those officers at the Department of State, the Department of Defense, or at the CIA who disagreed with the accepted knowledge—in other words who refused to accept the web of lies that made it possible to portray the war as a success—had their careers shortened or were passed over for promotion. Only those who willingly shut their eyes to reality, and for whom promotion was more important than the lives of countless Vietnamese and Americans, were able to play the game. No wonder the US lost the war in Vietnam, both the war for the hearts and minds of the Vietnamese *and* the actual military encounter. As James Risen notes in *State of War*, a similar fate was visited upon CIA operatives who attempted to provide a fairer assessment of the threat posed by Iraq before the 2003 US invasion.

I can think of a number of occasions where my immediate supervisor had committed blatant security breaches—revealing information to third parties who either did not have the appropriate clearance (a cab driver, for example) or simply did not need to know (other agencies). In fact, it was recognised within and outside the unit that she was a "talker." Given that exposing such violations would have pitted me, alone, against my supervisor and the entire system that backed her, I chose to remain silent. In other words, the system of intimidation prevailed, even if, in the end, to expose the matter would have been the responsible thing to do. This is compounded by the fact that there is no clearly defined channel through which security violations, or abuse, by supervisors can be exposed. As PERs are top-down only, meaning that supervisors rate their subordinates but not the other way around, the occasions to expose supervisory violations are extremely rare.[55]

Based on the above, it should be obvious that Alpha-type personalities are undesirable. The problem, however, is that the Service tends to hire a disproportionate amount of them (who should not to be confused with individuals of exceptional quality). Why there aren't more clashes, shouting matches or resignations on the spot can probably be explained by the system of fear that is in place: The Alpha is beaten into submission, and fearing for his career, he learns to shut up. This is yet another way by which what constitutes the individual—the traits that make him who he is—is expurgated by the Service. This, of course, cannot but make A-types miserable. But the angst is kept inside, and very few express their anger. People will choose depression or alcoholism before risking to compromise their career at CSIS. They will visit, in secret and shame, the in-house psychologists, who can only accomplish so much. Never mind the long-term consequences for one's health, both physical and mental, or what this means for the Service in the future.

The only part of the A-type individual that is allowed to survive is careerism, the unending quest for the promotion. A quite unsettling consequence of this is that individuals in supervising positions tend to lose sight of their mandate and responsibilities, which is to protect Canadians. When the object is promotion, and when the environment is not a meritocracy but, as we have seen, one that promotes durability, the tendency is therefore one of avoidance: do not make waves, lie low, follow orders, do not change things. This mode of thinking prevents the emergence of original, or "outside the box," thinking. Attempting new things implies risks; one had better stick to the proven methods, even if these, perpetuated over the decades, no longer fit the current needs.

Accompanying this desire for promotion is the requirement to ensure the survival of the investigation, which represents another negative pressure against change. The truly aggressive and original desk head could probably manage to wrap up an investigation in a few years—at least the targets that exist at the time. But what good would this do the Service? The last thing it wants is to find itself without a job. It's a bit like the chiropractor who ensures a clientele by never really fixing what is wrong with his clients. The inclination, therefore, is to maintain the status quo: The enemy lurks out there, we are actively investigating him, but he is proficient. Fear, the unknown, the lies, told and retold, at the Service and outside. Investigations are therefore transformed into never-ending quests, a mathematical hyperbole. Once again, Jack Hooper's McCarthy-like comments about future terrorists being "like us" come in handy, as we will never run out of people "like us."

In order to survive or thrive, a desk needs to demonstrate to the management that it is conducting an active investigation. While much of this is a smokescreen intended to mislead the higher-ups, who are responsible for attributing investigators to a desk, some supervisors mistake amount of activity for the health of an investigation. To them, lack of activity is a risk to the desk, as it holds the implication that come the next fiscal year it might lose some of its investigators to another investigation, or perhaps, in the rarest of occasions, even be shut down altogether. Year after year, the battle rages on. The pressure is on the desk head, and in turn on the analysts, to make things happen. Nothing that alters the balance or endangers the investigation, but just enough recycling of old techniques to prove that something is being done. When the assessment of an investigation is made in quantitative rather than qualitative terms, giving the impression that an investigation is alive and well, if not growing, is easily accomplished. Inaction—even when the opponent is himself inactive—is unacceptable. Faced with seeming inaction on the part of the enemy, it is therefore important for a desk to demonstrate that the enemy is in fact not inactive, but rather overly proficient. Absence of activity is construed as a sign that the opponent excels at what it is doing. The silent Soviet subs all over again. Furthermore, every mistake committed by the enemy that would make it look vulnerable or incompetent is also concealed. To ensure the survival of an investigation, if not its growth, what is needed is a strong, competent and ultimately dangerous enemy. After all, as a character in Le Carré's novel *Tinker Tailor Soldier Spy* puts it, by making one's opponent look a fool, one loses the incentive for engaging him. Moreover, given investigators' strong need to feel indispensable, no one wants to be seen to be pitted against a weak enemy. In the end, all of this creates an institutional philosophy in which operations exist for the sake of the operation, with assessments of the threat that are usually overblown.

Another variable that has an impact on how CSIS and its employees behave is the sense of inferiority that informs Canada's relatively young service vis-à-vis its bigger and more experienced allies outside the country. This gives rise to a situation akin to that of a ten year-old kid who wants to play with his teenaged brother and his friends. "Me too! Me too!" he shouts, knowing that he will need to prove his mettle if he is ever to be accepted by the older kids. In reverse, the older, bigger, better-financed agencies, seeing the kid striving for attention, look on amusedly and will occasionally propose that the upstart do things for it, all under the pretext of improving co-operation between the services. More often than not, the Service will be happy to oblige. As most other agencies operate in countries where civil rights regulations are more lax than in Canada, the pressure will be on CSIS to commit certain actions that, on its own, it would never have considered. By seeking to play with the giants, the Service may on occasion feel compelled to bend the rules by which it usually operates, or even break Canadian laws. In fact, the more aggressive agencies provide the incentive for CSIS to do so. Given all the reasons enumerated above, from a sense of being above the law to community-wide racism, added to the brainwashing of intelligence officers into believing that threats abound, bending the rules has become easier than ever. Over time and through repetition, this threatens to erode the system of laws that has been in place to ensure that CSIS does not act outside its mandate or overstep its authority. Certain operations that not only did not provide any quantifiable operational results but were also characterised by a total disregard for the consequences for entire families have been launched by CSIS as a result. For all intents and purposes, those operations were initiated at the behest of a foreign power.

While the media and academics usually portray threats to Canada's sovereignty in terms of trade, defence, and diplomacy, the sovereignty over intelligence matters has also been under siege. The bigger agencies, such as the CIA, the Department of Homeland Security and the Israel Secret Intelligence Service (ISIS), have pressured Canada to accomplish certain things in the name of co-operation and security, and as a result Canada's sovereignty has suffered. In the long run, what in the past had distinguished Canada from its bigger brothers—its capacity to act independently and to make political decisions on its own—could very well disappear. Ironically, one of the main reasons why Canada has been spared the pain of a terrorist attack on its territory is mainly the perceived independence abroad of Canada as a country that stands on its own feet and that does not unreasonably yield to the demands of the imperial giant or its handful of servants, like Britain and Australia.

But what if Canada is no longer seen under this light? What if rather than being perceived as a moderate voice, Canada comes to be regarded as nothing more than a participant, however unwilling in the past, in the American empire experiment, a mere subject of its immense power? What if CSIS practices become more and more aligned with those of the far less abstemious CIA? As a character in Le Carré's *The Honourable Schoolboy* exclaims after hearing of the British Secret Service's intention to nurture the "special relationship" with the American cousins: "*Top table* ... sacrificial altar if you ask me. We already burned the Middle East and half Africa on it. All for the special relationship."[56] Canada has no Middle East or Africa to lose, no remnants of its imperial foothold. But it has a sense of itself to protect.

By thus trying to demonstrate its capability to play in the intelligence "big leagues," the Service has lost sight of its mandate: to protect Canadians. In many ways, operations have become ends in themselves rather than the means to accomplish something. We should never lose sight of the fact that *intrusive investigations should always be an instrument of last resort, which is used only when the Canadian government has reasonable grounds to believe that an individual or an organisation represents a threat to the Security of Canada.* Any other use of investigative tools—as an instrument for self-glorification or to demonstrate to an ally that we are willing to participate at their level, on their terms—should be strictly forbidden. The one question, therefore, that intelligence officers should be asking themselves before launching an operation is, Will this operation *benefit* the current investigation *on Canadian terms*? This is not intelligence protectionism, or a failure to understand that the world is interconnected at an unprecedented level. It is only a way to ensure that our intelligence services continue to reflect the system of laws and values that characterises us as Canadians.

Intelligence officers whose moral resistance is already weakened could reasonably feel that they are now caught in an even bigger organism, which increases the level of permissibility. Once the line dividing Canada and other countries has been breached, and once an individual sees himself as being regulated not by Canadian laws but rather those of the much more permissive Global War on Terrorism (GWOT), the door has been opened for the commission of acts that, in

Canada, should be illegal. The less immediate the decision-making process becomes (in other words, the more it is seen as part of the GWOT rather than a Canadian policy), the easier it becomes for individuals at every level of the organisation to feel non-responsible for the consequences of their actions. The bigger the flock, the more anonymous its constituents become. The more aggressive the US intelligence apparatus has become, the greater the pressure has been on Canada to adopt similar tactics.

As noted in the 2004-2005 Annual Report, SIRC warns that since Sept. 11, 2001, the legislation contained in the *Anti-terrorism Act* seems to have allowed the Service to expand the definition of those groups and individuals it is allowed to investigate. Whereas in the past only groups and individuals representing a direct "threat to the security of Canada" could be investigated, it is now possible for the Service to obtain warrants against groups and individuals who have no presence in Canada and who have no intention of targeting Canadian interests. Thanks to the Act, CSIS is now in a position to demonstrate to its allies that it is a full participant at the international level, with the laws to back its actions. Never mind the repercussions on Canadian security; the objective is maintaining international alliances and appeasing foreign powers that relentlessly accuse Canada of being lax on security. In the process, and whether they are conscious of this or not, CSIS and its employees are helping spread the US empire, a whole enterprise that, as we shall see later, is making the entire world a less secure place.

Despite the fact that technology isn't, in and of itself, the answer to today's security and intelligence challenges, there nevertheless is a requirement for an understanding of the technological possibilities that exist, especially those that terrorists and other organisations can exploit to accomplish their objectives. With a few exceptions, the old guard at the decision-making and supervisory level at CSIS, however, is incapable of understanding these new technologies. Concepts such as virtual meeting rooms on the Web, or virtual money transfers whereby an individual can purchase Internet money with a debit or credit card and transfer that e-money anywhere in the world, are simply beyond the comprehension of the previous generation. Rather than turn to the new employees who grew up with and are using such technology, the old guard has a tendency, once again, to resist listening to the younger voices, lest it demonstrate their ignorance and therefore risk compromising their chances for a promotion. While it is already extremely difficult to keep pace with the new technologies, institutional resistance only makes matters worse. The cat-and-mouse game in which intelligence officers and terrorists are engaged is not unlike natural selection: Survival of a species is slanted in favour of the fastest—the fastest lion will eat, the slowest one dies; likewise with the prey. What happens if a lion consciously chooses not to strive for speed? He dies, and nature gets rid of him and his unborn descendants. The same applies to the world of counterterrorism: Agencies cannot choose, out of ignorance, resistance, or incompetence, not to evolve and to keep pace with the rest of the world. And yet, this is exactly what is happening at CSIS, at least in the operational, old-guard-run sector. We can only hope that as the new generation replaces the old this technological gap will be closed.

To be fair, there are some good supervisors at the Service. Not everything is bad. Some individuals, in spite of institutional pressure, do manage to retain their integrity. But they are, sadly, the minority. I remember one supervisor who had a tendency to explode in rage whenever he disagreed with the contents of a threat assessment. His outbursts were legendary, and expected. While expletives are certainly not the best way to communicate in an office environment, his anger nevertheless demonstrated that he actually cared about the product. Even if the recruit who was on the receiving end of that anger was yours truly, I was aware that he cared, and ultimately I came to have more respect for him, poor manners notwithstanding, than the numerous other supervisors who would "approve" my documents after barely glancing at them.

Unfortunately, the solitary voices of those who care or occupy a position because of their competence cannot counter the nefarious effects of an organisation that encourages mediocrity. The prevalent breed of supervisors, therefore, is more like the Examining Magistrate in Franz Kafka's *The Trial*; they look good and mighty in the portraits, but in reality they are but dwarves sitting on a kitchen chair. This brings to mind the Mossad agent who recruits Avner, the leader of a counter-terrorist cell in George Jonas's *Vengeance*, which served as the basis for Steven Spielberg's movie *Munich*. Selling the benefits of working hard throughout one's career within the Israeli service, the agent boasts that he, too, started at the bottom. But look at him now, look where he is. Avner cannot help but laugh at this "fifty-year-old schmuck, sitting on a wooden chair in a sweltering little room, interviewing raw recruits. Very exciting."[57]

I suspect that the great majority of the best ones simply packed up and left years ago. The few that are left are fighting an uphill battle they know they cannot win.

This is a world of the unhappy. It is rampant, and it is infectious. It spreads. Many of the new recruits I have stayed in touch with since my resignation admit to being unhappy. Some, only a few weeks out of training, have already realised that they do not feel comfortable in that environment. Many are waiting to see how it will be like in the region, and if they don't like it there, have admitted to me that they would quit. How healthy can an organisation be when a large proportion of its new employees is already looking for a way out?

Still, very few of the disgruntled will actually express their disillusionment openly, and almost never with supervisors or management. It is shared among intelligence officers, but given the system of fear, such expressions are made covertly, mere whispers in the office. Since expressions of dissatisfaction with the employer are, as we have seen, next to an act of treason, there is no mobilisation of employees as a force for change, no Solidarity or Chapter 77 to end the totalitarian regime. Everybody is on his own, and single voices alone simply are too weak to challenge the Goliath of the institution. The absence of open discourse on the general wellbeing of the workforce engenders self-doubt in the employee; he worries that the problem lies with him, a line of thought that, as we have noted, is encouraged by CSIS: The problem is not us. *It is you.* This inevitably leads to a descent into solitude. During training, we are even told to recognise the telltale signs that an intelligence officer may be losing his sense of purpose: The otherwise social butterfly—which most of use were—now avoids people, will spend an increasing, if not inordinate, amount of time on his own. We were also told to avoid these people, for they are dangerous, infectious. It is very revealing that the training staff would feel the need to tell recruits during the entry training course about this reality. Might it be that the management is aware that the problem is more common than it seems? It does not take extraordinary effort to realise that the malaise is widespread. But everybody fights, not wanting to let go. Some are good at lying to themselves and have repeated the lie so often—it is a great job, it is challenging, I love my job!—that they play back the chorus to whoever asks. In most cases, however, we can see through the lie. The enthusiasm sounds made-up. The army of sufferers, therefore, suffers in silence.

The institutional resistance to change, and the lack of respect for the ideas, experience, and worth of new employees, let alone its failure to recognize and fully address discontent within the ranks, means that CSIS will remain a monolithic entity, one that is ill-suited for the rapid social and technological changes that are occurring in the 21st century. The Service's inability to weed out incompetence, and its current self-defeating system of promotion, also means that it will have difficulty keeping pace with sub-national groups, such as al-Qaeda, that are quick to adapt to their environment and are not constrained by the crushing bureaucracy that often prevents the Service from doing anything. How can CSIS ever hope to compete with groups whose sole objective is to attain their objectives, groups without a fixed hierarchy? Moreover, within radical organisations, incompetence or lack of dedication to the cause results in an individual either being thrown out, or silenced in the most savage of manners. How can an intelligence service that does not rid itself of its incompetent elements ever hope to counter, let alone outpace, such groups? Can we conceive of bin Laden, seeing that an operative is not doing his job, moving that person from operational planning to, say, weapons acquisitions—in other words, that he would brook the incompetence and simply move the problem to another sector? Of course not, and most people in the private sector would agree.

The game of terrorism and counterterrorism is a deadly one, and the consequences of failure for the state and its people can be devastating. Can we, therefore, allow our intelligence service to take a gamble by retaining employees who have no place protecting the lives of Canadians, employees who do not have the skill sets, the knowledge, or the dedication? Can we allow employees whose sole concern is their next promotion to make decisions affecting the lives of Canadians? Are we willing to take that risk?

Some optimists at CSIS hope that change will happen, that once the gerontocrats go into retirement the Service will modernise itself. I am greatly troubled by this line of thinking, for two principal reasons. First, what about now? Is the requirement for security no less serious now than it will be five, ten years down the road? And furthermore, aware of how slow big institutions are at adapting and changing, if we wait half a decade or a decade, the benefits of change will only be felt fifteen to twenty years down the road. By that time, new sets of changes will be required. In a way, this slowness is similar to the problems in arms acquisition that modern military organisations are perennially facing, in that the process is so slow that by the time the equipment becomes operational, it is already obsolete and suited for the previous battle.

Secondly, through the system of pressure and fear, the old guard is ensuring its perpetuation by promoting officers who are willing to replicate their work habits. In other words, the new generation, forced to copy the old, will not generate the changes that are so desperately needed. This, again, is how authoritarian and totalitarian systems are able to continue functioning even after the "big man" has left the scene, as in the Soviet Union (Joseph Stalin) and China (Mao Zedong), to use but two examples.

For intelligence services to join the rest of the world—that is, the 21st century—they will need to be increasingly treated like private sector companies.

While, for obvious reasons, it is difficult to establish a bottom line or *profits* in the intelligence world, something can nevertheless be said about efficiency. Government cannot hide behind the difficulty of assessing efficiency as an excuse for inefficiency. Steps have been made in that direction, but unfortunately they tend to use quantity rather than quality as a benchmark. Who cares that an intelligence officer produces forty reports every month if most of those reports are useless? Would we not rather have an officer producing half as many reports but for those reports to actually contribute to the investigation, to the security of Canadians? Furthermore, while productivity is difficult to assess, dedication and professionalism can be evaluated. There are, right now and at all levels of the Service, people who the entire workforce could identify as sitting ducks. In other words, it is not difficult to name the rotten apples, and if the Service is ever to become the professional intelligence agency Canadians deserve, those bad elements will have to be removed, not when they retire, but now. They should not be given one more minute to cause damage to Canada and its people, or those who seek to start a new life with us.

Also, people with *managerial* skills should be put in positions of management. It is simply unpardonable for CSIS to have supervisors and managers who, were they in the private sector, would almost certainly be fired after a few weeks because of their incompetence. There are officers in managerial positions whose skills are limited to street intelligence; those people need to be out there, making contacts, meeting sources, and so on. It is irresponsible, and in fact counterproductive, to remove these individuals from the street and seek to transform them, probably against their will, into managers overnight because they have done their time or need to check the managerial box on their career progression chart. People without managerial skills will not only be a disservice to their subordinates and to the Service, but will also be miserable.

Finally, to return to our previous point, CSIS needs to ensure that it is effective *now*, not five or ten years down the road. I cannot conceive of Microsoft, or Sony, say, being complacent about their current state of affairs, with management telling the board members and investors that everything is ok, that profits will improve five, ten years from now, while Apple and Panasonic continue running. Investors expect profits now, and Canadian taxpayers should demand as much of their institutions. The key is accountability. Private sector companies are accountable to their investors and need to demonstrate efficiency on a regular basis. How can a federal institution claim as much when, in the name of security, it not only masks its errors but claims that it cannot reveal its successes? Can we imagine, again, the chief accountant at Sony, standing in front of board members in Tokyo, asking them, based on faith alone, to believe him when he says that the company is making profits—without ever showing them the numbers? Canadians have a right to know whether CSIS is doing its job or not. Without this requirement, without the appropriate checks and balances, failure and incompetence are allowed to become acceptable. In a world where failure can lead to substantial loss of life or, conversely, to the unwarranted destruction of a newly-arrived family in Canada, incompetence and unchecked careerism should be anything but acceptable. In the private world, heads roll, and so they should in government. In fact, in the private world, heads roll even *before* massive losses are experienced. We cannot wait for a bomb to go off on a subway, or in a shopping mall, before firing people. If they are deemed incompetent, they need to go, now. Firings are preventive; executives lose their jobs before the company goes under. Government should adopt this system.

CSIS, as we have seen, seeks anonymity. It somehow believes that the less the Canadian public knows about its activities—its existence, even—the better. A recent poll showed that nearly half of Canadians know little, if anything, about their spy agency. This is no wonder, as CSIS resents being talked about. In fact, it has a tremendous fear of its practices being exposed. The non-subtle threats that I received about writing a book on my experiences at CSIS are part of that aversion to exposure. While CSIS does have a public relations section, very rarely will CSIS provide anything beyond the usual "no comment" or "we cannot confirm nor deny." Playing dumb seems to be the operative philosophy. The Service, which in recent months has been under special scrutiny due to the Air India, the Arar and the Bhupinder S. Liddar case, is very inept at defending its actions, positions, and attitude to the Canadian public. In fact, it looks down at them with contempt, yet another sign, just as above, of its disconnect from reality. Its officers are isolated from each other, CSIS is isolated from its government counterparts, and though its mandate is to protect the real world out there, its actions are that of the ivory tower that deals with the unreal, that invents for itself, then seeks, ghosts, and begins to see them everywhere.

Lastly, it is imperative that we turn to the difficulty analysts and intelligence officers encounter when they have reached such a point of disillusionment as to consider resignation as the only remaining option. This is important because very few do it, which stems from the same mechanism that allows individuals with a strong moral foundation to willingly participate in something immoral. Despite providing an excellent analysis of what went wrong in the US defence and intelligence community apparatus before and during the Vietnam War, Daniel Ells-berg's *Secrets* fails to answer the question he asks himself as to why people helped wage an illegal war and, despite everything they knew, did nothing to stop it. The answer, I believe, lies in self-interest (career progression, earning a living) and participation in a project that is greater than the self, with all the religious undertones that it carries.

Compounding this is the mentality, beaten into the heads of intelligence officers from the beginning, that leaving the Service is akin to an act of treason. Since my resignation, the great majority of individuals I came to know during my stint at CSIS have refrained from getting in touch with me. The publication of this book—the ultimate act of treason, as I have been told—is sure to burn more bridges.

Following an officer's resignation, an interview is conducted to ensure that the employee has not taken classified information with him. I remember sitting in the lobby one Thursday afternoon, waiting for that post-mortem, during which I would be relinquishing the i.d. cards that granted me access to the building. Half of me wanted to see my former co-workers as they entered the building; the other half wanted to hide in the sofa so that I could avoid their judgment. Throughout the interview, the underlying theme was, Will you represent a threat to the Service? What will you do with the things you have learned, the things in your head? The accusation is tacit, but it is there. You are a threat to them because you broke the bond that tied you to the family. This was when, for the second time in my career at CSIS, I was warned against writing a book about my experiences.

Another factor that weighs heavily in an intelligence officer's decision whether to leave the Service or not is financial. At $38,600 a year (it is slightly higher now, though by no means appropriate), starting a career at CSIS represents a pay cut for many individuals. What exacerbates the problem is that in many cases, the recruit's spouse or companion will have been forced to make a difficult career choice: To quit his or her job and hope that, once they relocate to Ottawa, he or she will be able to find something.

What this means, therefore, is that the decision to resign has very real financial ramifications, and as such many disgruntled employees who have a desire to quit simply cannot afford to do so—at least not until they have found something else, which one must do in secret, as hunting for a job while one is still employed at CSIS does not sit well with management. Given that intelligence officers are, with a few exceptions, forbidden to hold a second job, recruits have no means by which to increase their salary. Many are therefore trapped, forced to stay at a job that, slowly but surely, is gnawing at their sense of self. The longer they stay, the more mired they become, until the place turns into a prison.

*   *   *   *

It is a beautiful end of September day in Ottawa, one week after my retirement. I am meeting a friend who works as an analyst at the Privy Council's Office (PCO), the secretariat of the federal Cabinet. My friend has been working with PCO for about as long as I had worked for CSIS. We are sitting outside a small Lebanese coffee shop, welcoming the warm rays of the autumn sun. Our discussion inevitably turns to intelligence. A year earlier, he and I had taken a course on Asymmetric Threats at the Royal Military College of Canada. We also talk about the reasons why I left CSIS. As it turns out, most of my grievances are a confirmation of what he has heard, or experienced, himself. The Service's condescension toward other departments of the Canadian intelligence community, and vice-versa, is no myth. In fact, my friend informs me that PCO no longer bothers to read whatever document CSIS sends it. Not only have the agencies historically disagreed on a number of points, he says, but oftentimes CSIS had no information to back its arguments with, or would not share what it had that could convince PCO. In other words, CSIS was also asking other departments to believe it on faith. I had seen this many times. You didn't argue or debate with CSIS. Employees couldn't, nor could other members of the intelligence community. It appears that my friend's feelings are shared within the community: CSIS doesn't back its information, it is oftentimes unreliable, does not care to discuss things with or explain its views to its allies, and therefore its products are of little value. This is a serious problem. How safe is a country when the agency whose mandate it is to inform government of potential threats to security is ignored by its customers? How dysfunctional can the system be when that same agency has become the object of community-wide derision? Perhaps more worrying was the fact that my friend, and by rebound PCO, seemed to accept this with a shrug. Within the intelligence community, as is the case within CSIS, mediocrity appears to have become acceptable. It is one thing for other Canadian agencies to disagree with CSIS, and for them to choose to ignore whatever information the latter has provided. It is quite another, however, to fail to raise the matter with the powers that be.

*   *   *   *

Five years ago, almost to the day, I, along with another 19 individuals, was on the brink of "graduation" from IOET. Back then, our trainers spared no effort drilling into our young minds that what we did in the course of our work, the places we visited—the very nature of our work—should be kept secret from others at all cost. Some took this directive to such a level as to hide everything from their families.

I experienced no small amount of surprise when, in the May 25, 2007, issue of the *Toronto Star*, I came across an article about the just-retired Jack Hooper, the former Director of Operations (DO) and for a short period Acting Director at CSIS.[58] Part of the surprise lay in the fact that a high-ranking official would have an article published about him in a national newspaper. So there he was, the former man at the top, revealing his identity to any Canadian—to the entire world, in fact, thanks to the Internet.

The second shocker in the article was its candidness in describing some of the places Mr. Hooper had visited in the course of his work, places like Uzbekistan, Yemen, Kandahar and Lima. The heart of the matter is that readers are fully aware Mr. Hooper visited these locales in the course of his professional activities and not, as it were, as a private citizen—in other words, he wasn't on a personal vacation there. Again, during our training, it had been drilled into out heads that under no circumstances were we to divulgate trips to or contacts with operational areas, as we were to maintain the myth (a pretense that had many holes in it) that CSIS only operated domestically. So here he is, the spymaster boasting about his exploits in some of the world's hot spots. This makes me wonder if this article was ever cleared by CSIS—as all CSIS employees, current or retired—are supposed to do, or if perhaps some of its members are just above the law. Maybe the explanation is simpler. Maybe, as is often the case, CSIS is being inconsistent, if not altogether incompetent.

For many months after I resigned from CSIS I would avoid revealing where I had worked and be cautious in how I characterized my former employer when applying for a job. Part of me still wanted to play spy or simply wanted to respect the agreement that I had made with CSIS not to reveal where I had worked, what I had done. Some still do, choosing to hide behind a screen when testifying at the Air India inquiry, as did the director-general, now retired, of the section where I worked. But for the DO to open up the way he did, in an article where he is seen standing, hands in pockets, on a quay in British Columbia—that did it for me.

No more hiding. If a 22-year career intelligence officer can open up the way he did, there is no reason why someone who only practiced the same job for 29 months could not (I had always wondered, anyway, why former CIA officials, from Robert Baer all the way to former Director of Central Intelligence George Tenet, could publish their memoirs with such freedom while their Canadian counterparts were prevented from doing so).

Aside from epitomizing the greater liberties former CSIS officials now seem to enjoy in terms of talking about their former employer, what did the article in the *Toronto Star* have to offer? Sadly, precious little, aside from exposing a man who unfortunately stands as the perfect mascot for the macho attitude that guides CSIS and how it carries itself in the intelligence community. Hooper, for example, talks about CSIS and its dealings with governments that are known to disregard human rights: "Here's the deal. Everybody would like to believe that we have an array of choices that are good choices and bad choices. But we're going to a dance where every girl is ugly, okay … They're all ugly. And all we can do is get the least ugly girl to dance with. But you know, when you bring her home your dad is going to tell you, 'That is one ugly woman.' And you're going to say, 'Yeah dad, but she was the best looking of that lot.' Does that make you smart? Not in the eyes of your father."

The above quote was in reference to the Syrian government and how CSIS became involved in the Maher Arar case, the Syrian-born Canadian who, thanks to information given the US by the RCMP, was deported to Syria, where he is believed to have been tortured. Besides being a repugnantly misogynistic and elitist analogy, Hooper's "ugly girl" is indicative of the mindset that prevails at CSIS, one in which the consequences of one's actions are discarded. The proverbial man in the bar always has a choice, and if all the girls are too "ugly," he can just leave. He doesn't have to dance—especially when he knows that choosing to dance will harm innocent people.

Speaking about Justice O'Connor, who presided the Arar Commission, Hooper then demonstrates another undercurrent at CSIS, that of the agency that knows better than everybody else: "Nobody knows what the right thing is to do [,] so it's left to us to make the decision about who the least ugly girl is."

Therein lies the danger for all Canadians, when CSIS is left to decide what is best for Canada, without, as we have seen, the accountability and checks that can ensure the survival of a democracy. Unfortunately, these two lines perfectly describe the aversion and contempt that CSIS has shown the court system as well as SIRC and the IG, the two supposed independent yet fangless accountability bodies charged with monitoring how CSIS conducts its operations.

But accountability isn't the object of the *Star* interview. It is about the man. And above all, the one impression it leaves the reader with is that of an unpolished bully, whose comments, such as "I would never let my guys drink Merlot [wine]. It's not allowed. It's a sissy wine ... It's light and girls drink it. And it sounds funny when you say it. Mer-lot. Men should never say that," cannot but—to pun—leave a bad taste in the reader's mouth. Why would any self-respecting career official say such things in a "first-time" interview with a national publication? How unrefined a mind must one have to use such derogatory terms to make a point (about what, one wonders)? Beyond that, if CSIS can allow such a person to climb to the top, what does this entail for the minority groups that will be targeted by the organization in Canada? If Hooper can show such flagrant disrespect for women and homosexuals, how does he treat Muslims, Sikhs, Aborigines, Africans, to name a few?

In my 29 months at CSIS I did not have much interactions with Hooper— "the CSIS chief who has a lot to learn about the Middle East but talks far too much," as veteran reporter Robert Fisk wrote on June 10, 2006. When I did, however, I was sitting at a long oblong table on the fifth floor of the headquarters building in Ottawa. Next to me was my supervisor, or head, and at table with us were lawyers and a handful of other officials. At the opposite end, oozing cowboy-like confidence, was Jack Hooper. Every time we went in that room, it was to renew a warrant or request to add targets to our investigation. We would make a short presentation, followed by a mockery of a question-and-answer session. Usually, Hooper would have the final, or next-to-final, word—a blessing of sorts— and we would leave, added powers granted.

The uncomfortable question is, given the man that has been exposed in the article—and by rebound the organization that permitted him to reach the pinnacle of power—how confident can we be that the individuals we asked to target in that stuffy room *should* be targeted?

Perhaps, like ugly girls and Merlot wine, targets can just as easily be spit out.

The above presents a very bleak picture of the Canadian intelligence community. Bright-eyed recruits filled with ambition are quickly beaten into submission, and instead of doing what they thought intelligence officers do, they are transformed into little more than unthinking, document-generating secretaries. Though it would be immature to expect that a day in the life of an intelligence officer has anything to do with how it is portrayed in books and movies, recruits nevertheless deserve a better treatment. But that isn't so. As long as an officer is capable of using copy-and-pasting functions, change dates, and use prefabricated document templates, he will be considered a proficient desk officer with potential for career progression. Godot haunts the halls of the building. There is little original thinking; this is, rather, a business of recycling, of mimicking, of helping congeal the past. At the structural level, CSIS shuns other Canadian agencies, other opinions. It is an isolated world, and the Truth, as it is understood by the Service, is under siege. Thanks to secrecy and unaccountability, this situation is allowed to persist. The machine feeds on young recruits, transforms them, spews out the recalcitrant few and the game goes on. Officers are broke, broken, and a few months after beginning their career they already feel the budding of despair as they enter the building in the morning. How can one be expected to serve his country under such circumstances?

CHAPTER 2

▼

CSIS AND THE WORLD

Pundits and armchair specialists the world over were quick to claim that the multiple terrorist attacks of Sept. 11, 2001, had changed the world. The heart of the US had been attacked, and if New York City and Washington were no longer off limits to the savagery that, until then, the Continental US had been spared, then no one was safe anymore. It was one thing to have your embassies in East Africa, or destroyers in North Africa, bombed; it was another for the attacks to take place on North American soil.

But what do these experts mean when they say that the world changed on Sept. 11? What, in fact, had changed? For nearly forty years of Cold War, the East and the West had been under the constant threat of, and on a few occasions came dangerously close to, nuclear annihilation, and there is no question that New York City, Washington, London and Madrid, which I do not name by accident, would have been incinerated had the US and the Soviet Union ever made the Cold War a hot one. Thankfully, cooler heads prevailed, and the superpower confrontation did not end in Armageddon. Running parallel to the Cold War—and sprinting ahead once it was over—the forces of globalisation were increasingly bringing the world together. Technologies were developed that greatly facilitated communication and travel. And the very technologies that permitted the miniaturisation of the world were also travelling, leapfrogging into third-world countries that still couldn't manage to feed their populations. Suddenly, cell phones were showing up in the remotest corners of the planet, and increasingly, field workers and local populations in every country, regardless of poverty or conflict, were getting access to the Internet. Thanks to hand-held cameras and portable audio-video editing suites, journalists no longer required a team of assistants to bring back images from distant or war-torn countries.

It is those technologies—cell phones, the Internet, debit cards, the easy transfer of money, airplanes—that allowed nineteen individuals to commit the attacks of Sept. 11. And box cutters. The new world was meeting the old. But the world didn't change on that day. Rather, the Western world joined the rest of the world. The awakening was a rude one, and it shattered the false sense of security that had installed itself in Western cities since the collapse of the Soviet Union. Starting in the 1990s, wars were small-scale, intrastate, and humanitarian intervention aside, their repercussions in the West were, at worst, modest. Or so we thought. What it took us a long time to understand, though, is that nations cannot cherry pick when and where they want to be global, and when they would rather stay isolated. Either you participate in the global experiment, or you don't. In other words, you cannot become global when it suits your needs to do so, only to return to a state of isolationism when that need has been fulfilled. A country like the US, for example, cannot trade at the international level, spread its culture, maintain military bases the world over, and hope, in return, to be left alone. The footprint is much too great. Moreover, the ethnic fabric of the US, Canada, and many European countries prevents this sense of isolation, as conflict or emergencies in poorer countries will almost certainly prompt members of those ethnic groups exiled in the West to act, either by demonstrating, calling for action, raising funds, or clashing with members of the other side within the country they emigrated to. This last point has often been neglected by the West, and only recently have academics started mentioning the risks inherent to this new reality.

In a way, this is what the West is experiencing with the current wave of terrorism, but the lack of foresight and preparation has led our governments to react in panic, and as we have seen, instead of addressing the problem logically, they have turned to racial and religious profiling, illegal detentions, outright racism, and the use of deadly force on a large scale. Individuals of Middle Eastern origin living among us are now, in the paranoid CSIS view, all potentially terrorists. Worse, if we are to believe CSIS, second-generation individuals who were born and raised in Canada are now starting to embrace radical ideologies, as if they were somehow predisposed to do so. They are like the Professor at the end of Joseph Conrad's *The Secret Agent,* passing unsuspected and deadly, like a pest in the street full of men.

What we must realise, though, is that all the elements that on Sept. 11, 2001, combined to "change the world" had been there for a long time, and the Niagara, to use Carroll's image, had finally taken us to an end of sorts. Like chemical compounds that, alone, are harmless, once combined they make for dangerous explosives. In its post-Cold War, US-led hubris, the West had lagged behind the rest of the world for over a decade, unaware that its exploitative actions and its neglect of the rest of humanity were creating resentment. Western countries reaped the benefits of exploitation in the Middle East, had access to relatively cheap oil, installed military bases close to sensitive areas in Saudi Arabia, and supported regimes in Israel and Egypt and Pakistan that repressed their populations, in Israel's case Palestinians under its occupation. As their economies boomed, Western countries failed to see that a storm was brewing.

The backlash could have been a pandemic emerging from Africa, or an early strain of the Asian Flu. Instead, it took the form of what *New York Times* journalist Thomas Friedman calls super-empowered angry individuals, individuals who, thanks to technology, now have the means at their disposal to act upon their grievances, whether they are real or imagined. What *did* change on Sept. 11, therefore, was how the West came to understand its place in the world, and with it, the strategic template decision-makers use to plan their moves.

For Canada, the attacks changed our world, but did so in a subtler way. We were not a primary target. Few Canadians died in the Sept. 11 attacks. The Canadian intelligence community, seeing the opportunity at hand and aware of the pressure that would soon come from Washington, requested budget increases and emergency funds, and obtained them. Ministers are always hungry for budgets, and following a decade of budget cuts, the Solicitor General, under which CSIS fell at the time, was handed a golden opportunity to sell the idea that more money, more people, were needed. The proposition that the world had changed—believable in the weeks immediately following the attacks—compounded the apparent logic of investing in security. But as the ashes in New York and Washington settled, the cool heads didn't prevail. Instead, the reaction remained one of panic, and CSIS began hiring left and right, with little consideration for the quality of the individuals it was bringing in. Failing to understand the origins of this new threat, CSIS hired a number of individuals who did not fit the new analytical requirements. Instead, it continued to hire individuals who were, at best, only fit to fight the last war.

For Canada, the greatest and most nefarious repercussion of Sept. 11 was the loss of Canadian sovereignty. Immediately after the terrorist attacks, the Canada-US border was shut. Not long afterwards, American politicians and the media began blaming poor border protection for the attacks, claiming that some of the 19 terrorists who had hijacked the four aircraft had come from Canada. It took months, if not years, of political information campaigns by Canadian diplomats to dispel that illusion, for in reality, not a single one of the hijackers had come from Canada. In spite of this, accusations of Canadian laxness at the border by American politicians—and by former US Ambassador to Canada Paul Cellucci, who should have been kicked out of Canada long before his ambassadorial mandate expired—have been frequent, relentless, and at times have come in the form of threats or dictates rather than dialogue. We have entered a new era of McCarthyism, one in which allies of the US must constantly prove how dedicated they are to combating terrorism, how trustworthy they are. Listening to the Prime Minister or the Minister of Public Safety in the months after the attacks, more often than not the discourse was meant to appease US fears rather than the Canadian public.

In that same vein, it also seems that any challenge directed at Washington in terms of a strategy for fighting terrorism results in accusations of being "soft" on terror, just like the Democrats had been accused of being soft on, or even supportive of, communism in their time. In fact, ever since the Bush Administration came to power, it has become increasingly difficult to be critical of anything the US does without suffering the consequences. A good example of this was the reaction of US Ambassador to Canada David Wilkins, who replaced Cellucci in 2005, to comments by Prime Minister Paul Martin during a conference in Montreal on climactic change, where he raised concerns over the lack of US participation in the environmental process. The rhetorical backlash was a furious one and was nothing short of Washington, via Wilkins, a Republican hack, dictating what the leader of another sovereign country could and could not say on his own soil. The right-wing media joined the chorus, with a pundit comparing Canada to "a retarded cousin,"[59] while a press secretary to former Republican senator Bob Dole rehashed the claim that Canada harbours terrorists. As these comments coincided with the beginning of an electoral campaign in Canada, they may very well have represented a covert attempt by the US, along with the right-wing media, to influence the outcome of the elections. This would not unheard of, as Washington behaved in similar fashion when it tried to manipulate Canadian elections during the Diefenbaker and Pearson years. Despite denials that Washington was insinuating itself into the Canadian electoral process, the temptation must have existed to rid itself of Paul Martin, who in the tradition of Pierre Elliot Trudeau had charted a path that was truly Canadian, even if it was one that flew in the face of US ambitions. Martin, with all his faults, had a vision for the future and should be commended for his commitment to internationalism. Now that the US-friendly Stephen Harper is Prime Minister, we are less likely to experience wild divergences in how Canada and the US interpret the threat of and deal with terrorism. This development, however, is not necessarily in Canada's best interest.

Throughout the Martin years, and to a certain extent today still, the US played the age-old political trick: Whenever there is a problem at home, blame others, deflect accusations. The truth is often a casualty of politics; it doesn't matter whether accusations of incompetence on the Canadian side of the border are valid or not. But within the US, it creates an image of siege, with the impression that others are to blame for their insecurity. After all, the US Government invested billions of dollars creating the Department of Homeland Security (DHS), reforming its institutions, and waging wars overseas. The CIA is more active than ever, with recruiting campaign ads appearing in *The Economist* and other magazines. New powers, tremendously intrusive powers, were given to a number of agencies, including the National Security Agency, which is now monitoring domestic phone calls and e-mails in the US—without warrants.[60] Alliances were made, or strengthened, with states like Pakistan, the Philippines, and a handful of Central Asian countries. Oftentimes, those deals came with the deployment of US soldiers and financial aid. Given all this action, all this investment, hardly anyone can accuse Washington of complacency. It therefore follows that if something went wrong, if the US homeland, in spite of this flurry of action, continued to feel threatened, surely it was Canada's, or Mexico's, fault. After all, comparatively speaking, Canada has spent but a fraction of the amounts the US has invested in national security. And didn't Ahmed Ressam, the alleged LAX Millennium bomber, come from Canada before he was arrested, in 1999, *on the US side of the border*, by an alert customs inspector? Didn't the former director of CSIS himself state, on a number of occasions, that every terrorist organisation in the world has a presence in Canada, prompting accusations on all sides that Canada is some sort of Club Med for terrorists? The sad truth is that in spite of all the money invested by the US Government into homeland security, in spite of all the alterations that were made to the intelligence system, the naming of a Director of National Intelligence, and pre-emptive wars abroad, the US has enough incompetence, both in terms of personnel and within its institutions, and has enough enemies dedicated to their cause, to allow for another catastrophic terrorist attack to occur on US territory. In fact, Michael Scheuer, the former head of the bin Laden Unit at the CIA and author of the helpful *Imperial Hubris*, is convinced, for reasons we will touch on later, that more, even deadlier attacks against the US are almost inevitable. The US Government knows this, hence the deflection onto allies north and south.

In spite of all the changes made to the US intelligence community, it still takes the FBI months, and sometimes years, before it will reply to a inquiry from another agency. In spite of all the changes, FBI regional offices still fail to share information with FBI headquarters. In spite of all the changes, the FBI some-times fails to see the difference between Sunni Muslims and Shiite Muslims. In spite of all the changes, and in spite of all the recommendations that were made by the 9/11 Commission, the FBI and the CIA still fail to talk to each other. In my dealings with these agencies, I have seen numerous instances of intellectual sloppiness, a total lack of judgement, no knowledge of history, poor writing skills—in other words, what Scheuer characterises as the "incompetence and der-eliction of some agencies."[61] The situation at DHS, the clearing house and, in many ways, the spokesperson for the entire US intelligence community on threat-related matters, is no better. It is a huge, lumbering beast, and it tends to over-react every time it receives threat information. To quote Scheuer again: "Fixed on protecting their posteriors, U.S. officials are determined to warn every American about every threat they can lay their hands on."[62] On more than one occasion, at great cost to both economies, parts of the Canada-US border were shut down due to threats which, upon closer inspection, were ostensibly fabrica-tions.

So why, then, the repeated accusations that *Canada* isn't doing its job? The reason, I believe, is that in addition to deflecting attention and not wanting to admit that despite the billions of dollars spent the US intelligence community remains a mess, the US Government intends to dictate, to lead the war on terror-ism *on its terms*. The US does not have allies in this war: it has subjects. Canada has received so much pressure from its southern counterpart that it had little choice but to create its own DHS, known as Public Safety and Emergency Pre-paredness (PSEP), invent the position of National Security Advisor, and to restructure its intelligence community. All that this accomplished, aside from appeasing fear-mongers in Washington and give Canadians the illusion that things were being done to ensure their security, was to create more layers to the Canadian intelligence community, so many layers, in fact, that most members of that community have little understanding of who does what. However, as Hay-den B. Peake, in his review of *Transforming US Intelligence*, lucidly observes in The Intelligence Officer's Bookshelf, "organizational changes ... seldom solve operational problems."[63] The reason for this is simple: The problem with intelli-gence lies in the analysis—in other words, it is a *human* problem—and no amount of structural reshuffling will ever address that issue. Based on my own experience, the only thing that these organisational changes have managed to accomplish is to make the distribution of information more cumbersome, and therefore lest timely.

The following example illustrates this point. In April 2005 I was invited to represent CSIS at a Canadian Forces' Officers' training course. Over three days, the participants, all majors and up, role-played how the different Canadian agencies would react during a scenario involving a fictitious three-pronged emergency on Canadian soil. My responsibility, aside for assisting the person who stood-in for CSIS, was to generate the threat assessments and situation updates that were distributed among the players. It soon became evident that the future leaders of the Canadian Forces had no idea who did what within the community, and I am not sure that the three-day exercise shed any light on what is, in essence, a complex system of systems. In fact, most analysts at CSIS do not understand it fully either. The "simpler" version of the community organisational chart we were briefed on during IOET had already proved too complex for some of us. With the creation of PSEP, the super-government agency, things have become more convoluted, and since Sept. 11, 2001, the fact that every branch of the federal and provincial governments has expressed a desire to play a role in combating terrorism has only made matters worse.

A surprising number of agencies are involved in security intelligence in Canada, including CSIS, the RCMP, PCO, the Canadian Security Establishment (CSE), and the Department of National Defence (DND). Other agencies, such as Immigration Canada, Customs, Transport Canada, Health Canada, Foreign Affairs and others, also have intelligence branches. One recurrent conclusion drawn from the tabletop exercises—a simulated terrorist attack on Canadian soil—the government holds annually is that communication between agencies is slow; there are too many layers, and the players are ill-informed as to which agency does what in case of an incident. In fact, were a real attack, say, a biological weapon incident in Toronto, or a chemical weapon release in the port of Montreal, to occur, the response would most likely be ad hoc, and in the name of effectiveness most of the layers that were created after Sept. 11 would be bypassed.[64]

Another tabletop exercise I participated in, this time involving an electronic attack on the Canadian infrastructure, led to hours of confusion as officers from various agencies tried to understand where to call and who to get in touch with. We all left the PSEP building less than confident that we would know how to react should a real attack occur. As an American political analyst recently wrote about the US intelligence community but could as well have been writing about its Canadian counterpart: "Can the notoriously dysfunctional interagency process ever be fixed by organizational tinkering alone, without the elaboration of a common conceptual ground?"[65] Another commentator on national security matters in the US recently compared the DHS to "a bureaucratic Frankenstein, with clumsily-stitched-together limbs and an inadequate, misfiring brain."[66] If an incident were to occur on Canadian soil, I would hope that most of these layers would be skipped over, as failure to do so would most certainly result in untimely response and additional loss of life. In fact, I would much rather put my life in the hands of the dedicated first respondents on the ground, or the soldiers, than in the gigantic and unnecessarily cumbersome system that has been put into place, a castle in the air, really, to reassure Canadians and Washington.

The March 11, 2003, multiple bombings in Madrid, Spain (also known as the 3/11 Madrid bombings), provides a perfect example of how quickly government structures are circumvented in time of crisis. Back then, I was an analyst at the Threat Assessment Unit, the perennially-understaffed section of CSIS that advises the Service and the rest of the community on potential threats to the security of Canada. That day, both my supervisor and her superior (in other words, the Head and the Chief) were out of the office, so as the senior analyst on the desk I was acting Head of the unit. Shortly after the bombings in Madrid, a call to my supervisor was rerouted to my phone. The person on the other end of the line was no less than the deputy National Security Advisor, and he wanted to know *immediately* what the Service's position was on the issue. He needed it now, as he was on his way to an emergency meeting with the National Security Advisor and other very high-ranking officials within government. The fact that supervisors two ranks up were absent didn't seem to worry him, nor was he aware that the *Service's* position was being given to him by an analyst who had less than a year's experience. As he was pressing me to provide a line or two on the Service's assessment of the attacks, I did not have time to turn to people higher up within the organisation. I did my best to give him as much information as I could, which was next to nothing, as the attacks had just occurred and we had yet to obtain information from other agencies. In fact, I did my best to rephrase the information that, like any other Canadian, we had obtained from the wires and on television. On that day, the CSIS "position" on a terrorist attack in Spain had boiled down to the information obtained and analysed by a single rookie analyst. That day, *I* was CSIS. While challenges such as this one were what I was seeking, it is nevertheless disconcerting that something like this, such a breakdown in the chain of command, would be allowed to happen. And during my time in the unit, it would happen again.

What was done to the Canadian security apparatus after Sept. 11 made the community more complex, heavier, and consequently slower. It certainly did not result in more security for Canadians. It did, however, serve as political ammunition: Canadians needed to know that their government was doing *something* to combat terrorism. And the strategy may have worked, as some critics of the Canadian response to terrorism have admitted that Canada has done a few things right. This includes the Frasier Institute, which in a report titled *Canada's Inadequate Response* writes that "various bodies were created to provide better coordination of intelligence, threat assessment, and response. These bodies include the Department of Public Safety and Emergency Preparedness, the Integrated Threat Assessment Centre (ITAC) and Integrated National Security Teams (INSETs)."[67] Obviously, critics that Canada was not doing enough to combat terrorism, which is the Frasier Institute's contention, nevertheless bought the concept of restructuring as action. Conclusions such as this one could only have been reached by individuals who, with all due respect to them, probably never worked in the security intelligence environment. The smokescreen of the super-agency had worked.

Among the reasons why governments all over the world have been restructuring their national security apparatuses is the "we might be next" syndrome. After all, one repercussion of terrorism is that after the event everybody seems to think they might be next. If them, why not us? How are we different from them? If, as some specialists—including numerous heads of state—have noted, the terrorists are against who we are, our values, our liberties, democracy, then surely there is nothing preventing al-Qaeda from attacking us next (as we shall see later, however, the perception that bin Laden and his cohorts are attacking the conceptual West because of these things is a complete, and perhaps self-serving, departure from reality).

It is fascinating to watch how the media and governments react after a terrorist incident, as it offers us precious insights into human behaviour and the psychology of the masses. Immediately after the London bombings in July 2005, all the media in Canada began focussing on the Toronto subway system, creating fears—based on no evidence whatsoever that a plot was afoot—that it might be next. Is the subway safe? How much security is there in the Toronto public transit system? Understandably, the Minister of Transportation publicly called for increased security measures for the Canadian transportation grid, but a side effect of this was that it exacerbated fears that we were next and that transportation would be the target. The Toronto subway was hammered into the minds of Canadians. In spite of absolutely no evidence that terrorists were targeting the Toronto subway, we were conditioned into believing that it was. The fear campaign seems to have paid off: In a poll conducted in fall 2005, Canadians viewed the Toronto subway as the most probable target of a terrorist attack.[68] This fear spread to the government as well, which in the weeks following the London bombings commissioned a number of threat and risk assessments against public transit—mostly city buses and subway systems.

Such focus on a single possible target, however, represents a security risk, in that all the attention is drawn to that one sector and all the resources are pulled in that direction, to the detriment of other possible targets such as landmarks, shopping malls, dams, and so on. By focussing on a single item, society could in fact force would-be terrorists to look somewhere else and give them an opportunity to exploit the fact that all eyes are turned elsewhere to launch a successful attack. Conversely, one could also argue that so much attention on a single target could make it even more appealing to terrorists, in that a successful terrorist attack following all that attention would further erode people's confidence in the ability of their government to protect them.

The Canadian government responded to Madrid and London with meetings and press conferences where, as noted above, more money was requested for transportation safety. The same happened shortly after 17 individuals were arrested in Ontario in June 2006. We need more money, CSIS' Hooper said. The objective was to soothe the apprehensions of Canadians, both the public and the members of government who are fed intelligence assessments. Faced with the unknown, and fed a poor intelligence, fear-mongering product whose contents cannot be disproved, the Canadian government is compelled into action. After all, as CSIS has often repeated, it's no longer a question of "if." As the attacks pile up in the rest of the world, surely, in their view our time will come. Because the media, which tends to focus on one crisis after another, perpetuates this sense of inevitability, the government must convince Canadians that it is doing everything in its power to prevent terrorism. So more money is spent. The government simply cannot be seen to be doing nothing; when there is nothing to act on, when the enemy is a ghost, the only thing it can do is spend money.

The restructuring of the Canadian intelligence community occurred relatively quickly, at least as far as government goes. In a matter of a few years, Ottawa had created, out of nothing, its very own DHS. We now had a National Security Advisor, had thrown millions of dollars into our intelligence community, CSIS was recruiting like never before, and DND was dispatching soldiers in Afghanistan. But it didn't stop there. In late August 2005—one month after the London bombings—there were talks in Ottawa of creating an intelligence panel of experts, most likely grey heads meeting on a weekly or monthly basis to discuss matters of national security. More layers. More meetings. The Canadian government was being proactive on public safety. What many failed to understand, however, is that no matter how many layers there are to our national security apparatus, if the agencies that comprise it are ineffective, or if the officers who comprise its workforce are incompetent, security will continue to suffer. In fact, by adding layers, we are making things more complex, and response potentially slower.

We are also adding noise to the signal: There is already so much information circulating out there, the last thing the intelligence community needs is more reports. But with every new agency comes additional reporting. Having noted earlier that under the current system evaluation of performance is determined by the number of reports generated, the incentive is therefore to produce more, which leads to output competition among agencies. Some even go as far as lift a report by another agency and affix their logo on the front page, then distribute that report, which ultimately ends up on the desk of the officer who created the initial report. I was once asked to highlight all the information that was included in another agency's report that had been copy-and-pasted from a threat assessment that we had distributed a few days earlier. Nearly two-thirds of that report had been taken, verbatim, from our document, without mention that the agency had obtained this information from us. In addition to needlessly adding to everybody's "to read" pile, someone could mistakenly conclude that the recycled information, if it is not properly attributed, is corroborative (that it confirms similar information) rather than what is, a cut-and-paste job.

Everything is distributed, up the chain, down the chain, and laterally. The good products get lost among the sea of not so good, and sometimes mediocre, ones. Human brains, given time constraints and physiological limitations, are unable to cope. The good information slips through the cracks. Things unclassified and therefore deemed unimportant, are not even read. The reaction is a natural one: Given, say, 100 documents to read in a day, but with time and energy only to read 60, human beings will inevitably be attracted to those documents that are deemed "secret." It gives one purpose and the impression that he has access to things that are beyond the reach of ordinary people. The loss of context that results from this failure to read open-source material is now community-wide and getting worse with every new report that is circulated.

Report writing has turned into a business. Like the law of supply-and-demand in the business world, agencies are now competing with each other over a limited customer base. Reports now need colour, logos, and an appealing layout if they are to be read. Content, alone, no longer suffices. About six months after I had begun working in the Threat Assessment Unit, we learned during a meeting with other agencies that CSIS threat assessments were for the most part unread by the rest of the intelligence community, not because what they contained was of no value, but rather, the other agencies indicated, because the threat assessment documents were not "sexy" enough. They were text only, black-and-white, and as a consequence they lost to other reports that looked better. In order to elevate the document from the literal bottom of the pile, CSIS threat assessments received plastic surgery in early 2004. Hours, weeks were spent consulting, preparing blueprints, versions and layouts. Threat Assessments now had a crest, were in colour, and were now distributed as electronic .pdf files. They were also given a catchy name, which also required weeks of consultation and debating. As expected, readership went up. The content remained the same, but the documents looked good. No one seemed to care that it took us more time to prepare them (and consequently had less time to analyse intelligence), or that they occasionally made our computers freeze, or proved too difficult to produce by some people with limited computer skills. Management liked the way they looked. Other agencies upped the ante, however, and began including maps and photos in their reports. (I never understood why, in its documents, Transport Canada, an agency that is responsible for public transport security within Canada, felt the need to include maps of, say, Colombia.) I imagine that the next step will be soundtracks, animated objects, jingles, or perhaps smells. Nothing would drive the message home like the smell of cordite in a threat assessment!

Another means by which agencies allied with the US hoped to calm the fears of the injured giant was to adopt what is known within the community as "integrated threat assessments." Integrated means that various agencies sit at the same table and, drawing (in theory at least) from their respective expertise and sources, generate timely, all-encompassing threat assessments, which are distributed within the community. In the US, this threat assessment centre is known as the Counter Terrorism Centre (CTC); in the United Kingdom, it is known as the Joint Terrorism Analysis Centre (JTAC). In Canada, it was first known as the Integrated National Security Analysis Centre (INSAC), subsequently renamed the Integrated Threat Assessment Centre (ITAC). ITAC is seated in brand new and high-tech office space within the CSIS headquarters building. It has representatives from a variety of Canadian agencies, including CSIS, the RCMP,

PSEP, Transport Canada, and others. Some agencies, such as PCO and Foreign Affairs, have been reluctant participants at best. ITAC also has liaison arrangements with its counterpart organizations in Britain, the US, Australia and New Zealand. INSAC and its successor, ITAC, have been hailed as examples of the more substantive developments that, since Sept. 11, have contributed to the security of Canadians. After all, "integrated" implies dialogue, and dialogue is what is required to ensure that no information is missed. In press conferences, Canadian government officials never miss an occasion to emphasise the role and successes of the integrated centres, always counting on keywords such as "timely" and "integrated" to impress the audience, and Canadian taxpayers.

The true story behind integrated threat assessments, however, is that they don't work. The principal cause of this failure stems from the inherently different mandates of the various agencies that comprise the Canadian intelligence community. Similar problems have been encountered in other countries. How can analysts representing different agencies—and who therefore have different mandates—manage to produce a document that respects everybody's needs and desires? To make it work, analysts have little choice but to make concessions, which results in watered-down assessments, or documents that skirt certain contentious issues on which consensus cannot be reached. In other words, the analysts at ITAC are being asked to square the circle. We are asking someone who represents International Trade, for example, to sit down with a representative from CSIS. One's mandate is to encourage trade and foreign investment. The other's is to ensure security. One wants to encourage Canadian investment in, say, Colombia; the other claims that travelling, let alone investing there, is dangerous. CSIS claims that entity X is a terrorist organisation; PCO disagrees while Foreign Affairs intends to enter into a dialogue with that group, hoping to play a role in a possible peace process.

These are but a few examples of the tensions that inherently exist whenever you force disparate agencies to work together. This occurs on a daily basis at ITAC. The two main casualties of these differences are content and timeliness. Content, as we have just seen, suffers from the requirement to speak in one voice. Timeliness, for its part, suffers because analysts spend hours haranguing. After the semblance of a document has been produced, it needs to be agreed on by the chain of command at all the agencies involved, proof-read, edited, translated, and finally distributed. In all the time I was at CSIS, I never saw a single *timely* INSAC or ITAC document. While the Threat Assessment Unit had, at any given time, three to four analysts, ITAC had dozens, which serves to demonstrate that manpower wasn't the issue. During my last months with the organisation, ITAC contented itself with redistributing threat assessments produced by its foreign counterparts, whose content rarely had any implications for Canadian security. Millions of dollars were poured into the creation of a Canadian integrated threat assessment centre. Numerous people were forced to divide their time between INSAC/ITAC and their office back at the agency they worked for. Many did not want to participate in the experiment in the first place. Several didn't have the training, knowledge, or skills to produce threat assessments. Writing by committee is an excruciating and frustrating endeavour. Before I left, the plan was for ITAC to have as many as 40, perhaps even more, employees by the end of 2005. But the more people are involved in the production of those documents, the slower and therefore increasingly insignificant they will be. Canadians are being deceived when their government tells them that ITAC is a success. It is anything but, and it is difficult to conceive of it being of any use to the intelligence community. Millions of dollars were thrown into the INSAC/ITAC project. The return on that investments made by Canadians is, sadly, much less than anticipated.

The role of CSIS' small Threat Assessment Unit is to produce assessments for everything ranging from foreign dignitaries visiting Canada to threats to Canadian soldiers deployed in Afghanistan. Because of the politicisation of threat assessments, however, many are produced for no better reason than to please certain foreign patrons, which needlessly burdens the small staff at the unit. Severely understaffed (at last count the Unit consisted of four novice intelligence officers), the Unit produces dozens of reports, in timely fashion, every week. Every single report needs to be bilingual; nothing can be distributed before being translated (in theory, reports can be distributed in French only, but never the reverse. As a French-only document would be of little use in a community that is only nominally bilingual, CSIS has little choice but to sacrifice timeliness for the sake of official bilingualism). The Unit serves as the conduit between CSIS and the rest of the community; it is the voice of the Service, and it does not have a staff that is commensurate with the task at hand. If, as the former director of the Service stated, a terrorist attack on Canadian soil is a near certainty, then only having a handful of inexperienced intelligence officers on its staff makes no sense. While management claims that ITAC will eventually fulfil that mandate, it is doubtful that the centre will be able to do this in the foreseeable future. Furthermore, as we have seen, timeliness is an immediate casualty of writing by committee. The Threat Assessment Unit at the Service will therefore continue to play an important role for years to come.

As was mentioned above, intelligence officers are bombarded with information. The situation at the Threat Assessment Unit is no different; in many ways it is worse. It gets reporting from all sides, in addition to various threats received in Canada or abroad, via fax, phone, walk-ins, and e-mail. No threat is ignored. Sometimes, in order to calm the community (and our southern counterparts), *negative* threat assessments must also be produced, reporting "no known threat," or "false information." Moreover, for every foreign dignitary who visits Canada, a threat assessment must be generated. For some countries, dignitaries residing in Canada—ambassadors, for example—also receive such a treatment, meaning that every time those individuals travel, whether it is within Canada or abroad, a threat assessment is produced. This even includes fishing expeditions by former US presidents and personal travel by other members of a foreign government. As certain dignitaries travel three, four times a week, from one city to another, this means that three or four threat assessments are generated. Even if the threat level remains unchanged, or is nonexistent, documents are written, with dates and destinations changed, and distributed community-wide. Phone calls to whoever needs to know are not sufficient. Proof is needed, something in writing, just in case. In case something happens. CSIS cannot afford to look bad. In fact, to ensure that Canada is seen to be taking security seriously, a "high" threat level is ascribed to certain individuals, even if, in reality, there are no known threats against them. Readers will not be surprised to learn that there exists a correlation between the unrepresentative threat levels we give to such diplomats and the countries they are from. One need only think of who the colonial masters are, or which countries get special treatment, to identify them. The ramifications in terms of resources—both at CSIS for those who need to produce those threat assessments, have them translated, etc, and within the community at large, including RCMP detachments and law-enforcement officers who provide protection—are substantial. What this highlights, therefore, is that many threat assessments are produced for nothing more than political reasons. While these reports are written, the intelligence officers at the Threat Assessment Unit are not looking at potential threats to *Canadian* interests. While translators work on these politicised documents, they are not translating reports that are of important operational value. The energy spent on producing these reports, the documents read preparing them, take away from the real analytical work officers should be doing.

Many other threat assessments are produced on topics that are hardly related to Canadian security. But everything needs to be covered. Just in case. One way to recognise what I like to call a "stretched threat assessment" is to look for a conclusion that reads something like "Should Canadians be in area at the time of an attack, they could be implicated or injured." As an analyst on the unit, I was forced to use that line, or a variation on that theme, on more occasions than I care to remember. Aside for stating the obvious, these reports serve absolutely no function. If someone, anywhere in the world, is within proximity of an attack, he or she indeed risks getting injured. Canada does not need intelligence officers and a multi-million dollar intelligence service to know that.

The tremendous workload, combined with the astounding lack of resources for so crucial a department, results in analysts having neither the time nor the energy to read up on history, to put things in context, and to *understand* what they are writing about. What makes matters worse is the fact that recruit intelligence officers will only spend one year in that Unit before being transferred. All the knowledge is lost, and the new recruits, and sometimes pre-recruits—people who have yet to complete their entry training course—are in charge of producing threat assessments that may, one day, have implications for the security of Canadians. Would Canadian citizens sleep well at night knowing that so few resources are committed to informing the rest of the Canadian community on potential threats to Canadian security? Would Canadians feel safe taking the subway in downtown Toronto knowing that ITAC, the vaunted success of the past years, is incapable of producing timely, valuable threat assessments?

In a November 2004 presentation at the University of Toronto, Michael Ignatieff, then of Harvard University and now a member of the Liberal Party of Canada, reflected that what he calls Islamic fascism (or "Islamofascism")—the al-Qaeda movement and other like-minded groups—is a real threat to security. As we saw in Chapter 1, marrying Islamic with fascism, extremism, terrorism, or radicalism, is more a sign of intellectual sloppiness than a helpful characterisation of a phenomenon. The cataloguing of human activity, such as what Mr. Ignatieff did with this comment, puts groups of people into boxes and, as a result, the world seems to make a little more sense. Newsmakers do it, as do politicians. It is reassuring and gives us the illusion that we can, based on which group an individual belongs to, predict his behaviour. However, regardless of whether it is occurring at the conscious or at the unconscious level, this is a racist view of the world, and it is sad that Ignatieff, a respected scholar, would fail to make such a distinction. Not to beat a dead horse, terrorism is terrorism. In very few instances is religion the motivator for terrorism. There is nothing in Islam, or in any other religion for that matter, that instructs individuals to hijack airplanes and crash them into commercial buildings, or to pack rucksacks with explosives and detonate them on board a train. *Individuals* with political or nihilistic motivations, however, do manage to convince, coerce, and instruct certain people into committing terrorism, and these people may, as is the case with al-Qaeda, use religious rhetoric. But by no means does this make the act of terrorism an *Islamic* one. As Graham Fuller, a former vice chairman of the National Intelligence Council at the CIA, observed in a recent article, "It wasn't Islam that made Middle Eastern states resist the colonial project, with its drastic redrawing of borders in accordance with European geopolitical preferences. Nor would Middle Eastern Christians have welcomed imperial Western oil companies, backed by their European viceregents, diplomats, intelligence agents, and armies, any more than Muslims did."[69] What if a deranged leader were to use, say, a Burger King menu to convince his followers to commit terrorism. What if, instead of Allah, the name of the Burger King founder were used? Would we call this Burger King terrorism? Of course not. Rather, we would look into the motivators and at the origins of the grievances that led to violence. The same applies to the current wave of terrorism. Islam has been hijacked—or rather the rhetoric of the Islamic religion has been hijacked—and it is a distinction that the world has yet to make. But it will have to if we are to avoid a bad situation from turning into a catastrophe.

I have hinted at it throughout this book, and now is the time to state it openly: bin Laden and his followers did not launch a war against the West because they despise who or what we are. Despite what the numerous pundits, scholars, reporters, politicians and heads of intelligence services have been drumming for years, al-Qaeda's objective is not a nihilistic one. It does not seek to destroy Western civilisation. It is not led, as some would claim, by an irrational megalomaniac who recoils whenever he hears about democracy, freedom of expression, or the emancipation of women. As Michael Scheuer eloquently puts it in *Imperial Hubris*, the bin Laden threat

> is neither a simple but lethal lashing out against all things non-Islamic, nor an inchoate eagerness to indiscriminately damage the many in an effort to hit the few who offend Muslim sensibilities. One of the greatest dangers for Americans in deciding how to confront the Islamist threat lies in continuing to believe—at the urging of senior U.S. leaders—that Muslims hate and attack us for what we are and think, rather than for what we do. The Islamic world is not so offended by our democratic system of politics, guarantees of personal rights and civil liberties, and separation of church and state that it is willing to wage a war against overwhelming odds in order to stop Americans from voting, speaking freely, and praying, or not, as they wish.[70]

Instead, and very few Canadians have realised this, al-Qaeda has very clear strategic objectives, aims and goals that it has expressed more than once. Again, Scheuer:

> The threat facing America is the defensive jihad, an Islamic military reaction triggered by an attack by non-Muslims on the Islamic faith, on Muslims, on Muslim territory, or on all three … The focused and lethal threat posed to U.S. national security arises not from Muslims being offended by what America is, but rather from their plausible perception that the things they most love and value—God, Islam, their brethren, an Muslim lands—are being attacked by America.[71]

Scheuer concludes by writing that bin Laden and his allies are waging a war

> against a specific target and for specific, limited purposes. While they will use whatever weapon comes to hand—including weapons of mass destruction— their goal is not to wipe out our secular democracy, but to deter us by military means from attacking the things that they love. Bin Laden et al are not eternal warriors; there is no evidence they are fighting for fighting's sake, or that they would be lost for things to do without a war to wage.[72]

But what, exactly, is it that the US and its allies have done that would leave Muslims fearing for the things they most love? It is, simply put, neo-colonialism, the military garrisons, and the economic and political support given to repressive regimes in the Middle East and other Muslim countries in South and Southeast Asia. It is the invasions of Afghanistan and Iraq, support for Israel in its repression of Palestinians and illegal wars in Lebanon, support for the hated Saudi regime,[73] assistance to the Philippines in its battle against a Muslim insurgency in the South, muted response to Russian atrocities in Chechnya, silence in the face of Chinese repression of Chinese Muslims, and sanctions programs against Iran, Sudan, and Libya. It is also the indiscriminate manner in which Muslims in Western countries have been detained, investigated, and treated generally.

The argument that Spain and Great Britain were not targeted because of their support for US operations in the Middle East, but rather because they are liberal democracies, is wrong. Those countries were attacked because of their direct or indirect role in assisting the US as it colonises the Middle East. Madrid and London were bombed as part of bin Laden's military plan to put an end to that perceived colonialism. It was all part of the defensive war. It is also a backlash against the failure of the US to demilitarise itself after the Cold War had ended, to close its network of military bases around the world, to take the nuclear option off the table once and for all. And it is a shout of anger at the seeming incapacity of the West, more specifically the US, to tolerate systems of belief that do not coincide with its view of how things should be run.

So far, and despite claims to the contrary by Canadian officials, Canada has been spared because it has not yet been perceived to be a participant in the US experiment in colonialism. Because of the pressure that Canada has been subjected to since Sept. 11, however, and because it needs to demonstrate to the world that it is fully involved in the "war" on terrorism, Canada has gradually been sucked into a war that isn't its own. Historically, Canada has had little, if any, footprint in the Muslim world, and for the most part Canadians have benefited from the generally positive image of the country abroad, even in the Muslim world. Canada's advanced democracy—it is, in many ways, more mature than that of the US, which supposedly "gave" democracy to the world and has since been its defender—has not resulted in al-Qaeda targeting its cities. In fact, if we were to follow the logic of hatred for democracy as a motivator for terrorism, Canada and some Scandinavian countries would have been attacked *before* the US.

Despite the manner in which the right-wing media worldwide and the US neocons have portrayed them, Muslims are not idiots or nihilistic lunatics, and they certainly can distinguish between countries in the West, and between political systems and behaviours. But as Canada becomes more aggressive in its targeting of Muslim individuals, and as it deploys soldiers in Afghanistan for a mission that is dangerously starting to look like war-making rather than support for reconstruction, as was originally planned and explained to the Canadian public, there is a very real risk that al-Qaeda will revisit its perception of Canada and add it to the list, just as it did Spain and Britain, of countries that are threatening to conquer and colonise the Muslim world. This, too, can cause "blowback," a repercussion, at some point in the future, of our choices and actions.

The misnamed "war" on terrorism is like every other war that has come before: It is fought in the name of a *cause*. In fact, it is only by seeing it as a cause that countries like Canada can join the US in its war against al-Qaeda. In the West, that cause is "freedom," a word used so liberally by President George W. Bush that it is under threat of losing all meaning. Others—and they would be right—could argue that we are fighting for Capitalism, "modernity," or even Western values, whatever those are.

There are consequences to sweeping generalities, however, for they tend to blunt the imagination and leave no room for divergence of opinion. Like in Koestler's *Darkness at Noon,* the cause, in his case Communism, is "without scruples." The cause "rolled towards her goal unconcernedly and deposed the corpses of the drowned in the windings of her course ... The motives of the individual did not matter to her, neither did she care what went on in his head and his heart."[74] What if we were to ask an intelligence officer at CSIS, sitting at his desk in Ottawa, what it is that motivates him, that allows him to suspect an individual because he has the wrong surname, country of origin, or religious beliefs. The answer would be "security" or "freedom"—in other words, some overarching ideology. A cause. As with religion, most people find it impossible to go on without believing in something that is greater than the individual. One therefore puts his faith in the cause and rides upon its waves for a sense of purpose and security.

At home, there is a grave risk that the incessant and increasingly aggressive targeting of individuals of a certain religion—Sunni Islam—by Western agencies, will lead to individuals of that faith believing that their *religion* is under attack, at which point its defence will act as a motivator. The great risk that comes from the failure to make the distinction between motivation and religion is that the cataloguing of a brand of terrorism as "Sunni Islamic" could very well become a self-fulfilling prophecy: what began, as we saw, as politically-motivated terrorism with a few thousand hardcore adherents could become, by dint of irresponsible targeting and endless bigoted punditry, truly Islamic terrorism with hundreds of thousands of individuals feeling they need to lash out to protect their identity. The more individuals of the Islamic faith are the object of invidious accusations, the more such individuals are denied their rights, arrested at the border, expelled, detained for long periods of time, made to feel that their religious identity is a problem, or killed or maimed in wars to "liberate" or "free" them, the greater the danger that the political persuasions of a few will, indeed, turn into a war of religion or civilisations, as Samuel Huntington would have it. This response to a sense of siege does not mean that it would be justifiable for them to target civilians in retaliation, but it would certainly be symptomatic of the grievances that have been accumulating for years, just as it explains why bin Laden and others have turned against the West.

Perhaps this is what Osama bin Laden, a far better observer of the West than most, was hoping to achieve by declaring war against the US. Perhaps he understood the bluntness of the Western intelligence agencies and governments, and how their response would lead to the birth of thousands of potential candidates for his war. Perhaps he knew, too, that following the demise of the Soviet Union, the US would be in search of a new Nemesis, a new opponent to mobilise against.

If those indeed were his objectives, bin Laden is on the brink of accomplishing that objective, and the consequences could be nothing short of cataclysmic.

Let us imagine a scenario. A suspected terrorist is targeted, and after a long investigation he is expelled from the country. The lead piece of information came from a foreign agency, and the damning intelligence that led to the individual being targeted came from a single source, which was never corroborated. As a result of all the cognitive biases, racism, weakened moral boundaries, institutional ineptness and the fog of intelligence that we discussed in the previous chapter, it turns out that this individual wasn't a terrorist. But it is too late, and that person, along with his terrorised family, are forced to return to their country of origin. Whether it eventually recognises the mistake or not, CSIS does not do anything to remedy the situation, as this would be an admission that it committed a mistake. Better to use and hide behind the wall of secrecy. No one will know. Who cares, anyway? What is this individual to us? What recourse does he have? During the process, the target was dehumanised, attributed a file number, and was probably referred to as "scum," a "cancer." There are no consequences to CSIS resulting from the deportation, and thanks to the surgeon's distance from his subject, no one will have connected emotionally with the case, so no one from the inside will fight for the targeted individual and his family.

But the target's problems are only beginning. In all likelihood, CSIS shared with and received information from the intelligence service of the country to which the target and his family have been returned. Now that he has been a target of an intelligence service, that he bears the stigma, this individual, and perhaps his family members, will likely be unable to find work. He may be arrested, tortured, or disappeared, and his family shunned by friends who fear being subjected to a similar treatment, thus losing access to a social network that could have come to their assistance.

Will this individual, or his family, after all the suffering that is in store for them, accuse the intelligence service back in Canada of "Catholic terrorism"? While no Canadian detonated a bomb, lives were nonetheless destroyed. If we were to interview the intelligence officer who handled the case, would he agree to the accusation that he and his supervisors conducted religion-based terrorism? Certainly not. What was his motivation, then? Security, freedom, liberty, Western values. The officer did what he thought was right, in the name of the cause he serves. Even if he had doubts, he felt that those could safely be swept under the carpet. The cause of the GWOT provided that sense of protection. As we noted earlier, the adherence to the intelligence community involves a religious belief in the cause; there is no detracting from it, it is faith-based, it is not to be questioned. Whoever dissented was moved aside, transferred, or beaten into mute submission. The rhetoric, rather than coming in the name of Allah, is derived from the language of security, freedom, and all the other aspects of our civilisation we think we are defending.

Let us imagine, for the sake of this argument, that the deportee's view of his persecutors—unlikely a flattering one, at this point—were to spread. People in the village he originated from, his family, learn of his treatment in Canada, and later on of his persecution in his home country, which, rumour has it, resulted from information that the Canadian government shared with the target's new persecutors. The villagers, family and human rights and religious groups turn to the Internet and spread the news. Over time, all the cities in that country talk about what they could justifiably call, if we adopted our own skewed logic, "Catholic Terrorism" or "Freedom Terrorism." The fire keeps spreading, until other countries adopt this belief. The media seizes upon this and fuels the flames. Suddenly, Catholics, Canadians, Westerners, are arrested pre-emptively, detained without due process, expelled, their belongings are seized. Since Canada is a product of the same civilisation as the US, shares some its values, ideologies, religion, and is within geographical proximity, the conspiracy theories spread, and the rhetoric of radical leaders gains more traction. The US attacked Afghanistan, invaded Iraq, assassinated individuals in Yemen, threatened Iran, supported and armed Israel as it killed thousands of Palestinians and injured tens of thousands more. Canada, so close to the US, must have had a hand in the plot. In fact, they are one and the same. Furthermore, Canadian soldiers have been killing people in Afghanistan, some of them civilians. And its soldiers may have been complicit in the torture of Taliban detainees whom it handed over to Afghan authorities. Incriminating evidence is presented before underground committees. As the evidence against Canada piles up, some members begin to wonder if perhaps the time might not have come to teach Canada a lesson.

This is what the sweeping, reductionist view of the world that comes from the cause can lead to. Errors of cognition, in judgment, or downright incompetence and carelessness are hidden from the public. It is a looking-glass war, and the unjust generalisations of one are in turn used against the perpetrator in a vicious circle. The victims remember. Over time, seemingly inconsequential blunders made years ago may come back with a vengeance, using a form that, if we only had enough imagination, would seem very familiar to us.

Another shortcoming of intelligence services is their failure to distinguish between nationalism and religion. Again, what confuses analysts is the use of religious rhetoric by leaders of certain organisations. Immediately, the *political* actions made by those organisations are seen in the light of religion. For many of the less-educated analysts, Islam is a monolithic entity. As we have seen, certain officials at the FBI still fail to differentiate between Sunni and Shiite Islam. Canada is not exempt from this failure. To such people, Islam is Islam. And when Islam becomes, in the mind, coterminous with terrorism, whether we are talking about Sunni Islam or Shiite Islam makes no difference, which could perhaps explain why some specialists continue to this day to refer to a Sunni-Shiite axis, or that Hezbollah or Iran or Iraq may have played a part in the Sept. 11, 2001, attacks. The soldiers, whether they wear uniforms or not, practice Islam, ergo whatever they do is terrorism. This would explain why the Lebanese Hezbollah, a nationalist movement that seeks to defend its homeland from invasion and that in 2005 entered politics, continues to be seen as a terrorist organisation by countries like Israel, the US and Canada. That the movement's leadership maintains a paranoid view of the threat that Israel represents to the sovereignty of Lebanon is indisputable. That the Hezbollah leadership reflects this skewed perspective in its rhetoric is beyond doubt. But this doesn't change the fact that Hezbollah is primarily a *nationalist* movement. Undeniably, certain individuals with links to the organisation, such as the late Mugniyeh, were involved in incidents that occurred outside Lebanon proper, but the movement as a whole is primarily engaged in the defence of Lebanese territory. Which serves as a strong argument against the proposition, made by some, that Hezbollah was involved in the Khobar Tower bombing, an act whose benefits to Hezbollah and Lebanon are difficult to imagine. Still, at CSIS, the Hezbollah organisation falls under the Shiite Extremism rubric, while other agencies have simply placed it under the even wider Islamic Terrorism catchphrase. Even more so than al-Qaeda, Hezbollah is political, and religion has far less to do than realism as a motivation. Israel's relentless description of all things Hezbollah as terrorist—even when the organisation targets Israeli soldiers—certainly doesn't help to dispel that notion.

So, instead of making religion a motivator for terrorism—which it is not—we should use the phenomena themselves to describe human activities. If things truly need to be put into boxes, why not speak of al-Qaeda-ism, bin Laden-ism or, if we must, Hezbollah-ism? In so doing, we could counter the noxious belief that it is normal for Islamic and Terrorism to appear side-by-side in newspaper articles, textbooks, and intelligence reports. By doing this we would inoculate ourselves against intellectual irresponsibility that, in the long term, could very well give rise to the so-called "war of civilisations," a war that we absolutely must avoid and that can be avoided. Unfortunately, there is little indication at present that the Canadian intelligence community, let alone its allies, are prepared to move in that direction. Mired in the tactical, day-to-day nature of their work, intelligence services are myopically failing to ask the hard, strategic questions that, in the long run, will have a far bigger impact on the lives of citizens than whether poor Mohammed was carrying one or two brown paper bags as he walked out of a Tim Horton's in downtown Calgary.

Finally, it should be understood that terrorism is a tool, a form of behaviour, by which individuals with certain aims try to achieve results. The *political* cause, say, the liberation of Palestinian territories, is indisputably intellectual and political. Painting movements that strive for the liberation of Palestine under the all-encompassing umbrella of Islamic Terrorism, or Levant Terrorism or Sunni Terrorism is simply wrong. It is the means—the targeting of civilians—that should be investigated, not the individuals who believe in, and support, the cause, which by standards of international law is a just one. Understanding the difference between political aims and means would save CSIS and other members of the intelligence community tremendous amounts of time, money, and potential headaches. But they will only be able to do this if they abandon the generalisations that so far have characterised their (mis)understanding of the world.

Another fallout of the current emphasis on Islam and terrorism is that, with a few notable exceptions, all the other investigations have been suffering. This is not to say that those investigations have been abandoned altogether, but resources for those tend to be secondary and available only when the Sunni Islamic Terrorism section doesn't need them. This reaction can be explained by the fact that the Sept. 11, 2001, terrorist attacks, and to a certain extent the 1998 US embassy bombings in Kenya and Tanzania, along with the Madrid and London bombings, were ingenious and serious enough to grab everybody's attention. This is what terrorism is all about: It must be big, it must beat the last incident in terms of scale and complexity, and if you manage to do that the world will be your audience. The human brain constantly needs to be impressed; absent a stimulus, it falls into fatigue. This phenomenon operates in movies and explains why movie studios constantly strive to overdo whatever degree of violence, shock, or special effects had been achieved in the movies that came before. The same occurs with natural catastrophes: famine in Africa leads to an outpouring of media coverage and humanitarian aid. Band Aid concerts are organised. Two years later, a similar catastrophe in another African state will be met with tepid donor enthusiasm. From Somalia to Rwanda, on to Sudan and the next calamity. Of course, geopolitical interests will also be a factor as to whether states will provide assistance to a country or not. A recent example of this is the lack of funding for the 2005 famine in Niger while citizens of New Orleans, in the wealthiest country in the world, received help from various countries, including Canada, through concerts, direct assistance, and so on. This phenomenon is known as *compassion fatigue*.[75] Terrorism operates the same way, and as psychiatrist Frederick Hacker notes, terrorists seek to "frighten and, by frightening to dominate and control. They want to impress. They play to and for an audience, and solicit audience participation."[76] Terrorists, therefore, must outdo themselves. In recent years, al-Qaeda has been very adept at doing this. In the process, it gained an audience, both with the public and the government agencies that oppose it. This, in turn, has led to a tremendous focus on that threat alone, and to a reorganisation of the various intelligence communities that are mandated with countering threats to national security.

With the exception, perhaps, of Chinese espionage and Iran, all other investigations at CSIS have suffered as a consequence of the focus on al-Qaeda, which could create problems if, at some point in the future, terrorism were replaced by some other form of activity as the greatest threat to national security. All this focus means that when that next threat comes, our agencies will still be fighting the previous war and will need years to shift their ossified foundations and reorient themselves to address the present danger.

The al-Qaeda-related terrorist attacks of 1993, 1998, 1999, 2001, 2003 and 2005 were only the initial shots in the *malaise du jour*. As the world continues along its iniquitous North-South progression, as issues of poverty and repression remain unresolved, other voices will, in time, emerge, and most intelligence services will be unprepared to face, let alone understand, them. Retired Lieutenant-General Roméo Dallaire, who headed the United Nations Assistance Mission For Rwanda (UNAMIR) during the 1994 genocide and is now a member of the Canadian Senate, recently stated at a conference at the University of Toronto that at some point in the future, other disgruntled groups who live among us will start calling for attention to their own sets of problems. What the Western world had failed to understand before Sept. 11—that the world was more connected than it ever had been before, and that fortresses were no longer sufficient to protect ourselves against the proverbial barbarians—it still fails to understand as pertains to the rest of the non-Islamic world. Most people within the security intelligence community, as well as our politicians, seem unable to understand this looming threat, much as their predecessors failed to shift their gaze from Moscow in the 1990s to the Middle East. The focus at the moment is simply too fixed on the Islamic world to allow for other threats, some emerging, some on the horizon, some already here, to be conceptually understood. Large minorities that immigrated to Canada to flee persecution, war, and human rights abuses in their home countries may, one day, resort to various forms of violence to be heard, or turn their communities into a microcosm of the battle back home. And unlike al-Qaeda, whose grievances are mostly limited to the Greater Middle East, other groups are fighting for causes that happen to be much closer to home.

A lurid example of this reality is the ongoing turmoil in Haiti. The poorest state in the Americas, Haiti's history is marked by instability, poor governance, outside intervention, and civil unrest. According to the United Nations Development Program (UNDP), life expectancy for a Haitian male in 2005 was 49 years,[77] while that of neighbouring Cuba, for example, is 74.8.[78] The current political conflict in Haiti involves the pro-Jean-Bertrand Aristide movement, and those who were opposed to the dictator, who was deposed in 2003. A large number of Haitians live in Canada, and most of them are concentrated in French-speaking Montreal. Given Canada's participation in the United Nations Stabilisation Mission in Haiti (MINUSTAH), if anything goes wrong back in Haiti, Canada is bound to feel the repercussions. It is, in a way, a lose-lose situation for Canada, for it is also quite possible that failure to participate in MINUSTAH would prompt the Haitian community, which would rightly accuse the Canadian government of neglecting its responsibilities as a citizen of the Americas, to use increasingly violent measures to make itself heard. We must never lose sight of the fact that terrorism is a means to draw attention to a political problem, to force engagement where engagement is absent. Palestinians, and before them Jews, to use another example, did not start blowing things up just for fun or because they have a genetic predisposition to violence; they resorted to terrorism after their political demands had been ignored for too long.

Existing, as is currently the case, or absent, Canadian participation in Haiti, the two factions involved in the conflict could also clash on the streets of Montreal—in other words, conflict "over there" could be imported "out here." Canada, with such a large ethnic composition, is not immune from these problems. Other areas of the world—Latin America, Eastern Europe, Africa—also have a substantial representation in Canada. And as the world draws ever closer together, Western states will be even less in a position to ignore wars, famines, epidemics, injustice and the other ills occurring within those countries. Given our tendency to imagine ourselves as "outside" or "above" the system, however, there is the real possibility that someday, someone or a group of individuals will reach the conclusion that they have little choice but to awaken us to reality, either because they need our help or as a result of our actions, government or corporate, in that part of the world. If everything fails, if appeals to governments, to the United Nations, do not lead to action, nothing works like a bomb. It is this failure in Western society to realise that the al-Qaeda phenomenon is but one iteration of the many dangers we face in this united world that should keep us awake at night. This failure of vision and of leadership is made very real when, as we saw earlier, an intelligence officer desiring to learn Spanish is denied her request for reimbursement of tuition and is told she should rather be learning Arabic. There is too much focus on the immediate, on that which one hears and reads about in the news, and too little on all the other aspects of a world that, in the not-so-distant future, could also threaten us. This is why CSIS and the intelligence community in general continue to be reactive rather than proactive. And this is why they will fail to protect us if the next blows comes from outside the Islamic world.

As with the al-Qaeda threat, Canada must never lose sight of the fact that wars and security threats, whatever their origin, do not pit civilisations against each other: Rather, they are very country-specific, and as such politicians and intelligence services should strive to customise their actions to address the problems as they affect *their* country. In other words, the threat that al-Qaeda, for example, poses to the US is very different from the one it poses to Canada. As a result, countries should refrain from standardising their security apparatuses or basing their policies on those adopted by Washington or Israel as they wage their own wars. In fact, it is the very copying of other countries' systems that threatens to suck countries like Canada into a great war of civilisations. Given the US' militarised approach to terrorism, a copy of that model could force Canada to deal with the issue in a way that does not fit its needs and interests. Failing to realise that, Ottawa's response has been similar to the US', which explains why, seven years after Sept. 11, 2001, Canadian vessels are still patrolling the Persian Gulf and Canadian soldiers are still getting killed and injured in Afghanistan.

Whether Canada should be in Afghanistan, or should have gone to Iraq, is debatable. Despite the tremendous capabilities of the unit, it is unlikely that JTF-2, Canada's special forces, made much of a difference in the immediate response to the Sept. 11, 2001, attacks, given the size of the US response. Canada's participation in the International Security Assistance Force (ISAF) and in the provincial reconstruction teams (PRTs)—at least before that mission turned into one of chasing and killing Taliban militants—was based on sound judgement and the belief, not unfounded, that Canada's experience in peacekeeping and stabilisation missions elsewhere could bring added value to what is being attempted in Afghanistan. The current deployments of Canadian personnel in

Haiti and in the Congo are equally worthy enterprises, as will future deployments in Sudan. Canada is mature enough to choose its battles, and should be able to say no to US bullying when it sees that participation does not serve its interests and those of the global community. Obviously, even when it picks its fights, there will be consequences, and some of those consequences could include terrorism at home. But this is a risk that as an active global citizen Canada must take. Failure to act, failure to abide by our responsibility to protect those in need, can only make matters worse in the long term.

It goes without saying that as Canada ventures out into the world to protect its interests as well as those of the global community, its intelligence services will also need to play a greater role, which as we saw has led to much debate in Ottawa over who should be responsible for intelligence collection abroad. With the risks inherent to intervention, intelligence agencies will need to lend a hand and to prepare against whatever backlash there might be at home. The presence of Canadian soldiers in Afghanistan, in Haiti, in the Congo and perhaps some day in Sudan, could radicalise certain elements within Canada, mostly individuals who originate from those countries. Another possibility is that groups over there that stand to lose from Canadian intervention could sponsor attacks against Canadian interests, at home or abroad, in retaliation, or to pressure Ottawa into pulling its troops.

It is very easy to understand that CSIS has a role to play in this, but in its current form, and with its current myopic focus on the Middle East, it is in no position to provide that support. Even if CSIS wanted to become more active abroad—as it already is, according to recent statements—it currently does not have, as we have seen, the ability to train intelligence officers in preparation for deployment to conflict zones. In fact, it hardly has the capacity to train its officers on culturally-sensitive issues that exist in Canada. For the time being, training for missions abroad is bound to be provided by more experienced allied agencies. This, for obvious reasons, also diminishes Canada's—and should it come to this CSIS'—ability to act in its own interest, for not only will the agencies that give the training likely become privy to the operations that Canada is preparing for, but it also provides them with an opportunity to "shape" our officers in their image, with their own world view. Lastly, CSIS' current workforce being what it is, most operatives being deployed abroad would stick out like sore thumbs. Not only would they be Caucasian, but they would also know next to nothing about local languages, customs, religion and history. Some day, the Canadian public will learn the scope of CSIS' involvement abroad when, as the result of poor preparation and lack of proper support, one of its officers is either caught red-handed, or killed.

Having said all this, where does Canada stand in the world, in the "war" on terrorism? What should the Canadian intelligence community, and CSIS, seek to accomplish? First and foremost, it is incumbent upon us to be aware that terrorism is a reality. It is also important to understand that terrorism is not an end in itself, it is not about causing pain and destruction for the sake of pain and destruction, but that it is a symptom of an underlying problem. And that underlying problem can only be resolved through a honest look at, and eventually a substantial change in, our policies vis-à-vis the Middle East and the rest of the world. Failing to do so, the upward cycle of terrorism could haunt us for a very long time. As Michael Scheuer observes: "A policy status quo, in essence, leaves America no choice but a war of annihilation."[79]

Terrorism is an instrument. Despite the recent upsurge in its use, it has always existed, although in recent times the means by which to commit terrorism have been refined, making it deadlier and more spectacular. But in the end terrorism continues to consist in blowing things up, and in so doing, creating a state of fear. In an increasingly complex world, targets with a denser concentration of potential victims, and the effects of a successful attacks on the economy, could prove very inviting to would-be terrorists who seek escalation, who want to up the ante. Taller towers to be brought down, bigger aircraft to be hijacked, denser public transportation systems to be blown up. We are told, as well, that terrorists could one day use biological, chemical, and nuclear weapons against us, that they seek to acquire them or develop them.

But it is extremely important to keep in mind that in the end these means all aim to achieve the same objective: to disrupt the normal course of societal life, and to draw attention to a cause. Following this logic, we must also understand that there is nothing inevitable about terrorism—provided that we address the underlying causes and deny terrorists the argument they need to justify an act of terror. An exception to this rule might be nihilistic groups, such as the Aum Shinrikyo, which in March 1995 launched a successful, though more disruptive than deadly, sarin gas attack in the Tokyo subway. Other than seeking to destroy the world and by doing so ensure their own survival, members of the Aum did not have political aspirations, and were not seeking to ameliorate the lot of a repressed people through terrorism. Such groups, however, are aberrations rather than the rule, and terrorism remains a tool—not an end in itself—for groups like al-Qaeda, the Palestinian Islamic Jihad, Hamas and Hezbollah, that have political needs, grievances, and goals. Once it is understood that politics is at the root of terrorism, it is easier to come to terms with the fact that addressing terrorism alone, in other words, attacking a *tactic*, which has largely been our response to Sept. 11, will at best be but a temporary solution. As Anatol Lieven writes in *America Right or Wrong*: "The darkening of the American mind was worsened by Bush's identification of the enemy as 'terrorism'—a bizarre formulation, as has often been pointed out, equivalent to declaring 'aerial bombing' or 'tanks' the enemy."[80] One cannot cure someone's diseased heart by removing it. Terrorism is a symptom, the expression, as we saw, of an existential malaise that has been allowed to fester for too long. By no means does this make terrorism acceptable, or that those individuals who are inclined to use it should not be trying to find other ways to communicate their anger. But it is, so far, the most potent tool the downtrodden have had at their disposal to be heard, when the world often chooses not to pay attention to them. As the modern world, despite the vaunted virtues of globalisation by the IMF and other trade organisations, doesn't look like it is about to become more egalitarian, the weak will increasingly feel the need to shout, and to shout loudly. And the weak are increasingly among us, no longer isolated in some remote African, Southeast Asian, or Latin American state. They walk among us in the global community, and the means to be heard, in other words the means to commit an act of terrorism, are increasingly within reach, and deadlier.

"We live in a world where [terrorism] is inevitable," Keith Weston, the former head of the counterterrorism unit of London's metropolitan police force, said during a disaster management conference in 2006

Of course terror is inevitable, as are dropping bombs or firing bullets in war. When Israel fires missiles into Gaza, some people on the ground are bound to feel terrorized. Is that inevitable? Yes; violence terrorises. As long as there are asymmetrical conflicts, people to be swayed, governments to be intimidated, and political ends to be achieved, terrorism will continue to be resorted to, no matter what shape or form it takes. As a technique, it is but one of the multiple heads of the hydra, one among the many means by which humans can visit ills upon their brethren. Uppercuts, karate kicks and head butts are inevitable, too. Methods and techniques are nothing more than intellectual concepts transformed into action to achieve an end. They always have been and always will be with us.

Conversely, there is absolutely nothing inevitable about *where* terrorism will occur, and this is what really matters, especially to us in the West. To reiterate: The technique of terrorism *is* inevitable; it is part of the multi-pronged arsenal we have at our disposal. However, there is nothing teleological about the method of terrorism, as if it were some type of cancer that will only stop proliferating after it has enveloped the entire planet. *Where* and *why* terrorism occurs is predicated, as we have seen, on the actions of states and specific circumstances. There was nothing inevitable, for example, about the London bombings. It was, rather, a response to policy choices made by the British government. Everything depends on how our governments, our intellectuals, the media and the public play the game. The choice is ours (or should be ours) to create the political space that will prevent terrorism from being visited upon Canada.

How, then, do we address terrorism and its underlying causes? In his November 2004 lecture at the University of Toronto, Michael Ignatieff pointed out, as we saw earlier, that the threat of Islamic fascism is real, and that it concerns us. Despite the fact that al-Qaeda does have a political agenda—to put an end to the West's underhanded colonisation of the Middle East—it is, at best, a defensive, short-term strategy. Until the day that the al-Qaeda executive proposes a viable socio-economic system of governance to replace the existing one, it and its allies worldwide will remain marginal, even in the Muslim world. In other words, they will continue to receive moral support for their actions against the US, but when it comes to running countries, they will remain on the sidelines. Though these organisations were partly inspired by the Iranian Revolution of 1979, where a clergy overthrew a secular, corrupt and repressive ally of the US, they have nothing in common with the Ayatollahs and their cohorts who, in the years before the revolution, proposed a political *alternative* to the way things had been under the Shah. The Islamic Republic of Iran, despite its faults and numerous accusations that it is tinkering with nuclear technology, is still a working state, and while the Ayatollahs may at times be anachronistic in their views, Iran remains a viable state that is run by professionals. Bin Laden and his friends, however, have little in the sense of running a modern, viable state to propose to their followers. Few people, even in the Middle East, would imagine, let alone seek, a return to the caliphate. This, therefore, leaves the door open for Western countries to propose an alternative, one that would substantially diminish the support that al-Qaeda has so far been receiving. The reason why so many have wed themselves to the deadly focus on the immediate proposed by bin Laden is that the status quo has become untenable and that these people have lost faith in the honesty of Western governments and multinational corporations to help them create a better, just future. For many, Western governments want to maintain that status quo and are therefore an obstacle to the better future they want for themselves and their children. Hence the image of destitute Palestinians living in refugee camps their entire lives, while next door the main reason for their condition, Israel, enriches itself, remains a potent symbol of the universal suffering of Muslims, and why it is so important that the Israel-Palestine conflict be brought to a just conclusion, one that is based on international law rather than through a "negotiated" peace in which one side has an overwhelming advantage.

Only engagement, accompanied by a thorough revamping of Western policies in the Middle East, can avoid the continual descent into ever-deadlier violence. Unfortunately, as Michael Scheuer points out, "because frank debate on the changes needed is unlikely, America will literally have to stick to its guns."[81] That is a choice for the US to make. It doesn't have to be Canada's.

As we have noted, Canada has been sucked into a war that isn't his. It is a war that, according to a recent survey of terrorism experts carried out by the magazine *Foreign Policy*, isn't being won by the West. With 86% of respondents saying that the world is much or somewhat more dangerous today than it was immediately after Sept. 11, and 79% saying that an attack on US soil on the scale of Sept. 11 within the next five years is likely to occur, the great majority of people now understand that despite claims to the contrary, and despite an investment by the strongest military power in history of billions of dollars in intelligence and war-making, the "war" on terrorism is actually being lost.[82]

Seeing that war is a failure, we could choose, instead, to adopt the honest road in the Islamic World, and to act in our self interest. Countries like Canada are still in a position to propose an alternative to the two clashing systems—US colonialism and al-Qaeda—that can only lead to perpetual violence or annihilation. Some "radical" organisations, such as the Egyptian Muslim Brotherhood, made attempts in the past to abandon violence and engage their governments politically. It was the firm and intransigent response to such organisations by those governments that led organisations like al-Qaeda to conclude that there was no point in considering the political approach. In states like Pakistan, Saudi Arabia and Uzbekistan, to name a few of the US-supported regimes that have been targeted by al-Qaeda and its allies, there is no, or very little, room for political opposition. Seeing that the political option did not exist, underground organisations felt they had no choice but to turn to violence to be heard. It is in our nature: We want to be heard, one way or another. And we want our voice to be treated as equal to that of others, not in the humiliating manner of the Palestinian negotiator forced to accede to unjust Israeli demands only to lose the respect of his Palestinian constituents. People want justice. In its absence, violence wins. Dialogue, intriguingly, is not an option that has been considered with the Taliban in Afghanistan. While there are signs that some less "radical" elements would be amenable to a political solution to the insurgency, that door has been closed by NATO and the US, which is dooming us all to war unending and lends credence to the radicals' contention that force is the only option.

One role Canada could play in the campaign against terrorism is to create room for dialogue and to assist the repressed populations as they try to change their societies. But absent a radical change in how the US engages the world, countries like Canada can only accomplish so much. Without a reorientation of US foreign policy, global terrorism is bound to stay with us for a very long time, much as did the Cold War, which, largely as a result of US intransigence, did not have to last that long.

While the US stays the course and until it exhausts itself, what Canada can do is minimise its exposure to the backlash against the US and its allies.

It would therefore be in the interest of all Canadians for the Canadian intelligence community to refrain from adopting the behaviour of its southern counterpart, which, as James Risen wrote, has become "militarised."[83] Just as intelligence should not be politicised or militarised, we cannot allow it to become a stand-in for policy, or an end in itself. Just as terrorism is only a tool and cannot, in the long term, generate the ideas that are needed to build society, so is counterterrorism. It, too, is only an instrument by which certain changes can be brought about. But it is, ultimately, an instrument that can only be used to address symptoms and tactics. The real change, our real chance of surviving this conflict, is diplomacy. As Canada, a so-called middle power, does not have enough diplomatic and economic weight to resolve the problems of the Middle East, the least it can do is avoid being dragged into Washington's self-defeating war over the region.

But this is easier said than done, and seven years of partnership with the US in its worldwide campaign against terrorism has almost congealed into a political *fait accompli* that will be difficult to overturn. Thanks to the skilful rhetoric that followed Sept. 11, subsequent attacks and the occupations of Afghanistan and Iraq, we have been led to believe that terrorism affects us as *global citizens,* and that as a consequence this threat must be confronted through a common front, a shared cause with the US in the lead. Unfortunately for countries like Canada, who were faced with the choice of being "with" the US or "against" it, this so-called coalition is nothing more than an exercise in unilateralism and political bullying. Moreover, throughout all this the US has perceived its allies as nothing more than appendages, forcing them to do certain things that are not necessarily in their best interest, and castigating them when they refused to do so. Just to please its master, Japan went as far as to reinterpret its pacifist Constitution, written after its defeat in World War II, so that it could participate in a supporting role in the campaign against terrorism. When domestic politics threatened to end Japan's contribution, Washington warned of "serious consequences" to the US-Japan relationship.

While these countries recognise that international terrorism poses a threat to security, stability, and the global economy, and agree that it should be stopped, they nevertheless have sovereign needs of their own, and as such their participation in the common front should reflect those interests rather than be shaped by the single needs and expectations of the US. States must respond to terrorism in light of the threat that it poses to their interests and to the international community, and not to the US (or Israel) alone. In recent years, US allies that have been targeted by al-Qaeda-inspired terrorism—the United Kingdom, Spain, Turkey, Saudi Arabia—were all perceived to be servants of the US. They were seen as having lost their independence, and in the eyes of bin Laden and his followers they had become nothing more than instruments of US colonialism, worst among them those located in the Middle East. But who could blame them? Beyond the touching moniker that on Sept. 11, 2001, we were all Americans, we were subsequently all forced into one big family through political and economic pressure and threats. So much so that countries with little to contribute militarily nevertheless participated in the campaign in Afghanistan. Others even more ludicrously joined in the invasion of Iraq. In reality, though, the coalitions of the willing were rather coalitions of the compelled: join us in Afghanistan, in Iraq, in Iran, or else. Either you're for Freedom, or you're against it. There was no middle ground. Trade became linked to the issue of terrorism. Countries that, out of their sovereign right, refused to participate in the invasion of Iraq were kicked out of alliances and could no longer receive certain intelligence products. These were dubbed "Old Europe" and "traitors." In the popular press, France became the US' "oldest enemy." On the other hand, countries that decided to join the US bandwagon were showered with investment, business deals, American military bases, and defence alliances. Even murderous authoritarian regimes like Uzbekistan's, or states that had failed to comply with the Non Proliferation Treaty, like Pakistan, were befriended by the Americans and were adopted by Washington as trustworthy allies in the "war" on terrorism, further congealing the oppression in those countries.

Such pressure and political bullying compelled certain states into taking part in operations that they were either unsuited for, or for which they didn't have the support of their constituents. Canadian participation in the invasion of Iraq would have been such an instance. In Washington, the Bush administration seems to equate the world's willingness to lend a hand with abject acceptance that things ought to be done "the American way." It is as if the US were a super-computer and its allies mere plug-and-play devices that, once they are connected to the CPU, are forced to accomplish their specialised tasks in accordance with the US software. This is very much the way the "war" on terrorism has been fought so far. The US has chosen to go it alone, and while it seeks the cover of multilateralism by going to the UN and by inviting countries to join in the Coalition, it acts like Hobbes' famous Leviathan. For those groups and individuals on the receiving end of that political-military-intelligence alliance, it becomes very difficult to distinguish between the targets: they are Americans, or its imperial subjects. Thus Madrid and London—and perhaps, one day, Toronto, Montreal, or Ottawa. Not because of who we are, but rather what we became.

Alliances alone were not sufficient for Washington. Allies needed to demonstrate their willingness to play in the big leagues, to prove their mettle, and to push the envelope. Whether doing so actually contributed to a state's security—or in reverse, made matters worse—didn't matter to the White House or the Pentagon or Langley. Play ball, go the extra mile. In the name of the alliance; in the name of Freedom. Thus pressured, some states sent token troops into Afghanistan and into Iraq. Aside from the US and the United Kingdom, however, few had the military capabilities to wage modern, high-intensity war in Iraq, or to face the complexities of the deadly insurrection that followed. Some countries, such as Spain, suffered the consequences of that deployment, and wisely pulled out their troops after the 3/11 bombings. Despite claims to the contrary, those lives that were lost in that attack were a direct consequence of the Spanish government's decision to send troops into Iraq, regardless of the fact that this deployment contributed absolutely nothing to the well-being of Iraqis or to mission success in Iraq. It was a political decision stemming from diplomatic pressure and, perhaps, from the promise of economic benefits to such participation. The cost to Spain for regaining its sovereignty and independence, sadly, had to be paid in Spanish blood.

Canada, though it decided not to participate in Iraq, has played a role in other areas linked to the "war" on terrorism. As we saw, it deployed its elite JTF-2 unit soon after the attacks on Sept. 11, and its mission was to kill. Subsequently, Canada deployed more than 2,000 soldiers to Kabul, the capital of Afghanistan, and in 2004 ISAF was under Canadian command. In 2005, Canadian soldiers were deployed to Kandahar to support the PRT, but since then their mission has shifted from supporting reconstruction to fighting a high-intensity war against insurgents, which has resulted in severe loss of life. At this writing, 78 Canadians soldiers and one diplomat have paid the ultimate price in Afghanistan. And many hundreds of Afghans, some non-combatants, have been killed by Canadian soldiers. While we like to think that we are doing good in Afghanistan, our presence there is not necessarily a welcome one, given the country's long history of resistance to foreign intervention.

In the realm of intelligence, similar pressure to comply with American demands has been applied. Soon after the invasion of Iraq in 2003, intelligence agencies worldwide were bombarded with requests from the CIA on Iraq-related matters. All were expected to provide the FBI and the CIA with what they needed in terms of information. But the alliance was a one-way street: while agencies were expected to provide assistance and reply to requests from their counterparts, the US response to queries by those agencies was something else altogether. They were not a priority, and they would wait. As we have seen, the FBI can take months, and sometimes years, before replying to a request. No matter how improbable and unfounded the threat information is, however, American agencies will send urgent requests to allied agencies, expecting a response in the briefest of delays. A mixture of panic and incompetence on the American side often results in requests for information that do nothing but add to the high workload of intelligence officers in allied agencies. But they respond, to the best of their abilities. After all, imperial subjects do not talk back, and do not question the wisdom of whoever their master is.

We have noted that countries with experience in espionage and counterterrorism and whose agencies are at the top of the food chain exert tremendous pressure on lesser powers like Canada. The main sandbox does not have much room, and for those who want to play in it, they need to demonstrate their willingness to abide by the rules set by the Big Boys. Failure to comply results in the toddler being kicked out, perhaps with a bloody nose. As the milieu is extremely competitive and hierarchical, intelligence services all aim to be in the big leagues, and CSIS is no exception. Careerism and self-promotion, as we saw in the previous chapter, is alive and well within the Service. The pressure is therefore on the various intelligence services to jump through the fiery hoops set by the CIA and the handful of other Big Players. In so doing, agencies tend to lose sight of their mandates. Operational objectives that, first and foremost, ought to be the protection of their constituents, are transformed by the need to strike alliances and the hope of landing a seat at the adults' table. One grave consequence of this—and I have seen it in action—is that sometimes agencies will launch an operation that not only is of little value to the country but that ultimately *increases* the threat against it.

This situation is all the more worrying when one reads in the news that high-ranking CIA officials, seeing that the Pentagon is positioning itself to do so, are asking for the Agency to embark upon increasingly aggressive covert measures. Following Sept. 11 and accusations that the CIA misled Washington on terrorism and weapons of mass destruction, the CIA has been under siege and has sought ways to prove its necessity. Not unlike allied countries of the US, the CIA has also come under tremendous pressure from the militarised White House. Porter Goss, who after George Tenet's resignation was appointed by the White House to become the CIA's director, was reputedly one of the most aggressive directors in recent years. In the words of a former CIA operative, Goss "[was] probably more aggressive than most of the senior officers in the clandestine service." Former agents, disgruntled at the lack of operational efficiency, have been publishing their memoirs, and many have recommended that the clandestine branch of the CIA be more aggressive.[84]

This, in itself, should make one pause, for reasons that are self-evident. As the CIA becomes more aggressive and as it adopts techniques that historically have been associated with ISIS, other agencies, including CSIS, may feel the need to do so as well. In the process, through a mix of speedy action and inexperience (not to mention unwise decision-making), certain agencies could endanger national security rather than bolster it.

Already, many countries, including Canada, have greatly expanded the powers and reach of their intelligence and law enforcement agencies, and given the pressure that agencies like the CIA and ISIS bring to bear on their allies, those powers will feasibly continue to grow. But, as the preceding pages have hopefully made clear, this increase in powers has not been accompanied by an increase in brain-power, so the gap between permissibility (what we're allowed to do) and capability (the intellectual power we have at our disposal) has widened, which exposes society to grave dangers. Recently, as James Risen reported, soon after Sept. 11, 2001, Washington secretly approved measures that allow the NSA to eavesdrop, without a warrant, on US citizens suspected of being connected to terrorism, in the hope of gaining additional information on the structure of the al-Qaeda network.[85] (In February 2008, the US Congress voted in favour of an amendment to the Foreign Intelligence Surveillance Act that provided retroactive legal immunity to telecoms companies that allowed the NSA to eavesdrop on phone calls and e-mails against terrorist suspects without a warrant.[86]) Unconstitutionality aside, this relaxing of regulations protecting the individual, combined with the lack of brain capital to support such added responsibilities, not only opens the door to abuse, but also severely increases the likelihood of error. This "slide" will result in innocent people, or people targeted through guilt-by-association, being monitored by the NSA and other agencies. And as these issues are rarely debated in the courtroom, what constitutes a "suspected terrorist" is open to interpretation. Once the legal system has been removed from the equation, the potential for abuse becomes very real.

This is why the only real system of accountability that remains today is the media. It is newspapers that, when at their best and facing the threat of legal action, nevertheless choose to go ahead and publish a story that the government would rather keep secret. Nevertheless, while some news outlets may be commended for exposing abuse at home, the media also shares its part of the blame when it comes to coverage of events abroad, which oftentimes provides a view of conflict that, by design or omission, minimises the suffering of people like Palestinians and other groups and clearly favours the US, Israel, or the stronger party. If, as a society, we are to mobilise and ask that our government truly act in a responsible manner, we must request that our media serve us news that are complete and balanced, and that take international law into account. Coverage that masks the suffering of a people, that dehumanises human beings or, as we have seen, that fails to call to account government officials who do so, makes it more difficult for Canadians not only to understand what is going on elsewhere but also diminishes our capacity to empathise with groups whose grievances could one day find an expression in our own backyard.

As in the media, the language that is used in the reports that accompany exchanges with allied agencies is also reflective of the Service's political position vis-à-vis the world: For example, any form of attack by Palestinian groups against Israeli interests is referred to as "terrorism"; conversely, any attack by the Israelis against Palestinians, however wanton, will be "military" or "in retaliation." On that issue, I remember becoming extremely angry with our service's turning a blind eye to the savage acts that Israel was committing in retaliation to "terrorist" attacks against it. I could no longer bear the bias and informed my supervisor at the time, in writing, that from now on I would refuse to participate in the preparation of threat assessments for that particular country. My letter found its way up the ladder, and by accident I came upon the reaction of a senior analyst who had been consulted by my supervisor as to how she should react. His comments were to the effect that I was being juvenile and that the continuance of such behaviour could in the long run reflect negatively on my career. In other words, I was to willingly allow my employer to shape the language that I used, even if that language went counter to everything I believed in.

The Canadian government's relationship with the state of Israel deserves additional remarks. As I soon realised through my own experiences, there is no room at CSIS for questioning Israel's policies or the actions of its intelligence services. Whenever I raised the issue or expressed my disagreement with Israel, my supervisors would ignore me or accuse me of ignorance. Others would accuse me of anti-Semitism, or of moral relativism. Israel was beyond scrutiny, its actions untouchable. As John Mearsheimer and Stephen Walt noted in the *London Review of Books*, however, this lack of criticism may in fact increase the threats to our security.[87] Given that Israel's treatment of Palestinians in every sector is hardly just and that its security and intelligence apparatuses tend to act aggressively, groups on the receiving end who perceive those actions to be supported by Western powers could eventually decide to strike in the West. Even if only Israeli interests were to be attacked in Canada, the risks of collateral would be very real. Whether we like it or not, support for, or muted response to Israel's harsh and unjust treatment of Palestinians is one of the pillars upon which rests bin Laden's war against the US and its allies.

These double standards do not go unnoticed. This brings to mind a controversy that emerged when I was an undergraduate student in Montreal. The hall in the main building was always filled with booths, plastered with banners and posters, representing a number of causes, from AIDS to women's rights. Given that university's ethnic composition, some of the booths were for political causes. Palestine was prominent among them, and the movement gained the university a certain reputation for "radicalism" (that image was further damaged when, in 2001, former Israeli prime minister Benjamin Netanyahu's scheduled lecture at the university was cancelled after a handful of demonstrators, including a few students, turned violent and started breaking windows). One day, as I was on my way to class, one booth caught my attention. I usually did not pay too much attention to them, but this one stuck out: Israeli flags and colours in full display, this was an Israel Defence Force (IDF) recruiting campaign. Somehow I knew there was something not altogether right with a foreign army recruiting on Canadian university campuses. I wouldn't have minded it much if it had been the Canadian Armed Forces—or CSIS, even, which does have the occasional booth on university campuses across Canada. But an Israeli one? Though the second *intifada* was half a decade away, it was already evident, at least to those among us who were interested in political developments abroad, that the IDF was not dealing with the situation in the Occupied Territories with proportionality. Soon afterwards, that booth was gone.

Years later, by then working at CSIS, that university would often be mentioned as a nest of radicals.[88] Whenever I mentioned the IDF recruiting campaign, people at CSIS didn't seem to understand why there could be anything wrong with that. I wonder what their reaction would have been if, instead of the IDF, it had been Hamas or Hezbollah doing the recruiting. None of those entities should conduct recruiting on university campuses; that the IDF would not only be allowed to do so but to accomplish this overtly is a clear sign of preferential treatment, and one that, in the end, damages Canada's image both domestically and abroad.

The Canadian government's response to Israel's illegal aggression against Lebanon in the summer of 2006 can only have made matters worse. For the Canadian Minister of Foreign Affairs to stand by silently while a Vancouver rabbi called Hezbollah "a cancer that needs to be eradicated" and to use the same kind of language of hatred the very next day, when the "Hezbollah" at the receiving end of the Israeli bombing—which included banned weapons like cluster bombs—applied to undefended women and children, is not only unrepresentative of Canadian values but also endangers the security of Canadians. Again, for various reasons, the Canadian government was siding with Israel, to such an extent that it could not even summon the criticism that the savage military campaign so rightly deserved. Even when Hess-von Kruedener, a Canadian UN observer in Khiam, Lebanon, was killed, along with three other UN observers, by an Israeli precision-guided missile on July 25,[89] Ottawa failed to condemn the attack or call for an investigation. It issued no condemnation, either, when seven Canadian-Lebanese were killed when a house in Aitaroun, along the Israel-Lebanon border, was bombed by the Israelis.[90] As Israel was waging what it called a "defensive" war of aggression, it seemed that killing Canadians was also acceptable. These things, we must not forget, do not go unnoticed. While many Canadians may have disagreed with their government's silence on Lebanon, the message abroad was that Canada does not care about the plight of civilians caught in an unjust war.

It would be easy to blame CSIS for all the problems that currently plague it. It would be even easier to point fingers at individuals and recommend that they be removed from office. But the reality is, CSIS is only part of the problem. A lot of what is wrong with it is the result of systemic problems within the Canadian community that have been allowed to exist for far too long, as well as pressures, both domestic and foreign, that are beyond its comprehension or ability to change. Without a strong government that clearly and logically consolidates the *Canadian* position on terrorism and national security, on al-Qaeda and the other threats that are emerging in the 21st century, CSIS and the other agencies that comprise the Canadian intelligence community will continue to be shaped, pressured, and exploited by the greater powers. As long as this is allowed to continue, the ill-prepared, ill-trained and isolated body of intelligence officers and managers will take us ever closer to catastrophe. It is long time that Canadians realised that our security is contingent on Canada being able to act in its own interest rather than that of the US. There is an urgent need for debate on those issues within Canada, on topics such as what we expect from our soldiers currently deployed in Afghanistan, or whether CSIS really ought to become more aggressive or more involved internationally. Is war-making against insurgents, in a country that in its long history of invasion has never been defeated, not even after ten long years of occupation by the Soviets, what we believe Canadians should do? If it is really what we, as Canadians, believe is the right thing to do, then let's do it and let's provide our soldiers with all the backing that they need. But should this be our choice, we would have to accept that Canada's image abroad will likely change, and that as a result our security at home may very well be compromised.

✳   ✳   ✳   ✳

Despite US President George W. Bush's constant declarations to the effect that al-Qaeda has been weakened by the "war" on terrorism and that it is "on the run," analysts the world over are starting to revisit this assumption.

A clear indication of this failure to eliminate the threat can be found in recent comments by no less a player in anti-terrorism than Dame Eliza Manningham-Buller, the head of the British domestic intelligence service, MI5. In November, Manningham-Buller—well-known for her cool-headedness when it comes to discussing threats to the nation—said that since 2005 MI5 had identified 30 major terrorist plots in Britain and was monitoring the activities of—take a deep breath—no less than 1,600 Britain-based individuals from approximately 200 terrorist networks. This on the home front alone! Those exact same figures were repeated by London Metropolitan Police Deputy Commissioner Paul Stephenson at a security conference in Sydney, Australia, soon afterwards.

With the population of Great Britain at 60.7 million as of late last year, this meant that there was one terrorist suspect for every 38,000 British—an astounding figure no matter how one looks at it. To put things in context, for Canada, with its population of about 33 million, this would mean 868 terrorist suspects in its midst. If this were the case, CSIS would have to grow about eight-fold to be in a position to monitor the activities of all those suspects. And this excludes all the other groups targeted by intelligence services, such as China, Russia, Iran and others. Given, based on my experiences, the usual ratio of 2 intelligence officers for every target of an investigation, this would mean that in Canada, more than 1,700 intelligence officers would be working on the al-Qaeda file alone, a figure that excludes the communication intercepts specialists, translators, and other operational staff, not to mention pay and administrative staff, lawyers, and so on. (As of last year, the *total* workforce at CSIS, including administration, pay services and others, was approximately 2,400.)

But what those numbers truly show is that if they are true, the West is clearly doing something wrong, so wrong, in fact, that defeat in its "war" on terrorism is almost certain. Ever since they launched the campaign against al-Qaeda and other like-minded groups in 2001, the architects of the "war" on terror have repeatedly said that this new war is as much a military campaign as it is a war for the hearts and minds of people in the Muslim world. Given the MI5 numbers, it would appear that the hearts and minds part has either gone terribly wrong—or worse, that the leadership didn't mean what it said. This, of course, is not entirely impossible, as to this day former British prime minister Tony Blair still refuses to acknowledge that Britain's actions in Iraq and Afghanistan have an impact upon domestic security.

The most alarming part is that even if Manningham-Buller's figures are overblown, the intelligence community and the British government believe they are true and don't seem to grasp that they are indicative of a monumental failure on the diplomatic front. Absent such an understanding, such figures—real or inflated—can only go up.

CHAPTER 3

▼

THE JUNE 2006 'GROUP OF SEVENTEEN' INCIDENT

No event better encapsulates everything we have seen so far than the arrest, in early June 2006, of 17 individuals in Southern Ontario who, according to the authorities, were planning multiple terrorist attacks inside Canada. Although some references to this incident were made in the previous sections, this chapter looks at the matter in further detail. As this is, in many ways, an ongoing case, and given the fact that a publication ban was imposed soon after the arrests, it is difficult to know in full detail what transpired during that dramatic period. Nevertheless, based on our understanding of how CSIS and the wider community operate, we can make a few observations that should help us make better sense of the affair. I present it in a manner that shows, as honestly as I can put it, my own intellectual journey as a former intelligence officer, from the initial belief in everything we are told, to a sense that everything is not what it seems. In a way, this is how an intelligence officer *should* receive, digest, and analyse information—with an open mind, but also with a sense of criticism.

"We are a target because of who we are and how we live, our society, our diversity and our values," Prime Minister Stephen Harper said in Ottawa a day after 17 individuals in Southern Ontario were arrested in what was the country's largest antiterrorist operation since Canada's *Anti-terrorism Act* came into effect in December 2001.

Nearly three tonnes of ammonium nitrate (a fertilizer), we were told, were seized by authorities—three time as much as was used in the bombing on April 19, 1995, of the Alfred P. Murrah Federal Building in Oklahoma—along with a cell phone that may have been intended to be used as a makeshift detonator. No sooner had the arrests been made than officials and the media began speculating that a terrible attack had been foiled. As is usually the case in such situations, people have the end state in mind—a massive bombing somewhere in Canada, possibly in Toronto's metropolitan area, which is likely inspired by the precedents set by the Bali, Madrid, and London bombings—before we are apprised of the details. Logical case-building, however, should start from the bottom and find its way up; in other words, we cannot assume a conclusion and make the evidence fit that picture. Far too often, the reality is quite different from what it might have looked like initially. In a society like Canada, which is based on a system of laws and individual rights, we cannot simply put intentions in a suspect's head, or use a few items as evidence of those intentions. Only time and hard work by intelligence and law-enforcement officers can give us the right to accuse individuals of a crime that has not been committed.

A few days after the arrests, parts of the alleged terrorist plan were leaked to the press: A plot to kidnap parliamentarians with the intent of forcing the government of Canada to pull its troops out of Afghanistan; to behead the Canadian Prime Minister; and to blow up public buildings, including the Canadian Broadcasting Corporation (CBC) Broadcast Centre in Toronto, which is across the street from where the CSIS regional headquarters are located (I am not revealing any secrets here; a plaque clearly identifies it in the lobby).

As coverage of the arrests continued, with a prominent display of force, SWAT teams and all, the list of potential targets for the alleged planned attacks kept growing. First, it was the Parliament building in Ottawa, but then that target had been dropped, we were told, due to the terrorists' unfamiliarity with Ottawa, a city whose layout, for anyone who has visited it, is anything but difficult to figure out. Unless the suspects were supremely incompetent (which, according to at least one source, they may very well have been), Ottawa should not have been too daunting a challenge, certainly not enough to drop an operation by professionals. Then it was the CN Tower, followed by the CSIS office in Toronto, the Toronto Stock Exchange (TSX), and an unspecified military base. We heard about truck or car bombs (called vehicle-borne improvised explosive devices, or VBIED, a term that, because of the insurgency in Iraq, has entered the everyday lexicon). It then emerged that one of the suspects may have enrolled in flight school, indicating, perhaps, that a plan for an attack from the air was in the offing, only to have been abandoned as well.

The problem with all these allegations, which came from a Crown synopsis, is that it was impossible to verify them. Defence lawyers also noted the dearth of details concerning the accusations against their clients.

It seemed like the list would never end, and soon people's imagination began filling the gaps. The Toronto Subway was soon added; the University of Toronto, Tim Horton's or any other landmark. Soon, all the possibilities were covered. Each new possible target that was leaked had sentimental value for a population that received the news with a sigh of relief, as if Armageddon itself had been averted. As the authorities provided potential targets one at a time, people reacted in different ways, depending on their relationship with those locations. For me, the CBC building had a special meaning, as my father, a career CBC employee who retired in 2000, was among those who helped build the studios in it. I also happened to know some people who worked there. The second potential target that made me pause was the building in which the CSIS regional office is located. As a former employee of that organisation, I had visited it— spent days in there, in fact—and knew many people in it, including friends. For others, the emotional link was to the CN Tower, the TSX, and so on, for a variety of reasons.

Two principal forces were at work simultaneously during those weeks, and both had the potential to awaken the imagination and exacerbate fear within the public. First, wittingly or not, the authorities were adding fuel to the fire by enumerating a list of potential targets. Either they didn't know which were the targets, or they knew but chose, for one reason or another, to widen the net. Regardless, the end result was the same—fear, and relief that the authorities had prevented a catastrophe, thus justifying the existence of the security apparatus and its growing budgets.

The second was the media, which fed on, interpreted, magnified and diffused, non stop, all the precious little information it was receiving from the authorities. When the latter closed up, the media turned to the so-called security "experts" (who also recognise a lucrative opportunity when they see one) and reported every rumour that emerged. This was the big news in Toronto—in Canada, even—and the occasion was not to be missed. We were making the news; we were being noticed. CNN was in Toronto; we were on Reuters, the BBC, perhaps even on Al-Jazeera!

Then the information started to dry up. As always, the reasons given as to why the government could not provide more information, or due process for the accused, in fact, were the same as always: Sources needed to be protected, and providing more information could jeopardise their security. Some of the information that led to the arrests likely had come from foreign agencies, which Canadian authorities were to refrain from revealing. Finally, the authorities argued that this was an ongoing investigation and that to reveal more now would have complicated their efforts.

Soon thereafter, while we all sought answers, the Supreme Court imposed a publication ban on the prosecution of the suspects. After feeding crumbs to the press for a little more than a week, the Crown decided that the proceedings should take place beyond the scrutiny of reporters, rights groups, the families of the accused, and the public. The reason given, as with all things secret, was the same old need to protect the sources—domestic and foreign—whose information had led to the arrests.

Following a preliminary hearing on June 4, 2006, on Sept. 24, 2007, the Crown called for direct indictment of the suspects, meaning that the defence counsel could not hear the testimony of the Crown's key witness, Mubin Shaikh, a police mole who had penetrated the suspected "terrorist" organisation, and that of another mole.[91] As it later became apparent, Shaikh had a well-honed knack for self-publicity and it is not impossible he would have misled some of the suspects—especially the five minors—to achieve his own ends. Based on the evidence and his own comments, Shaikh is hardly a reliable witness and has rather displayed a tendency to provide the authorities with information that supported their preconceived ideas. In other words, he told them what they wanted to hear.

The more one looks at the Group of Seventeen, the more obvious it becomes that they were, at best, a bunch of misguided youth who probably represented more of a danger to themselves than to Canada. On June 20, 2006, June, *La Presse*, a Montreal-based French-language newspaper, published an article on the subject, in which it revealed, among other things, that the group may have been "dangled," in the language of the trade, by a source who had infiltrated their group.[92] In other words, at the behest of Canadian authorities, the said source—likely Shaikh—may have encouraged (on his own, or with guidance from the authorities) the group members to aim for something bigger than they were capable of, or had intended to accomplish. In law-enforcement jargon, this is called entrapment, and it is illegal. Law enforcement officials cannot lead an individual to commit a crime only to arrest that person for committing, or attempting to commit, that crime.

What better reason would there be for a publication ban on the whole affair than the need to keep those facts away from the public? How else could we explain that, despite being aware that they were under surveillance, the Group of Seventeen continued planning whatever it is that they had in mind? The possibility certainly exists that they were led to believe that no action would be taken against them. These were, after all, impressionable youth, and if, as the authorities suggest, they were credulous enough to swallow an ideology of hatred, then what was there to prevent them from also swallowing whatever it is that the source wanted them to believe? Credulous individuals aren't credulous for one purpose but not for another. If they buy something idiotic once, chances are they will buy again.

The whole affair reeks of fabrication. The Group of Seventeen probably mattered little to the authorities; they were, after all, disposable, and the *Anti-terrorism Act* provided all the dispensations that made it relatively easy to do so. What matters to CSIS and others is the illusion that we are indeed facing a grave threat from terrorism. It justifies budgets and new buildings, and it inflates the ego. The incident also coincided, strangely, with a review of the Security Certificates, which have served CSIS and the rest of the community well since Sept. 11, 2001. Widespread fear was a sure way to ensure that the Certificates would not be abandoned, or their powers diminished.

Case-building, as we have noted, is mostly an exercise in interpreting innuendo and piecing together a jigsaw puzzle based on imperfect, incomplete, and sometimes downright wrong information. In other words, intelligence officers never work with a clear-cut piece of information. Then, individual and institutional biases arise, leading analysts to operate with the conclusion as a point of departure. This in turn engenders syllogism, which, as we saw in Chapter 1, intelligence agencies commit on a daily basis: X is a contact of target Y, therefore X must be involved too, as is Z, who knows X. The end state—guilt—is assumed for all three characters, and whatever piece of information is obtained on any of the three will be tainted by this. As a result, almost all intelligence material can be shaped to fit the model.

Compounding the challenges mentioned above is the fact that the institutions of power in Ottawa (and everywhere else, to be fair) are surrounded by walls. Nowhere are they thicker, however, than around and within the security intelligence apparatus. Walls have long existed between the authorities and the public, between the rulers and the ruled. But there are also walls between the authorities themselves, even within the organisations. As we saw in Chapter 1, those walls come mostly from the system of "need to know." If someone decides that you don't need to know, you won't, and if you try to access the information, you're bound to get into trouble. Such secrecy serves its function, which is mostly to ensure that no one will ever be in a position to criticise someone else's work, from the desk officer all the way to the organisation. What's worse, limiting the number of people who have access to the information inevitably reinforces "groupthink," whereby, through a process of self-reinforcement, everybody in the group becomes unable to depart from the prevailing view, with no chances of getting fresh input from the outside.

Based on all the deficiencies we have explored so far, there exists a very real possibility that some of the 17 individuals were nabbed as a result of guilt-by-association, shoddy intelligence work, syllogism, or institutional biases. Maybe this is not the case, but the possibility certainly exists. As we have seen, intelligence work is an imperfect art, and errors of commission cannot be avoided. Even the best, most experienced analysts make mistakes. They are, after all, human. Furthermore, when lives are believed to be at stake, the logical reaction would be to cast as wide a net as possible.

Where we run the risk of encountering fundamental ethical problems, however, is when the authorities' obsession with secrecy obviates the means by which those individuals could clear their name—in other words, due process. Absent such recourse, innocent people will be prosecuted and their lives destroyed. In certain cases, secrecy also provides a convenient way to cut corners and cover up investigative deficiencies. Individuals could be put behind bars, or expelled from the country, based on a less than airtight case.

For CSIS, law enforcement agencies and ultimately the government, failure to provide enough information about the proceedings of an investigation could backfire. The public needs closure and needs to know that those individuals were arrested for a reason. In other words, they need something to substantiate their fears. Failing to do so, doubts will linger, and some will wonder if the whole things might not simply have been orchestrated to please Washington or, more cynically, to justify the billions of dollars that Ottawa has so far spent on counterterrorism. The Harper government's resentment of the media could also be self-defeating, as without answers the public could reach the conclusion that is has been lied to, that the threat did not exist or that the suspects were not provided with all the legal protections that, as Canadians, they were entitled to. As a result, public confidence in the reliability of our government may have been harmed.

In this instance, someone high up in Ottawa seems to have decided that the public did not need to know what was going on. Or the defence lawyers and the defendants themselves, for that matter. Given the high likelihood that errors of judgment and inference were committed by the officers who worked on the case, this means that no one in Canada will be in a position to scrutinise the proceedings to ensure that those errors are heeded and taken into consideration. Absent an outside view, the unfortunate seventeen will be denied due process, and some of them will face sentences that, in a democracy, they should not be facing.

If the problems were limited to CSIS, we could expect that court authorities and the Canadian judicial system as a whole, have the means to review all the information that was used as evidence against the suspects, and thereby correct any mistakes that may have been committed. Unfortunately for the suspects, that is not the case. Vast amounts of information will be presented, and vast amounts will not. Court officials will only see what CSIS and its partners want them so see; only incriminating evidence, or intelligence that can be interpreted as supporting the case, will be submitted. Every piece of information that does not support the case will be omitted. In other words, secrecy within the system will ensure that even the checks and balances that would, in theory, protect us from abuse are circumvented. As a result, errors will remain hidden. What is even more alarming is that even if the whole thing was nothing more than a spectacle, a political tool to justify the existence of our security apparatus or to appease the US, the oversight system would be unable to reach that conclusion. In the end, the walls of secrecy ensure that the truth will never be known, not by the public, and not by the legal system.

Situations like these happen in police states like Uzbekistan, where people are seized in the middle of the night and disappeared forever. It happens in Guantanamo Bay, Cuba, where many al-Qaeda and Taliban suspects are held for extended periods of time. It happened in Abu Ghraib, where Iraqi insurgents were beaten, humiliated and tortured by American soldiers. And yes, shocking as it may be, our present system, the topic of this book, means that it could happen here in Canada.

There is no doubt that in recent years Canada may have begun showing up on terrorists' radar screen. Despite the objectionable fear-mongering approach that high-ranking officials in the Canadian security establishment have taken since Sept. 11, 2001, the possibility that, at some point in the future, a terrorist attack will be committed on Canadian soil does exist, especially if we continue to allow pressure from the US to guide our policies. However, the prime minister's reaction to the arrests in Toronto and his reiteration that we are a target because of who and what we are irresponsibly avoids looking reality in the eye. As we have seen, al-Qaeda does not hate us for what or who we are. We become a target when it and its followers start believing that our actions are threatening or supporting colonialism in the Muslim world.

Canadians must come to the realisation that there is a cost to engaging the world, and that we cannot deploy thousands of soldiers into Afghanistan, no matter how humanitarian we believe our actions might be, and not expect a reaction. Canadian forces in and around Kandahar have become increasingly proactive in their anti-Taliban operations. In the process, people are bound to get hurt. Eventually, someone—Taliban or otherwise—will get killed, and that someone will have a sibling, a friend, a cousin, in Canada. A would-be terrorist will not resort to violence because of some fundamental hatred for our system of values or our liberties; rather, violence will become an option when one feels that a wrong must be righted, a death avenged, or a point made. It will become justifiable, in the perpetrator's mind at least, when "terrorism" here is seen as no different from the "terrorism" committed by our troops abroad. Canadians like to see themselves as peacekeepers, and we like to think that what our brave soldiers are accomplishing in Afghanistan is welcomed by all. But it is not. It is war-making, and there is nothing clean about that. Bullets are being fired, people are being arrested, and errors are sometimes being made.[93] News that Canadians might have played an indirect role in the torture of suspects handed over to Afghan authorities—which Ottawa may have been aware of—could further hurt the reputation of our troops there.

This is not to say that we should not be in Afghanistan, or that Canada should shirk its responsibilities as a global player for fear that we will get a collective black eye at some point in the future. But a responsible prime minister should do his utmost to educate the population and prepare it for the eventuality that the battle we brought to someone else's shores could eventually be visited upon us. We are not innocent anymore, and the hatred that some individuals may feel toward us is the result of our actions. As the country debates whether to stay the course in Afghanistan or call it quits, to continue to fight a war or return to the initial mandate of providing support to the PRTs, these issues should be put on the table. If we are willing to take the risk, and if we believe that it is in the best interest of Canada to have 2,500 soldiers fighting a war that perhaps cannot be won in Afghanistan, then so be it. But there will be consequences, and we could very well see more June incidents as a result.

It is interesting to note that on certain occasions—usually when a terrorism "incident" has occurred on Canadian soil—CSIS will come out of its shell and openly discuss its foreign operations. On March 30, 2004, Momin Khawaja, a resident of Orleans, outside Ottawa, became the first individual charged under Canada's *Anti-terrorism Act*. Two months later, CSIS was approaching the media and explaining that given the change in the nature of the threat, the Service had in recent years become increasingly active abroad, which included dispatching Service assets (sources) to countries from which the threats emanated, or developing more relationships with foreign agencies.

No sooner had the June 2006 terror arrests been made than CSIS was once again making its case with the public. The tune sounded strangely familiar: Given the changing nature of the threat, CSIS needed to engage into more operations abroad, for which more money was required, et cetera et cetera. The one difference this time, however, was the admission, by Director Jim Judd himself, that CSIS was not only sending sources abroad, but that its very own home-grown operatives were doing the round trips, something that a few years ago no one at CSIS would ever have admitted.

This should not necessarily come as a surprise. Like any other intelligence agency around the world, CSIS was capitalising on the recent coup, just as the FBI, the CIA and MI6 (or BSIS) did after Sept. 11. This time around, the opportunity was there for CSIS, and the widespread fear generated by the events provided the momentum the organisation needed to make the final push toward becoming, at last, the foreign intelligence gathering agency it wanted to become.

Readers will note that CSIS' shift toward activity abroad has happened gradually, with the nature of the foreign-based intelligence collection being revealed little by little. First, two years ago, CSIS struck agreements with foreign agencies, or sent sources travelling. Now it was sending its own people. This is reminiscent of the story about the frog that the scientist drops in a bucket of water: If the water is boiling, the frog will jump out to save its skin; increase the temperature gradually, however, and the same frog will allow itself to boil to death.

In a way, the Canadian public is not unlike the unfortunate frog. Rather than being boiled to death, however, the instrument of fear is being used on it. Every two years or so, the sense of imminent danger is elevated a little, the screw turned a little tighter. While nothing happens and no attack is committed on Canadian soil, the sense that we are under siege, that an attack is always imminent, nevertheless lingers. Although the strategy is somewhat more subtle than the colour-based "treat level" system the US adopted, it operates in similar fashion.

Done long enough, the hitherto unthinkable possibility of Canada spying abroad becomes universally acceptable, if not necessary.

The same with the Security Certificates or the more intrusive powers CSIS constantly strives for; the greater the climate of fear, the likelier it is that CSIS and the rest of the intelligence community will obtain what they want. In all, the movie-like spectacular that the arrest of the Group of Seventeen turned into in June 2006 bears all the hallmarks of a public relations campaign waged against the Canadian public to make it easier for the authorities to pass laws that would otherwise have received tremendous opposition.

Given everything we have seen, the unqualified analysts, the incompetence, the insufficient training, the poor morale, the racism, the increasingly aggressive targeting, the lack of oversights, the walls of secrecy and the external pressure, how confident can we be that the authorities have solid enough a case against the suspects that they can be trusted to conduct a trial outside of public scrutiny, in secret?

CHAPTER 4

▼

FIXING THE SYSTEM

It would be presumptuous of me, having only worked at CSIS for a little less than three years, to claim to know everything that is wrong with the organisation and, additionally, what needs to be done to address these problems. After all, I have not experienced the life of an intelligence officer in the region, where things *might* be slightly different. Readers must also be reminded that the experiences described above are my own and that other people may have reached different conclusions. I have, however, been pondering my experiences for many months, and furthermore, many of the information I present in this work, along with some of the conclusions reached, comes from interviewing a large number of intelligence officers, both from my generation and those who came before. Armed with these, I feel well-positioned enough to make certain recommendations—ideas that, had they been in place while I was with the Service, could have changed my decision to leave.

- The Service must do everything it can to hire individuals who have the required skills and level of education. This may mean hiring fewer recruits every year, but in the end Canadians would get a far better return on their investment. With this, however, comes the responsibility of ensuring that the work that is expected of intelligence officers is challenging. It must also be kept as far away as possible from what is, in essence, secretarial work. Before being hired, officers are attracted to the intellectual challenges, puzzle solving and thinking outside the box that seem to be the responsibilities of intelligence officers. Making the job description fit those expectations would help address current retention issues. The sense of betrayal that comes from realising that one's job isn't what it was made out to be is a major factor in an employee's loss of a sense of belonging to an organisation.

- If the Service gets serious about hiring the right people, it will need to offer better salaries at the onset. At the current salary level for new intelligence officers, the best potential recruits will not even bother to apply and will look elsewhere. Being an intelligence officer should require rigour, and a type of knowledge and analytical skills that are not found in other individuals. In order to attract those individuals, the salary should be commensurate with the level of investment, both financial and intellectual, that a recruit has made to acquire those skills. The Service should strive to hire the best and to create an environment that is conducive to excellence. Failing to do this, it should avoid hiring highly educated, well-travelled and curious recruits, and limit itself to people who will be happy following orders and pushing paper.

- In order to work for the Federal Government, employees need to demonstrate basic skills in French and English. Failure to meet this requirement results in language training that, for most, takes nearly a year and is fully covered by the government. Other than people who originate from the Province of Quebec, very few Canadians know enough French to be able to claim they are bilingual. As a rule, only about five or six individuals, out of a class of twenty, come from Quebec. For the others, months are spent learning basic French. The problem with the program is that training prepares them to answer the exam questions—not to operate in a French-speaking environment. Moreover, once the recruits manage to pass the exam, many will never use French again. Thousands of dollars are spent training every officer; it is a really poor investment of Canadian taxpayers' money if, five years down the road, those individuals who passed the exam cannot write, let alone speak it, properly. Instead of focusing on making the trainees pass the French exam, the language program should aim at making them proficient in the language so that they can *use* it and *retain* it. The fact that the Service does not offer a bonus for bilingualism does not help.

- The training program for entry officers (IOET) needs to be rethought. The assumption that the way CSIS has done things in the past twenty-four years is the right way of doing things in the 21st century needs to be challenged. With the hiring of more skilled recruits should come a program that truly satisfies the requirements of professional intelligence officers. A substantial amount of time should be spent on information management and the preparation of intelligence products. Entry officers need to be acquainted with cognitive biases, false analogies, and the art of intelligence analysis. There cannot be an expectation, as there is now, that those skills will somehow develop on the job. Furthermore officers should be encouraged—in fact it should be mandatory—to read up on history, languages, and the humanities. Human problems cannot be understood, let alone solved, without a solid grounding in those.

- A dose of humility should be injected from the onset to prevent the god syndrome that is rampant among intelligence officers. Moreover, more openness within the various branches of the Service, and outwards into the rest of the community, is also required, as it is essential for learning from other people's successes and mistakes. Officers and institutions cannot be expected to learn in isolation; the spirit of being part of a common endeavour, rather than competing against other agencies, should be encouraged. Mistakes should be seen as opportunities to learn rather than a threat to one's chances of getting a promotion and as something that needs to be hidden from one's supervisor, management, review bodies, or the Canadian public.

- Managers should welcome the skill sets and knowledge that new intelligence officers bring to the organisation. As groups that may represent a threat to the security of Canada are relying on emerging technologies to plan and coordinate, CSIS should also tap into the generation that understands the uses and potential of those devices.

- Divergence of opinion, within and without the Service, cannot continue to be treated with contempt. Systems must be put in place whereby different opinions at least have a chance to be considered. This applies to investigations and official documents, such as affidavits, that are presented to court. Parallel to this, the habit of recycling information from one year to another should stop. While doing so could be time consuming, CSIS cannot be allowed to cut corners when people's lives are at stake.

- Non-intelligence officers at CSIS, such as subject matter experts (SMEs) in RAP, communications analysts and linguists should be given the respect that is due them and consulted more often. Their work cannot continue to be treated as bonus material that one can do without. Absent a culturally representative and well-travelled body of intelligence officers, these SMEs represent the Service's only window on, and therefore knowledge of, the outside world.

- Cultural sensitivity and the issue of racism need to be addressed, both during training and throughout one's career. Those represent what is probably the greatest threat to Canadian security in the long term. It is therefore capital, both morally and professionally, that all officers be made aware of the impact of a racist view of the world, and that measures be taken to ensure that racism does not become part of the accepted norm within the organisation. Short of a thought police, something must be done to prevent racism from becoming institutionalised and part of the language of the organisation.

- Intelligence officers should travel more and be encouraged to learn more about the groups and countries they are investigating. This will become even more important as the Service increases its activities abroad. Experience in a foreign country should be part of the training program.

- The new intelligence officers themselves, rather than management, should be asked to provide insights into the health of the organisation, and their grievances should be taken seriously. Instead of calling on outside "experts" to evaluate satisfaction levels at CSIS, the workforce should be encouraged to express its opinion freely, without having to fear that doing so will affect one's chances of getting a promotion.

- More heed should be paid to officers who show an interest for specialisation. Under the current system, officers are expected to be generalists and are accordingly moved from one investigation to the next every three to four years. This results in loss of information and mitigates long-term investigative cohesion. A service will never be able to keep pace with its opponents if, by design, it runs back to square one every half decade. Terrorist organisations constantly change and renew themselves, but do so with a sense of continuity. This does not mean that CSIS should only have experts, as doing so would limit the flexibility that an ever-changing world requires. However, intelligence officers who have special linguistic skills or sets of knowledge that are difficult to replace should be allowed to become specialists and to remain in that area for a good part of their career. It makes no sense for an officer who knows about China, speaks the language, has travelled or worked there, and is passionate about the subject, to be moved after serving three years on the desk. If he so chooses, that person should be allowed to become an *operational* SME.

- Given that most of the potential threats to the security of Canada come from other regions of the world, the Service should begin hiring individuals who are representative of those cultures as soon as possible. Less than 10% of the work-force identifying itself as a visible minority is inappropriate. The importance of doing so cannot be stressed enough. As we have seen, the combination of the wrong education, ignorance, and racism possibly represents the greatest threat to Canada. Hiring officers who not only understand a culture but who are its product would solve this problem. Such officers would be in as better position to approach communities with which they share affinities, and within the Service itself their presence could greatly contribute to the education of others. As things stand now, intelligence officers who have seen little of the world have few people to turn to with their questions about other culture, mores and religion. They need to seek out friends outside of work, which the Service discourages—especially when those friends happen to be from the community that the officer is charged with investigating.

- CSIS and the Canadian government should make it clear to the public that they are not involved in the rendition of terrorist suspects to countries where they run the risk of being tortured. In other words, they should distance themselves from such activities as were undertaken by US intelligence services. Canada will gain nothing from being a participant in torture and can only create enemies if the perception that it does endures. The Canadian government should also come clean on recent allegations that CIA planes, with suspected terrorist detainees on board, have on a number of occasions used Canadian airports for refuelling stopovers. To this end, appropriate public relations campaigns and more transparency should be implemented.

- As the intelligence community keeps expanding, the government of Canada should ensure that the appropriate oversight bodies are in place to monitor not just the activities of CSIS but those of its allied agencies as well. One likely positive outcome of the O'Connor Commission will be the creation of a monitoring body for the RCMP. Finally, systems should be implemented that facilitate the communication between these oversight bodies to ensure that no information falls through the cracks.

- Monitoring bodies like the Inspector General and the Security Intelligence Review Committee should be given the appropriate powers to impose change when change is needed. Recommendations in the Annual Report are not enough, as they are not binding. A true system of checks and balances, one that Canadians can put their faith in, is the surest way to avoid abuse.

- Efforts should be made within the community to address the deficiencies in communication. Great chasms currently exist between a number of agencies involved in the security intelligence community. The institutional turf wars cannot be allowed to continue. High-level meetings should be organised where grievances and differences in opinion are openly discussed. Agencies should not be allowed to ignore another agency's reporting, whether they agree with the findings or not. Simultaneously, the issue of reporting overlap should be addressed. Agencies that are merely cut-and-pasting another agency's assessments and putting their stamp on what now passes off as their own work should be reprimanded. Given the growing size of the community, special efforts should be made to reduce the amount of information that is generated. Reports should always be written with the consumers in mind, and the question, Will this reporting truly add to the body of knowledge the community needs to ensure the safety of Canadians? should always be asked. If the answer is no, the document should not be released.

- ITAC needs to become a functioning body and not just a political tool that makes the government look good. Emphasis should be put on timely, valuable and actionable intelligence products. The officers who are sent by the member organisations should participate in ITAC because of their abilities, not for what in many cases appears to be punishment. The process needs to be streamlined, with fewer layers of approval before a document is released to the community. Documents should be relevant to Canadians, not just a quantitative addition to the list of publications. Absent this, the Threat Assessment Unit at CSIS should be properly staffed.

- The management at CSIS should think of ways to incorporate certain best practices from the private sector. While the business of security intelligence cannot be defined in terms of profits and bottom line, there nevertheless is a requirement for effectiveness, and in order to be an effective organisation, below-par employee performance should not be tolerated. Rotten apples, rather than be moved from one position to another, should instead be fired. Furthermore, promotions should be granted based on merit and not for time served. Performance evaluations should continue to be top-down but should also be bottom-up and lateral. To prevent retaliation, the identity of the bottom-up reviewers should not be known to the supervisor. This could be used as an instrument to assess discontent and to ensure that supervisors are there on merit.

- CSIS, along with other agencies involved in the intelligence sector, cannot be allowed to usurp the decision-making role of policymakers by limiting the options on the table. Great consideration should be paid, therefore, to ensure that CSIS does not taint the information it provides to the National Security Advisor and the Prime Minister for self-serving ends. Policymaking must remain the remit of national governments, and no action should be taken by any agency behind the back of Parliament.

- The Canadian government must ensure that absolutely no intelligence collection is carried out without a proper warrant. Moreover, extra effort must be paid to ensure that warrants and affidavits, no matter how urgently they are required, are given the consideration that such documents require. Warrants have been and *should* continue to be refused if the information provided is not solid enough to permit the intrusive powers that are being sought. Rubber-stamping must not, under any circumstances, be tolerated.

- Decisions to investigate, or not, should be based on *Canadian* interests. Investigations for the sake of investigation, or that are carried out to demonstrate CSIS' willingness to play in the Big Leagues, should be stopped.

- Within government and beyond, an honest debate on what terrorism means to Canada, and what should be done about it, is needed. Divergence from the US way of doing things should not be painted as anti-American, unduly nationalistic, or "pro-terrorist."

- In light of the dangers they represent to Canadian national security, Canada's alliance with "problem" states like Israel should be reconsidered. Inquiries should also be launched to investigate the level of pressure CSIS and other organisations are receiving from those countries. The Canadian government should ensure that no operation is ever launched by CSIS at the behest of another country.

Some critics could accuse me of making unreasonable demands on intelligence officers, or of setting the bar too high. But I wonder how the population would feel if, for example, we were to lower the standards for, say, surgeons. Both professions have lives in their hands and, as such, both should only be practiced by well-qualified individuals, with the proper tools, and the proper oversight. Security intelligence, as a profession, is about saving lives—to protect Canadians from threats to national security. Just as important, security intelligence is also about protecting people from being unjustly targeted. It makes no difference whether the patient is lying on an operation table or is going about his everyday life somewhere in Canada: both deserve the very best.

Conclusion

When you look long into an abyss,
the abyss also looks into you.

—Friedrich Nietzsche

By no means is this work intended as a diatribe against all things government. Though imperfect, the Canadian governmental institutions are an achievement that every Canadian should be proud of. Most of the time, most of the civil servants who comprise its workforce are working toward the maintenance and the improvement of the values that define us as a country. In terms of social development, liberties, rights, openness and connectivity to the world, Canada is the envy of many nations. We must cherish that, and in turn each and everyone of us must ensure that those values and the institutions that are mandated with helping protect and define them continue to evolve. Unfortunately, certain institutions—those that are the object of this book—are failing us and are now using the events of Sept. 11, 2001, to further their obscure activities. While organisations such as CSIS undeniably have a role to play in a democratic society, they should not be allowed to go unchecked. In its present configuration, CSIS is a blemish upon Canadian society.

I was of two minds when I began writing this book, which after all criticises the organisation that employed me for nearly three years. Several months and an exile to another continent later, I am convinced, more than ever, that it was necessary for me to write this book.

Places tell their own stories, and if we are willing to listen, we can learn from them. I began editing this book while visiting Okinawa, Japan, an area that in the last battle of World War II suffered more casualties than were caused by the nuclear bombings of Hiroshima and Nagasaki. And yet, as I looked at my surroundings, I saw very little of the remnants of war. Life had resumed, people were prospering, and despite the still-fresh (to some) memories of war, the inhabitants of the small island had managed to look to the future and were able to shape it. Okinawa now has the highest life expectancy in the world. This demonstrates that even destruction on a scale that contemporary terrorists are unlikely ever to reproduce can be relegated to the past. Rather than continue fighting or holding a grudge against their conqueror, the Japanese decided to build anew, and what an accomplishment this was, not only on Okinawa, but throughout Japan. One can only hope that in spite of the atrocities of Sept. 11, the Western world can be strong enough to move and mobilize its immense talent and resources to improve the lot of mankind rather than engage in illegal wars, do away with human rights and weaken its own constitutions. Nearly seven years after the events of Sept. 11, it would appear that the US, along with the allies that it dragged into its wars, have regressed and become worse countries, mostly as a result of the choices they made in the name of security. But it is not too late, and humanity can be brought back on course, as long as enough people do not abandon hope that things can be changed.

New challenges, meanwhile, such as Iran's suspected and North Korea's proven attempts to develop atomic weapons, or continued instability in Israel and Palestine, with the old guard disappearing and new faces—considered terrorists by some—entering the political scene, will require our attention. Whether China emerges as friend of foe, and in the process deals peacefully with its neighbours Japan and Taiwan, will depend on diplomacy much more than balance of power. Under the current political approach of the US, which is now on the brink of sparking an arms race in space, chances are that the opportunities to deal with these challenges peacefully will be bungled, at great cost to all. Overemphasis on terrorism and a state of siege, along with the damage that this is doing to constitutions and international law, can only be detrimental to the much more pressing health, environmental, and population issues that we will be facing in the coming decades. The money that is being spent fighting in Iraq, which some estimates now put at US$2 trillion for the entire campaign, surely could have been put to better use elsewhere.[94]

These closing remarks are being written in a part of the world where the threat of international terrorism is much less immediate. In fact, terrorism rarely makes it on prime-time news. In the two years or so that I have been here, only once have I seen bin Laden on television. Instead, domestic politics and regional problems are what one sees on the news and what people argue over at the water hole. In other words, matters that pertain to national interests are what animates people locally.

This demonstrates that one's view of the world is very much defined by the media we watch and the discourse our politicians hold. Back in North America—and especially in the US—everything is about terrorism and its close relative, the occupation of Iraq. Eventually, it will be Iran, which could soon be followed by Hezbollah.

But not so here in East Asia. This step back, if you will, has provided me with an important corrective that, once applied to my worldview as a former CSIS employee, has made me realise that "international" terrorism the way it is defined in North America and Europe is anything but. The reality is, the world is still a system of regions. There is no "global" community in the real sense of the word. A such, the concept of "global terrorism," of a world threatened by and therefore united against al-Qaeda, is a complete fallacy. It is an illusion created by the US and its close allies to ensure that no one will ever question the wisdom of their actions. For East Asia, North Korea's test-firing of long-range missiles in early July 2006 and its nuclear detonation a few months later should be a much more pressing matter than al-Qaeda. A meek diplomatic effort was made by Washington, along with China, Japan and South Korea, but in the end it was nothing on the scale of, say, US efforts in Iraq or Afghanistan. Despite the nature of the threat, there is nothing global about the challenge that North Korea represents, nor is there anything global about al-Qaeda. Both are *regional* and *political* conflicts. They can only become global and military if we choose to make them so.

Still, Washington exerts immense pressure on the issue of terrorism, so much so that in March 2007, for example, the Taiwanese government proposed a new "anti-terrorism" act which, if passed, would give it very intrusive investigative powers with little oversight. Aside from the fact that this young democracy probably is not mature enough yet to adopt anti-terrorism measures of the type that have succeeded in stomping well-established democratic systems like Canada, Britain and the US, what is perhaps most alarming in this development is the fact that the draft was proposed not to address a need of the state, but rather in response to a perceived requirement to do one's part in the so-called "war" on terrorism. In other words, Taiwan was proposing far-reaching anti-terrorism laws so that it, too, could show which side it was on, that it was a participant in the US-led campaign again a-Qaeda and other like-minded organisations.[95]

The US presidential elections in 2008, in which the issue of pulling out US troops from Iraq has loomed largely, will also have repercussions on the rest of the world. As some sort of pullout is all but certain, the next president will never-theless be under tremendous pressure to demonstrate that he or she is dedicated to fighting terrorism. Consequently, regardless of who ends up in the White House, Democrat or Republican, the "war" on terrorism will continue, and so will the pressure on the US' allies.

As time passes, I have become more keenly aware of the destructive power of the anti-terrorism policies that, following Sept. 11, were adopted in Europe and North America. As former minister of Foreign Affairs Lloyd Axworthy wrote in his book *Navigating the New World: Canada and the 21ˢᵗ Century*: "It is such a contrast to see the billions of dollars being funnelled into military and bor-der-security expenditures as part of the anti-terrorist campaign while paltry sums are allocated for prevention and peace-building investments in areas where human security is at risk."[96] Should terrorism one day be seen as part of a series of contemporary concerns rather than *the* defining aspect of our time, it will lose some of its immediacy, and that drop in importance will allow for other pressing matters—the environment, gun control, AIDS and other infectious diseases, unemployment, substance abuse, education—to squeeze into the front seat. A great irony emerges when one thinks back on comments that then-CSIS director Ward Elcock made in May 2000, to the effect that Islamic terrorism was *the* lead-ing threat to Canada's national security. Just three years later, an outbreak of Severe Acute Respiratory Syndrome (SARS), which was believed to have origi-nated in China, would wreak havoc on Canada's largest city, and a year later, the same city would be hit by street gang violence that claimed about fifty lives—more lives, with the exception of the Air India bombing in 1985, than were ever lost as a result of terrorism on Canadian soil. Those two incidents alone, a disease and gang violence, have cost more Canadian lives and done the Canadian econ-omy far more damage than has terrorism since Mr. Elcock sounded his alarm. And yet, the focus in the news, in Parliament, remains on terror.

In September 2001, our leaders claimed that we had become one, that the world had become smaller. While it is true that events occurring in one corner of the world can, nowadays, affect us at home, it is important to keep in mind that the world is still an immense place and that local claims of universalism will more often than not constitute an attempt to give more importance than is warranted to an issue. The doomsayers in Washington hold that line of universal threat because it gives them access to almost limitless amounts of money to wage wars covert and overt and the justification for building bases in every corner of the world. Without that sense of universal doom and gloom, that money would be going elsewhere, and their little war would be seen for what it really is: a little war.

It is also important to keep some perspective. As we have seen, the media has a great capacity to captivate and, in the process, to define our world. If it's on the evening news, we tell ourselves, then it must be important. Since Sept. 11, no other issue has had more airtime than terrorism. In the five years since the attacks, thousands of books, articles, and movies have been produced on that issue alone. Billions of dollars have been poured into domestic security and wars fought under the umbrella of anti-terrorism. The last presidential election in the US was largely fought over the issue of terrorism and how dedicated the future president would be to protecting the country from terrorism, "rogue states" and weapons of mass destruction. Unfortunately, all this disproportionate focus on terrorism has misled us, and the daily bombardment has sucked so much of our mental energy that we have lost sight of the global priorities. The terrorist attacks that seem to have defined the past decade were indeed quite shocking, and they should be condemned. But in the grand scale of things, the devastation caused by them, and the resulting deaths, were small. While countries were busying themselves with the creation of new agencies, recruitment of new officers and anti-terrorism expeditions, hundreds of thousands of people were dying from civil wars in Africa. Numerous others were being displaced and forced to live in conditions that threatened their very survival and that of the states whose borders they had crossed. Famine, drought, AIDS, malaria and other communicable diseases, not to mention cigarette smoking, obesity, traffic accidents and substance abuse, kill more in a day than were killed by either side in the entire "war" on terrorism. Natural catastrophes, of which the recent years have provided ample examples, are much deadlier than any terrorist attack ever will be—and are far, far more likely to occur again.

And yet, a wealthy country like the US, wealthy enough to spend billions, or perhaps trillions, of dollars on defence and to fight "preventive" wars in every corner of the planet, cannot provide for residents of one of its poorest states after it is struck by a devastating hurricane. Our priorities are wrong, and the focus of our attention is out of sync. The people must request that their governments be more accountable, and part of this accountability runs through governments whose priorities are the right ones. Anti-terrorism has to be part of a government's policy; however, this should not be at the expense of attending to other, more pressing, issues. Would it not be ironic if bin Laden, which billions of military and intelligence dollars have failed to locate and arrest or kill, ended up being killed by an earthquake such as the one that struck Pakistan and India in October 2005?

It is unfortunate that in order to reap the financial benefits of trading with the US, countries like Canada will feel compelled to change who and what they are and to do things that are not in their interest. In the long term, that loss of identity may very well be far worse than anything would-be international terrorists could ever hope to achieve. Perhaps this is exactly what the terrorists sought when they attacked the US.

One cannot but be saddened when he sees the cancer of racism and intellectual stasis slowly crawl up on friends. It pains me to think that perhaps some of my friends at CSIS will be put in a position where they have no choice but to take the racist line, or play intellectual dead, in order to remain in the game. I resent the fact that the Service threatens to change the people that I know and care for into individuals who, in the workplace, are incapable of discernment and free will. If there is one thing that new recruits should always keep in mind, it is to retain their sense of morality, of who they are. Perhaps the CIA's William Nolte puts it best when he writes:

> The best defense for the analyst who feels pressure to reach a certain judgment, or the case officer pressured to "bend the rules," is the ethical recognition that no one—analyst, interrogator, or policymaker—is well served by such corruption. That may seem a strong word, no money changing hands or anything like that. But corruption it remains, of the intelligence officer's fiduciary responsibilities to speak truth to power and to understand that American intelligence, unlike traditional "secret services," exists within a structure of law and regulation. In the end, as professionals, we are left not just with an external check of such formal rules, but with an internal sense of right and wrong.[97]

Finally, I am greatly alarmed at the thought that refugees, immigrants and Canadians who, as a result of institutional carelessness and a racist view of the world at CSIS, will be made to suffer. Rather than see Canada for the open, welcoming society that it is, their opinion of the coveted haven risks being tainted by fear and a sense of betrayal.

Perhaps the O'Connor Commission and the Air India Report recently presented by Bob Rae are indications of a shift within the government of Canada in favour of accountability. But for them to succeed, the highest authorities *as well as the Canadian public* need to abandon their cynic view of matters of secrecy and truly request that whatever findings emerge from those commissions are acted upon. In other words, whatever the inquiries unearth, heads will have to roll. To date, the report card on the review of intelligence activity is not very promising.

SIRC and the Inspector General have been but fangless monitoring bodies. On the rare occasions when their reports were critical of certain practices at CSIS and recommendations were made, nothing was done at the Service to indicate that it was taking those recommendations seriously, let alone that it was implementing them. What is required is something unforgiving, a system in which there are consequences for inaction.

The Canadian government's official apology in early 2007 to Maher Arar for the role that some of its agencies played in his deportation, by the US, to Syria, where he was allegedly tortured, added to the $10.5 million compensation that it awarded him as part of a settlement, marks an encouraging departure, as does Ottawa's efforts—at least at some levels—to have his name removed from the US' terrorist watch list.

However commendable these developments are, they came after more than two years of investigation and a costly commission. The country—and potential targets of a CSIS or RCMP investigation—cannot afford such an aposteriori settlement to become the means by which intelligence blunders such as the one that led to Mr. Arar's deportation are solved. Prevention, better intelligence collection and how it is analysed and shared with foreign agencies, is key to ensuring that such errors will never be committed again.

The ruling in February 2007 by the Supreme Court of Canada that the anti-terrorism provision allowing the authorities to detain indefinitely suspected terrorists was counter to the Canadian Charter of Rights and Freedoms—coming less than a month after Maher Arar received his official apology—sends an encouraging signal to the world that Canada is in remission and that it recognizes, however belatedly, that some of the things it has done in the name of security have breached its age-old contract with its citizens.

At the heart of the issue are the Security Certificates, which under the Immigration and Refugee Protection Act (IRPA) are emitted against foreign nationals or permanent residents suspected of terrorism. The certificates allow for the detention, without a fair judicial process, of those individuals for extended periods of time, pending deportation. Ostensibly to protect intelligence sources (usually foreign) and methods of collection, the accused and their defence lawyers are given no access to the charges against them or the intelligence used to back those charges, making a proper defence in court virtually impossible. It is a system that, not altogether unfairly, has prompted comparisons to the manner in which the US has treated its prisoners in Guantanamo Bay.

Eight cases are pending, and twenty have been resolved since 1991. Of the latter, 15 have resulted in deportation. Of the 28 individuals, nineteen were of Arabic, Northern African or Persian origin. Unfortunately for the individuals whose cases are pending, the court suspended the February 2007 ruling for a year to allow for a rewriting of the relevant parts of IRPA. For the three most prominent cases—Hassan Almrei, Mohammed Zeki Mahjoub and Mahmoud Jaballah—this means a continuation of detentions that started in 2001, 2000 and 2001 respectively.

Were those individuals Canadians by birth and—let us be honest—Caucasian and non-Muslim, it is highly unlikely that the public, along with government, would allow their detention to continue for a single additional day without fair trial, let alone a year. But given the current state of affairs in the post-Sept. 11 world and the racist slant against individuals of Middle Eastern or Persian origin, Almrei, Mahjoub and Jaballah will remain incarcerated without provisions for a fair trial with access to the charges against them. Moreover, the ruling was accompanied by a caveat stating that prolonged detention would be allowed if the new version of the law conforms with the Charter. In other words, despite the seemingly path-breaking ruling, there is no assurance that those three individuals—and others to come—will receive a fair trial, let alone be freed and compensated.

A situation like this cannot be allowed in a democracy based on a system of law. Whether they are citizens or not, individuals suspected of participation in terrorism-related activities, both passive and active, deserve the full set of defence tools granted individuals suspected of other crimes. If found guilty in a fair trial, they should face the full consequences of their acts. But we cannot allow for the continuation of a system whereby suspects are detained for years without the means to defend themselves and cannot know the substance of the charges against them—especially when much of the intelligence used to send them to jail in the first place is, as we have seen, of questionable value, oftentimes based on innuendo, institutional sloppiness, false assumptions or outright racism.

Without provisions for a fair trial and respect for the Charter of Rights and Freedoms, the Security Certificates are only a tool used by authorities to conceal less-than-airtight cases against individuals who happen to be from the wrong ethnic or religious group.

*   *   *   *

Blaming the government is the easy part; what we need now, more than ever, is for Canadians to go beyond the usual resignation and do something. Canadians so far have been too complacent, their feeling of powerlessness overpowering. As long as disapproval of what is being done by CSIS and others is limited to scattered protests in front of the CSIS regional office in Toronto, change will not come. Canadians must remember that their government can and should be what they want it to be. Elections are one way of voicing one's opinion on a number of topics, including security matters. But much more can be done, starting with the realisation that certain things that the intelligence community has done since Sept. 11, 2001, are simply unacceptable, and that corrective measures are in order. This is a choice that we must make as a society. So far, the management at CSIS has not felt the need to change the way it does things because it has been able to shield itself from the meek criticism that has been directed at it. It knows, for the moment at least, that it is in a position of power. So far, the mention that information cannot be made public on the basis of national security has been sufficient to ward off the lonely critics who dared challenge the authorities.

In her assessment of the Liddar case, the former chairwoman of SIRC, Paule Gauthier, indicated that CSIS had played "semantic games to frustrate her probe by providing her with misleading answers to [her] questions in order to prevent Mr. Liddar or the review committee from having information … brought to our attention." Gauthier continues, "the committee was purposefully misled by the Service in the incident" in an attempt to shield itself from any embarrassing revelations that may have come from the review.[98] Such accusations clearly cannot be left unanswered. A concerted effort, by the public, academics and the media, to make them accountable should make CSIS and the rest of government pause. As someone who was on the inside for nearly three years, I can tell you that however powerful, shadowy, and remote these individuals may seem to be, they are still human beings, foibles and all. They all crave the same things, they all enjoy long breakfasts, apple dumplings, and a game of golf. In other words, they are not beyond the reach of citizens demanding accountability.

From the benefit of distance, it has become obvious that Canada is losing some of its hard-earned identity because, since Sept. 11, it has been forced into, and has failed to oppose, a war that isn't his. As Michael Scheuer writes: "U.S. forces and policies are completing the radicalization of the Islamic world, something Osama bin Laden has been trying to do with substantial but incomplete success since the early 1990s. As a result […] the United States of America remains bin Laden's only indispensable ally."[99] Can we allow Canada, by joining the US in its adventurism, to also become one of al-Qaeda's indispensable allies? In a way, Canadian authorities have failed to recognize that there is no "West" but rather a number of different countries located in this vague geographical area called "the West." By failing to do so, our leaders have made it easy from themselves to believe such falsehoods as al-Qaeda's purported hatred of that which defines Western societies—that is, democracy, freedom of expression, a capitalist system, equal rights for women and homosexuals (if only), and so on. Systems that believe they are under siege because of those values will be tempted to adopt the methods of their enemy to defend themselves, hence the growing resemblance in how Canada has been reacting to the perceived threat of terrorism on its soil. They hate "us," claim the powers that be, so the only option must be to rally behind the flag of Freedom through alliances, whether that be in intelligence sharing or war-making. To hate back.

I cannot emphasize enough the fact that despite everything the leaderships in Washington, Ottawa and London claim, bin Laden and his followers do not hate us for who or what we are; they hate us (or don't) for what we do, our actions. In its pursuit of alignment with Washington, which manifests itself in such incidents as how Canadian authorities have dealt with the Group of Seventeen to the increasingly belligerent activities of our soldiers in Afghanistan, Canada has only made it more difficult for the angry individuals in the Muslim world to see the distinctions between Canada and the US. If, at one point and as a result of its actions, Canada comes to be seen as a true participant in the US crusade against the Muslim world, then and only then can we seriously start thinking about the possibility that terror will be visited on the streets of Toronto, Ottawa, Montreal, or Vancouver, or the many Canadian interests abroad.

The Canadian experiment, with its rich diversity of peoples and ideas and ideals, immense resources both human and natural, and great fortunes of geography, stands as a precious example to the world. In all its imperfection, it is something that is to be cherished and which we must continue to improve upon. There are signs, sadly, that many of the elements that make this distinct societal and political entity so valuable are under attack. The damage, however, is not being caused by explosives going off in our public transit systems or inside our commercial buildings. Rather, that damage is being caused by something much more insidious: It comes from inside, from a failure to understand what it is that makes us different and, consequently, why we should be doing our utmost to protect that fragile gift. Who we bring to power, and what we allow our government to do in our collective name, for the sake of security, is ultimately how we define who we are.

*   *   *   *

There are still days when I wonder if quitting my job at CSIS was the right thing to do, that perhaps if I had stayed there I would have been able to change things. But I have since come to realise that I did the right thing. Firstly, my exile allowed me to do what I like best, write. The repercussions on my health, mental and physical, were nothing short of extraordinary, and my self-esteem, my sense of worth as a human being, have returned to normal after the many beatings they received at CSIS. My resignation was also a liberation; it broke the chains that hold every intelligence officer in a permanent state of bondage. Rather than have my employer dictate where and when I would be relocated, I became the sole master of my fate. That move allowed me, as was noted above, to see things differently and to gain a new perspective on what terrorism means to the world, and where Canada stands among the constellation of nations that comprise it. So in spite of the occasional "what if," I am confident that I did the right thing, and it is my fondest hope that this book, the result not only of my time at CSIS but also of my decision to leave the organisation, will enlighten Canadians and make them demand more accountability from the security intelligence community that acts in their name. Deep inside, my hope is that this book will help Canada save itself from the bogeyman that it risks turning into should it continue down the road that some cynical decision-makers in Washington, London and Ottawa, have drawn for it. We do not have to go that way—in fact, it is in our common interest that we do not. Let us therefore, to turn the epigraph I open this book with on its head, be human in defence of our humanity, compassionate in defence of compassion, and open-minded in defence of our disparity.

East Asia, March 2008.

End Notes

Introduction

[1] Suskind, Ron, *The One Percent Doctrine: Deep Inside America's Pursuit of its Enemies since 9/11* (New York: Simon & Schuster, 2006), p. 18.

[2] Sherry, Norman, *The Life of Graham Greene, Volume II: 1939-1955* (New York: Penguin, 1994), pp. 83-89.

[3] See Matthew J. Bruccoli and Judith S. Baughman, eds., *Conversations With John le Carré* (Jackson: University Press of Mississippi, 2004).

Chapter 1: The Totalitarian System

[4] Nolte, William, "Just War, Ethics, and Terror," *Intelligence in Recent Public Literature* (http://www.cia.gov/csi/studies/vol48no4/nolte_interviews.html)

[5] See, for example, William E. Odom's *Fixing Intelligence For a More Secure America* (New Haven: Yale University Press, 2003), and Bruce D. Berkowitz and Allan E. Goodman, *Best Truth: Intelligence in the Information Age* (New Haven: Yale University Press, 2000).

[6] Ibid.

[7] Baer, Robert, *See No Evil: The True Story of a Ground Soldier in the CIA's War on Terrorism* (New York: Crown, 2002), p. xix.

[8] National Commission on Terrorist Attacks upon the United States, *The 9/11 Commission Report: Final Report of the National Commission on Terrorist Attacks upon the United States* (New York: WW Norton, 2004), p. 339.

[9] The same problems have been haunting US counterterrorism efforts for years. For example, see "Elite US Troops Get Expanded Intelligence Role," Reuters, Tuesday March 7, 2006, which points out the "disorganization, even distrust, that critics in Congress and the academic world have said permeates the government's counterterrorism efforts."

[10] Baker III, James A. and Lee H. Hamilton, co-chairs, *The Iraq Study Group Report: The Way Forward-A New Approach* (New York: Vintage, 2006), p. 94.

[11] Lilley, James, and Jeffrey Lilley, *China Hands: Nine Decades of Adventure, Espionage, and Diplomacy in Asia* (New York: Public Affairs, 2004), p. 86.

[12] Packer, George, *The Assassins' Gate: America in Iraq* (New York: Farrar Strauss Giroux, 2005), p. 392.

[13] "MacKay calls Hezbollah 'cancer on Lebanon,'" *The National Post*, August 1, 2006.

[14] Kerbel, Josh, "Thinking Straight: Cognitive Bias in the US Debate About China," CIA Studies in Intelligence, Vol. 48 No. 3.

[15] Jonas, George, *Vengeance: The True Story of an Israeli Counter-Terrorist Team* (New York: Simon and Schuster, 2005), p. 376, n.1.

[16] Orwell, George, "Politics and the English Language, in *Essays* (New York: Everyman's Library, 2002), p. 964.

[17] Globe and Mail, September 14, 2005.

[18] Mr. Liddar was subsequently cleared, and under the Martin government was offered the job of Canada's deputy permanent representative to the United Nations Environment Program and UN-Habitat in Nairobi, Kenya.

[19] See Thomas Homer-Dixon, *The Ingenuity Gap: How Can We Solve the Problems of the Future?* (Toronto: Random House, 2000), pp. 208-13.

[20] Johnson, Chalmers, *The Sorrows of Empire: Militarism, Secrecy, and the End of the Republic* (New York: Henry Holt, 2004), p. 10.

[21] Mercado, Stephen C., "Reexamining the Distinction Between Open Information and Secrets," CIA Studies in Intelligence, Volume 49. No. 2.

[22] Ibid.

[23] Ellsberg, Daniel, *Secrets: A Memoir of Vietnam and the Pentagon Papers* (London: Penguin, 2002), p. 186.

[24] See, for example, Richards J. Heuer, Jr., *Psychology of Intelligence Analysis,* available at www.cia.gov/csi/books/19104.

[25] Packer, p. 107.

[26] Hutton, Will, *The Writing on the Wall: China and the West in the 21st Century* (London: Little, Brown, 2006), p, 186.

[27] Sagan, Carl, *The Demon-Haunted World: Science as a Candle in the Dark* (New York: Random House, 1995), p. 211.

[28] Canadian Press, April 2, 2006.

[29] See Isabel Vincent, "Charade in Havana," *National Post*, January 25, 2003.

[30] Canadian Press, April 2, 2006.

[31] Hutton, pp. 187-8.

[32] Johnson, p. 10.

[33] Ellsberg, p. 44.

[34] In "Governing Security, Governing Through Security," Mariana Valverde of the University of Toronto writes, "When politicians wave abstractions around like flags–abstractions like 'security,' or for that matter 'freedom'–citizens should be immediately suspicious." In *The Security of Freedom: Essays on Canada's Anti-Terrorism Bill,* Ronald J. Daniels, Patrick MacKlem and Kent Roach, eds. (Toronto: University of Toronto press, 2001), p. 89.

[35] Quoted in Delvoie, Louis A., "Terrorism: Global Insecurity or Global Hyperbole?" *Canadian Military Journal,* Vol. 6 No. 4, Winter 2006.

[36] Roach, Kent, *September 11: Consequences for Canada* (Montreal: McGill-Queen's University Press, 2003), p. 27.

[37] Readers interested in reading more on this issue are encouraged to look up Edward Said's *Covering Islam: How the Media and the Experts Determine How We See the Rest of the World* (New York: Pantheon, 1981).

[38] Rushdie, Salman, "What this cultural debate needs is more dirt, less pure stupidity," *The Times Online,* December 10, 2005.

[39] Nolte, William, "Just War, Ethics, and Terror," *Intelligence in Recent Public Literature.*

[40] Carroll, James, *House of War: The Pentagon and the Disastrous Rise of American Power* (New York: Houghton Mifflin Company, 2006), p. 508.

[41] Koestler, Arthur, *Darkness at Noon* (New York: Bantam, 1966), p. 208.

[42] Jonas, p. 50, 337.

[43] Le Carré, John, *The Honourable Schoolboy* (London: Penguin, 1977), p. 70.

[44] Kafka, Franz, *The Trial* (New York: Everyman's Library, 1992), p. 125.

[45] Ellsberg, p. 44.

[46] In all fairness to SIRC, however, in September 2005 it released its review of CSIS' handling of the Bhupinder Liddar case. The SIRC report was scathing in its remarks, indicating, among other things, that the Service had provided misleading information, that it had been biased in its assessment, and that the junior investigator who had handled the case had irresponsibly destroyed his notes. But the release of a report alone is not sufficient, and there is no system in place to ensure that CSIS complies with the recommendations made by SIRC. Public information campaigns and news coverage are likelier to have an impact on the Service's behaviour.

[47] Canadian Press, April 2, 2006.

[48] Immediately after the terrorist attacks of September 11, 2001, CSIS obtained a 30 per cent raise in budget and planned to hire as many as 300 new people (Roach, p. 192).

[49] See "CSIS Warns al-Qaeda May Target Canada," May 7, 2004.

[50] Quoted in Collacott, Martin, *Canada's Inadequate Response to Terrorism: The Need for Policy Reform*, Frasier Institute, February 2006, p. 82.

[51] Risen, James, *State of War: The Secret History of the CIA and the Bush Administration* (New York: Free Press, 2006), p. 76.

[52] Mitrovica, Andrew, *Covert Entry: Spies, Lies and Crimes Inside Canada's Secret Service* (Toronto: Random House Canada, 2002), p. 3.

[53] Public Report 2004-2005.

[54] Halberstam, David, *The Best and the Brightest* (New York: Modern Library, 2001), p. 75.

[55] In my view, no intelligence service is exempt from this phenomenon, as people in positions of authority use their reputation and secrecy to ensure that their faux pas are not exposed, and the organization, fearing any leaks to the public that would expose its deficiencies, will side with the supervisor in shutting down the subordinate. See, for an example of a similar situation within the Mossad (Jonas, pp. 159-60).

[56] *The Honourable Schoolboy*, p. 216.

[57] Jonas, p. 34.

[58] "Ex-top spy breaks silence," *The Toronto Star*, May 26, 2007.

Chapter 2: CSIS and the World

[59] MSNBC host Tucker Carlson made the comment. See http://mediamatters.org/items/200512160012.

[60] Risen, pp. 39-60.

[61] Scheuer, Michael, *Imperial Hubris: Why the West is Losing the War on Terror* (Washington: Potomac, 2004), p. xi.

[62] Ibid., p. 84.

[63] Studies in Intelligence, Vol. 50, No. 1, March 2006, http://www.cia.gov/csi/studies/vol50no1/12_Bookshelf.htm.

[64] See, for example, "7 July report highlights failings," http://news.bbc.co.uk/2/hi/uk_news/england/london/5046346.stm.

[65] Corn, Tony, "World War IV As Fourth-Generation Warfare," *Policy Review*, January 2006.

[66] Michael Crowley, quoted in Delvoie.

[67] Collacott, Martin, *Canada's Inadequate Response to Terrorism: The Need for Policy Reform*, p. 6.

[68] "Toronto subway most likely target of terrorist attack: federal survey," Canadian Press, March 21, 2006.

[69] Fuller, Graham E., "A World Without Islam," *Foreign Policy*, January-February 2008, p. 48.

[70] Scheuer, p. 8.

[71] Ibid, pp. 7, 9.

[72] Ibid, pp. 17-18.

[73] For an enlightening account of the US' dangerous relationship with the Saudi regime, see Robert *Baer's Sleeping with the Devil: How Washington Sold our Soul for Crude* (New York: Three Rivers Press, 2003).

[74] Koestler, p. 61.

[75] An excellent book on the subject is Susan D. Moeller's *Compassion Fatigue: How the Media Sell Disease, Famine, War and Death* (New York: Routeledge, 1999).

[76] Quoted in Hoffman, Bruce, *Inside Terrorism* (New York: Columbia University Press, 1998), p. 131.

[77] http://globalis.gvu.unu.edu/indicator_detail.cfm?IndicatorID=116&Country=HT.

[78] http://globalis.gvu.unu.edu/indicator_detail.cfm?country=CU&indicatorid=116.

[79] Scheuer, p. 85.

[80] Lieven, Anatol, *America Right or Wrong: An Anatomy of American Nationalism* (New York: Oxford University Press, 2004), p. 74.

[81] Ibid.

[82] "The Terrorism Index," *Foreign Policy*, July/August 2006, pp. 48-53.

[83] Risen, p. 221.

[84] See "CIA may need decade to rebuild clandestine service," Reuters, January 1, 2006.

[85] See "NSA eavesdropping wider than White House admitted: report," Reuters, December 25, 2005.

[86] Associated Press, Washington, Feb. 14, 2008.

[87] John Mearsheimer and Stephen Walt, "The Israel Lobby," *The London Review of Books*, Vol. 28 No. 6, 23, March 2006.

[88] It certainly does not help that in July 2006, Assem Hammoud, a suspected ringleader in a possible plot to bomb tunnels in New York, had attended the university in the mid-1990s, around the same time that I did.

[89] Howard Friel and Richard Falk, *Israel-Palestine on Record: How the* New York Times *Misreports Conflict in the Middle East* (London: Verso, 2007), p. 173.

[90] Human Rights Watch report, quoted in Friel and Falk, p. 179.

Chapter 3: The June 2006 "Group of Seventeen" Incident

[91] Teotonio, Isabel, "Homegrown terror case goes to trial," the *Toronto Star*, September 24, 2007.

[92] "Le SCRS a-t-il provoqué Toronto?" *La Presse*, June 20, 2006.

Conclusion

[93] See, for example, "Too many civilians killed by NATO in Afghanistan in 2006, official says," *International Herald Tribune,* January 3, 2007, in which the chief spokesman for NATO in Afghanistan admits that too many Afghan civilians had been killed by NATO forces in 2006.

[94] "Iraq War Could Cost US Over 2 Trillion, Says Nobel Prize-Winning Economist," *Guardian Unlimited*, January 7, 2006.

[95] Cole, J. Michael, "The Dangers of the 'Anti-Terror' Bill, *Taipei Times*, March 26, 2007, p. 8.

[96] Axworthy, Lloyd, *Navigating a New World: Canada's Global Future* (Toronto: Random House Canada, 2003), p. 283.

[97] Nolte, William, "Just War, Ethics, and Terror," *Intelligence in Recent Public Literature.*

[98] *Globe and Mail*, September 14, 2005.

[99] Scheuer, p. xv.

978-0-595-50344-5
0-595-50344-6

www.ingramcontent.com/pod-product-compliance
Lightning Source LLC
Chambersburg PA
CBHW020416290526
45785CB00002B/581